D0515334

It's **YOUR** country. Learn it. Love it. Explore it.

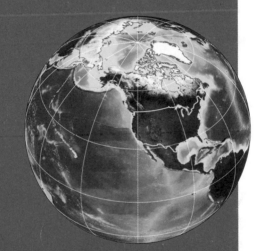

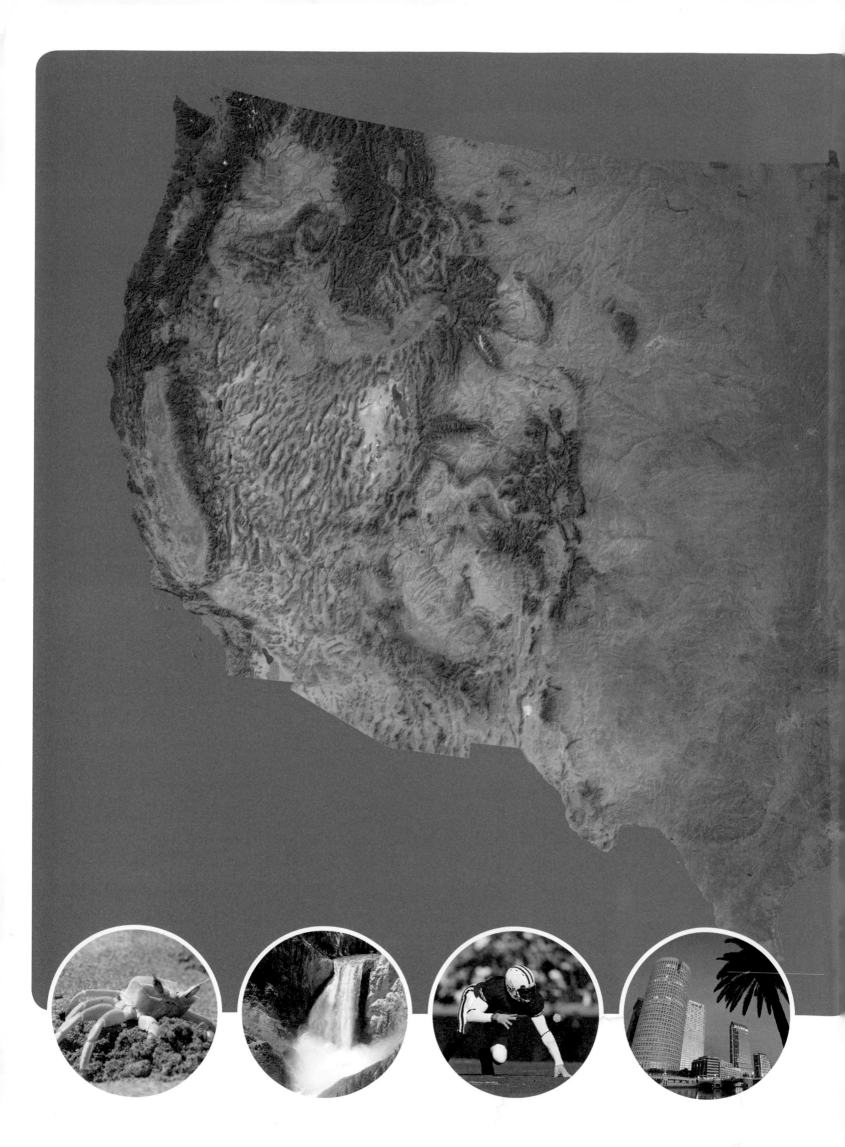

NATIONAL GEOGRAPHIC KIDS™

UNITED STATES ATLAS

NATIONAL GEOGRAPHIC
WASHINGTON, D.C.

TABLE OF CONTENTS

Northeast: Maine lighthouse, pp. 36–37

Southeast:
Florida manatee, p. 64

Midwest: Illinois hay field with tractor, pp. 90–91

Title page: Atlantic sand crab; Lower Falls of the Yellowstone, MT; football player; Tampa, FL;
sage grouse; skyline, Seattle, WA; Organ Pipe Cactus National Monument, AZ.

Territories: Festival dancers, American Samoa, pp. 158–159

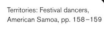

Southwest: Albuquerque balloon festival, p. 122

West: Wyoming ranch, p. 154

GETTING STARTED

HOW TO USE THIS ATLAS

This atlas is much more than just another book of maps about the United States. Of course you'll find all the things you'd expect to find—country, regional, and state maps, essays, photos, flags, graphs, and fact boxes— for the country as a whole as well as for each region and state (even the territories). But there's much more. This atlas, through a specially designed Web site (see pages 8–9), not only leads you to places where you can find more information and keep up-to-date about all kinds of things, it also allows you to go beyond the flat page and experience the sights and sounds of the country through the multimedia archives of National Geographic.

STATE FACT BOX
The fact box has all the key information you need at a glance about a state, its flag and nickname, statistics about area, cities, population, ethnic and racial makeup,* statehood, industry, and agriculture, plus some fun Geo Whiz facts and the state bird and flower.

*The ethnic/racial percentages total more than 100 percent because Hispanics can be included with any race or ethnic group.

WEB LINKS
Throughout the atlas you will find black-and-yellow Web link icons for photos, videos, sounds, games, and more information. You can get to all of these links through one URL: www.nationalgeographic.com/kids-usa-atlas. This link will take you to the Web site specially designed to go with this atlas (see pages 8–9). Bookmark it so you can use it often.

COLOR BARS
Each section of the atlas has its own color to make it easy to move from one to another. Look for the color in the Table of Contents and across the top of the pages in the atlas. The name of the section and the title for each topic or map is in the color bar.

The Northeast
The Southeast
The Midwest
The Southwest
The West
The Territories

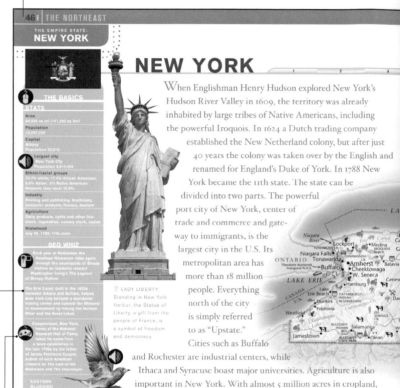

THE EMPIRE STATE:
NEW YORK

THE BASICS
STATS
Area
54,556 sq mi (141,300 sq km)
Population
19,297,729
Capital
Albany
Population 93,919
Largest city
New York City
Population 8,214,426
Ethnic/racial groups
73.7% white; 17.4% African American;
5.9% Asian; .5% Native American;
Hispanic (any race) 15.2%
Industry
Printing and publishing, machinery, computer products, finance, tourism
Agriculture
Dairy products, cattle and other live-stock, vegetables, nursery stock, apples
Statehood
July 26, 1788; 11th state

GEO WHIZ
Each year at Halloween the Headless Horseman rides again through the countryside of Sleepy Hollow as residents respect Washington Irving's *The Legend of Sleepy Hollow.*

The Erie Canal, built in the 1820s between Albany and Buffalo, helped New York City become a worldwide trading center and opened the Midwest to development by linking the Hudson River and the Great Lakes.

Cooperstown, New York, home of the National Baseball Hall of Fame, takes its name from a town established in the late 1700s by the father of James Fenimore Cooper, author of such American classics as *The Last of the Mohicans* and *The Deerslayer.*

EASTERN
BLUEBIRD

ROSE

NEW YORK

When Englishman Henry Hudson explored New York's Hudson River Valley in 1609, the territory was already inhabited by large tribes of Native Americans, including the powerful Iroquois. In 1624 a Dutch trading company established the New Netherland colony, but after just 40 years the colony was taken over by the English and renamed for England's Duke of York. In 1788 New York became the 11th state. The state can be divided into two parts. The powerful port city of New York, center of trade and commerce and gate-way to immigrants, is the largest city in the U.S. Its metropolitan area has more than 18 million people. Everything north of the city is simply referred to as "Upstate." Cities such as Buffalo and Rochester are industrial centers, while Ithaca and Syracuse boast major universities. Agriculture is also important in New York. With almost 5 million acres in cropland, the state is a major producer of dairy products, fruits, and vegetables.

⬆ LADY LIBERTY. Standing in New York Harbor, the Statue of Liberty, a gift from the people of France, is a symbol of freedom and democracy.

◁ NATURAL WONDER. As many as 12 million tourists annually visit Niagara Falls on the U.S.-Canada border. Visitors in rain slickers trek through the mists below Bridal Veil Falls on the American side.

URBAN GIANT
Figures are based on 2006 census projections and are for population within city limits.

8,214,426
3,849,378
2,833,321
2,144,491
1,512,986

New York · Los Angeles · Chicago · Houston · Philadelphia

With more than twice the population of the next largest city, New York—known as the Big Apple—is the country's largest city.

ABOUT THE WEST

The West
THE HIGH FRONTIER

The western states, which make up almost half of the country's land area, have diverse landscapes and climates, ranging from the frozen heights of Denali, in Alaska, to the desolation of Death Valley, in California, and the lush, tropical islands of Hawai'i. More than half the region's population lives in California, and the Los Angeles metropolitan area is second only to New York City. Yet many parts of the region are sparsely populated, and much of the land is set aside as parkland and military bases. The region also faces many natural hazards—earthquakes, landslides, wildfires, and even volcanic eruptions.

WHERE THE PICTURES ARE

WHERE ARE THE PICTURES?
If you want to know where a picture in any of the regional sections in the atlas was taken, check the map in the regional photo essay. Find the label that describes the photograph you are curious about, and follow the line to its location.

CHARTS AND GRAPHS
The photo essay for each state includes a chart or graph that highlights economic, physical, cultural, or some other type of information related to the state.

BAR SCALE
Each map has a bar scale in miles and kilometers to help you find out how far it is from one place to another on the map.

"YOU ARE HERE"
Locator maps show you where each region and state within the region is in relation to the rest of the United States. Regions are shown in the regional color; featured states are in yellow.

MAP ICONS

Maps use symbols to stand for many physical, political, and economic features. Below is a complete list of the map symbols used in this atlas. In addition, each state map has its own key featuring symbols for major economic activities. Additional abbreviations used in this atlas as well as metric conversion tables are listed on the endsheets at the back of the book.

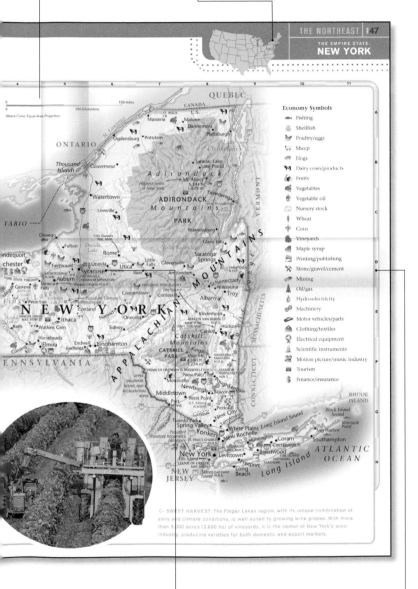

THE NORTHEAST | 47
THE EMPIRE STATE: NEW YORK

SWEET HARVEST. The Finger Lakes region, with its unique combination of soils and climate conditions, is well suited to growing wine grapes. With more than 9,000 acres (3,600 ha) of vineyards, it is the center of New York's wine industry, producing varieties for both domestic and export markets.

- •Aspen ....town of under 25,000 residents
- •Frankfort ....town of 25,000 to 99,999
- •San Jose ....city of 100,000 to 999,999
- •New York .....city of 1,000,000 and over
- ⊛ National capital
- ★ State capital
- ▪ Point of interest
- + Mountain peak with elevation above sea level
- • Low point with elevation below sea level
- —— River
- – – – Intermittent river
- ⊥⊥⊥ Canal
- ——— Interstate or selected other highway
- - - - - Trail
- ••••••• State or national boundary
- •••••••• Continental divide
- Lake and dam
- Intermittent lake
- Dry lake
- Swamp
- Glacier
- National Wild & Scenic River, N.W.&S.R.

- Sand
- Lava
- Area below sea level
- Indian Reservation, I.R.
- State Park, S.P.
  - State Historical Park, S.H.P.
  - State Historic Site, S.H.S.
- National Battlefield, N.B.
  - National Battlefield Park, N.B.P.
  - National Battlefield Site, N.B.S.
  - National Historic Site, N.H.S.
  - National Historical Area, N.H.A.
  - National Historical Park, N.H.P.
  - National Lakeshore
  - National Military Park, N.M.P.
  - National Memorial, NAT. MEM.
  - National Monument, NAT. MON.
  - National Park, N.P.
  - National Parkway
  - National Preserve
  - National Recreation Area, N.R.A.
  - National River
  - National Riverway
  - National Scenic Area
  - National Seashore
  - National Volcanic Monument
- National Forest, N.F.
- National Grassland, N.G.
- National Wildlife Refuge, N.W.R.

Economy Symbols

Fishing	Stone/gravel/cement	
Lobster fishing	Mining	
Shellfish	Coal	
Poultry/eggs	Oil/gas	
Sheep	Hydro-electricity	
Hogs	Machinery	
Dairy cows/products	Metal manufacturing	
Beef cattle	Metal products	
Fruits	Shipbuilding	
Vegetables	Railroad equipment	
Vegetable oil	Motor vehicles/parts	
Peanuts	Rubber/plastics	
Nursery stock	Chemistry	
Wheat	Food processing	
Corn	Clothing/textiles	
Rice	Leather products	
Soybeans	Glass/clay products	
Sugarcane	Jewelry	
Cotton	Electrical equipment	
Tobacco	Computers/electronics	
Coffee	Scientific instruments	
Vineyards	Aircraft/parts	
Maple syrup	Aerospace	
Timber/forest products	Motion picture/music industry	
Furniture	Tourism	
Printing/publishing	Finance/insurance	

INDEX AND GRID
A grid system makes it easy to find places listed in the index. For example, the listing for Syracuse, New York, is followed by **47** D5. The bold type is the page number; D5 tells you the city is near the point where imaginary lines drawn from D and 5 on the grid bars meet.

HOW TO USE THE ATLAS WEB SITE

As you can see by flipping through the pages, this atlas is chock full. There are photographs, statistics, quick facts, and—most of all—lots of charts and detailed maps. Plus there is a companion Web site that adds even more. You can watch videos of animals in their natural surroundings or of a volcano erupting; listen to the sounds of people, places, and animals; find lots of state information; download pictures and maps for school reports; and play games that allow you to explore the United States. You can even send e-postcards to your friends. The

Web site provides added value to specific subjects in the atlas and also helps you explore on your own, taking you deep into the resources of National Geographic and beyond. Throughout the atlas you will find these icons.

PHOTOS

VIDEO

AUDIO

GAMES

INFO

The icons are placed near pictures, on maps, or next to text. Each icon tells you that you can find more on that subject on the Web site. To follow any icon link, go to www.nationalgeographic.com/kids-usa-atlas.

⇨ **START HERE.**

There are three ways to find what you are looking for from the Home Page:

1. BY ATLAS PAGE NUMBER
2. BY TOPIC
3. BY ICON

NATIONAL GEOGRAPHIC © 1996–2008 National Geographic Society. All rights reserved.
Kids Home | Animals | Games | Stories | Activities | Videos | My Page
GeoBee Challenge | NG Explorer Classroom Magazine | NG Kids TV | NG Little Kids
Parents, Students, and Educators: Kids Atlases Shopping | NGS Books
nationalgeographic.com | Kids Privacy Policy | Contact Us | Magazine Media Kit | Customer Service | Subscriptions | Education Guide | Email Newsletters | Shopping

www.nationalgeographic.com/kids-usa-atlas

1. SEARCH BY ATLAS PAGE NUMBER

⇐ **PAGE NUMBER PULL-DOWN MENU.** If you find an icon in the atlas and want to go directly to that link, use the page number pull-down menu. Just drag and click.

2. SEARCH BY TOPIC

⇒ **LIST OF TOPICS.** If you want to explore a specific topic, click on the entry in the topic list. This list is your portal to vast quantities of National Geographic information, photos, videos, games, and more, all arranged by subject. Say you're interested in Animals. One click takes you to the Animals choice page (below).

⇓ **CREATURE FEATURES.** Click to go to the National Geographic Kids' animal site. Click on an animal, and you will find a full feature about it, including photos, video, a range map, and other fun info.

⇐ **ANIMALS A–Z.** This choice takes you to the animal site for adults and older kids. Use the list of animals in the upper right-hand corner of the page. Clicking on an animal name takes you to the profile of that animal.

⇓ **CRITTERCAM.** Scientists put video cameras on animals to learn about the animal from its point of view. Click to see those videos, learn about the project, play games such as exploring the virtual world of a seal, and more.

3. SEARCH BY ICON

⇐ **SELECT ONE OF FIVE ICONS.** If you want to find all the videos referenced in the atlas, or all of the audios, photos, or games, click on one of the icons. A list will drop down. Choose from the list, and you're there! Clicking on Blackbeard takes you to a trailer for a National Geographic Channel film.

THE PHYSICAL UNITED STATES

Stretching from the Atlantic in the east to the Pacific in the west, the United States is the third largest country in area in the world. Its physical diversity ranges from mountains to fertile plains and dry deserts. Shading on the map indicates changes in elevation, while colors suggest different vegetation patterns.

⇨ ALASKA AND HAWAI'I. In addition to the states located on the main landmass, the U.S. has two states—Alaska and Hawai'i—that are not directly connected to the other 48 states. If Alaska and Hawai'i were shown in their correct relative sizes and locations, the map would not fit on the page. The locator globe shows the correct relative size and location of each.

San Francisco

Coast Ranges   Sierra Nevada   Great Basin   Rocky Mountains

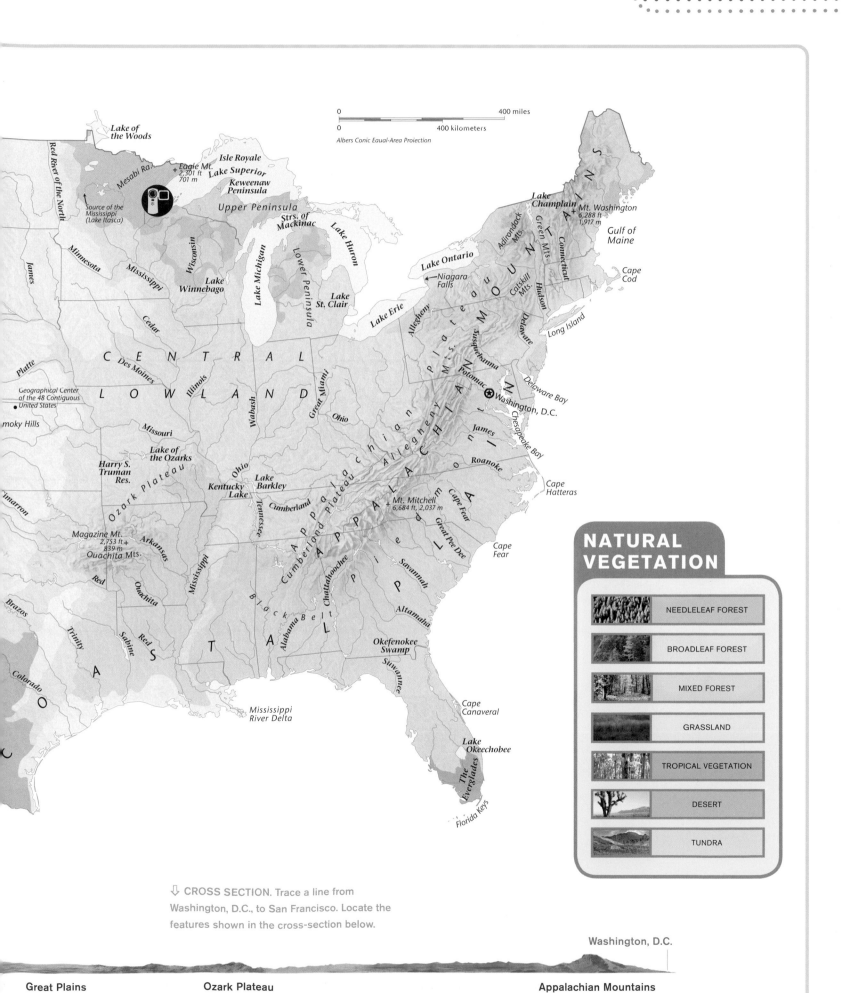

0   400 miles

0   400 kilometers

Albers Conic Equal-Area Projection

Lake of the Woods

Red River of the North

Isle Royale

Eagle Mt. + 2,301 ft 701 m

Mesabi Ra.

Lake Superior

Keweenaw Peninsula

Source of the Mississippi (Lake Itasca)

Upper Peninsula

Strs. of Mackinac

Lake Huron

Minnesota

James

Wisconsin

Mississippi

Lake Winnebago

Lake Michigan

Lower Peninsula

Lake St. Clair

Adirondack Mts.

Lake Champlain

Green Mts.

Connecticut

Mt. Washington + 6,288 ft 1,917 m

Gulf of Maine

Cape Cod

Catskill Mts.

Hudson

Lake Ontario

Niagara Falls

Long Island

Allegheny

Platte

Cedar

Des Moines

Illinois

C E N T R A L

Wabash

Great Miami

Ohio

Allegheny Mts.

Plateau

Susquehanna

Delaware

Delaware Bay

moky Hills

Geographical Center of the 48 Contiguous United States

L O W L A N D

Missouri

Lake of the Ozarks

Harry S. Truman Res.

Ozark Plateau

Kentucky Lake

Lake Barkley

Ohio

Tennessee

Cumberland

Appalachian Plateau

Cumberland Plateau

Potomac

Washington, D.C.

Chesapeake Bay

James

Roanoke

A P P A L A C H I A N

M O U N T A I N

Cape Hatteras

imarron

Magazine Mt. 2,753 ft + 839 m

Ouachita Mts.

Arkansas

Mississippi

Red

Ouachita

Mt. Mitchell + 6,684 ft, 2,037 m

Black

Chattahoochee

Cape Fear

Great Pee Dee

Savannah

P

i

e

d

m

o

n

t

Cape Fear

Brazos

Trinity

Sabine

Red

C O A S T A L

Alabama Belt

Altamaha

Suwannee

Okefenokee Swamp

P L A I N

Colorado

Mississippi River Delta

Cape Canaveral

Lake Okeechobee

The Everglades

Florida Keys

NATURAL VEGETATION

	NEEDLELEAF FOREST
	BROADLEAF FOREST
	MIXED FOREST
	GRASSLAND
	TROPICAL VEGETATION
	DESERT
	TUNDRA

⇩ CROSS SECTION. Trace a line from Washington, D.C., to San Francisco. Locate the features shown in the cross-section below.

Washington, D.C.

Great Plains   Ozark Plateau   Appalachian Mountains

NATURAL ENVIRONMENT

A big part of the natural environment of the United States is the climate. With humid areas near the coasts, dry interior regions far from any major water body, and land areas that extend from northern Alaska to southern Florida and Hawai'i, the country experiences great variation in climate. Location is the key. Distance from the Equator, nearness to water, wind patterns, temperature of nearby water bodies, and elevation are things that influence temperature and precipitation. Climate affects the types of vegetation that grow in a particular place and plays a part in soil formation.

CHANGING CLIMATE

Summer Arctic Sea Ice Boundary in 1979

Scientists are concerned that a recent warming trend may be more than a natural cycle and that human activity may be a contributing factor. An increase in average temperatures could result in more severe storms, changes in precipitation patterns, and the spread of deserts. Rising temperatures may also play a part in the melting of glaciers, which could lead to a rise in ocean levels and the shrinking of the Arctic ice cover. NASA satellite images indicate that Arctic ice is shrinking as much as 9 percent each decade. Many believe that this puts polar bears at risk, since they normally hunt and raise their young on ice floes.

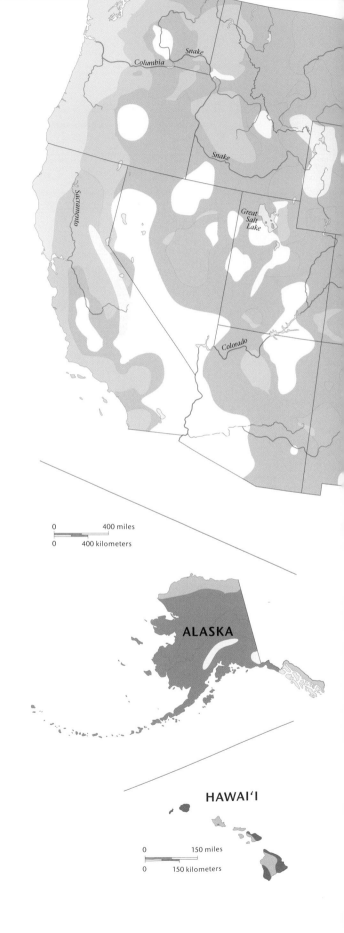

0 — 400 miles
0 — 400 kilometers

ALASKA

HAWAI'I

0 — 150 miles
0 — 150 kilometers

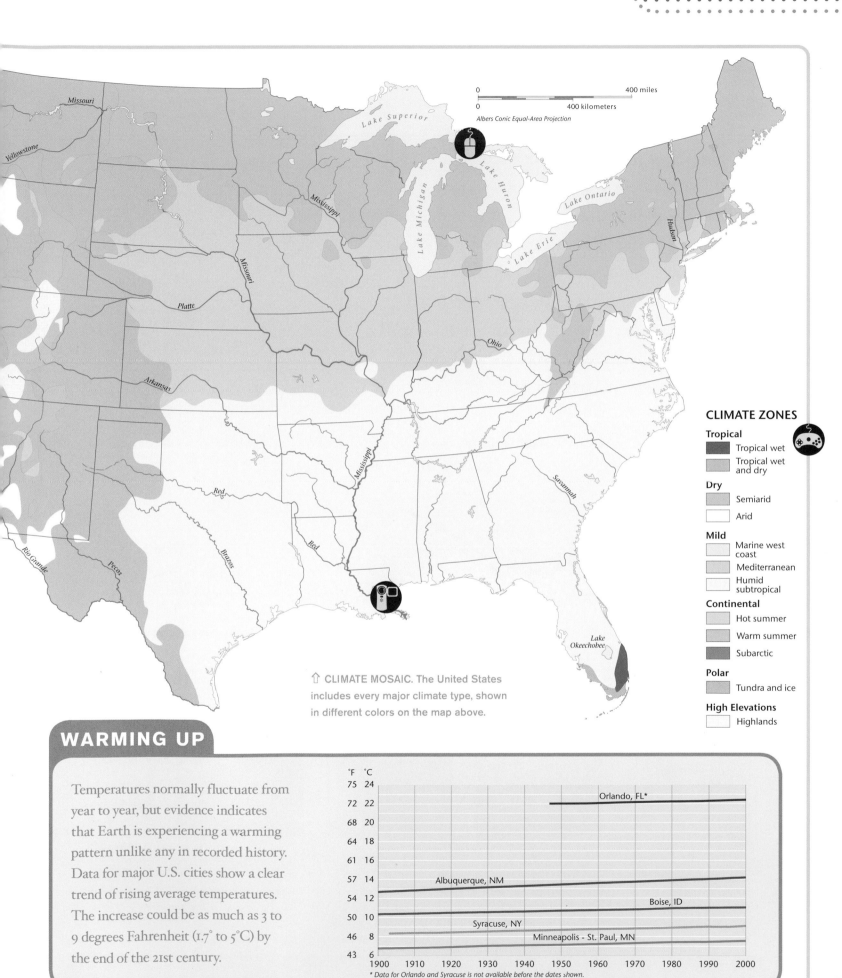

⇧ CLIMATE MOSAIC. The United States includes every major climate type, shown in different colors on the map above.

CLIMATE ZONES

Tropical
Tropical wet
Tropical wet and dry

Dry
Semiarid
Arid

Mild
Marine west coast
Mediterranean
Humid subtropical

Continental
Hot summer
Warm summer
Subarctic

Polar
Tundra and ice

High Elevations
Highlands

WARMING UP

Temperatures normally fluctuate from year to year, but evidence indicates that Earth is experiencing a warming pattern unlike any in recorded history. Data for major U.S. cities show a clear trend of rising average temperatures. The increase could be as much as 3 to 9 degrees Fahrenheit (1.7° to 5°C) by the end of the 21st century.

Orlando, FL*

Albuquerque, NM

Boise, ID

Syracuse, NY

Minneapolis - St. Paul, MN

°F	°C
75	24
72	22
68	20
64	18
61	16
57	14
54	12
50	10
46	8
43	6

1900 1910 1920 1930 1940 1950 1960 1970 1980 1990 2000

* Data for Orlando and Syracuse is not available before the dates shown.

NATURAL
HAZARDS

NATURAL HAZARDS

The natural environment of the United States provides much diversity, but it also poses many dangers, especially when people locate homes and businesses in places at risk of natural disasters. Tornadoes bring destructive winds, and hurricanes bring strong winds, rain, and more; shifting of Earth's crust along fault lines rattles buildings; flood waters and wildfires threaten lives and property. More than one-third of the U.S. population lives in hazard-prone areas. Compare this natural disasters map to the population map on pages 18–19.

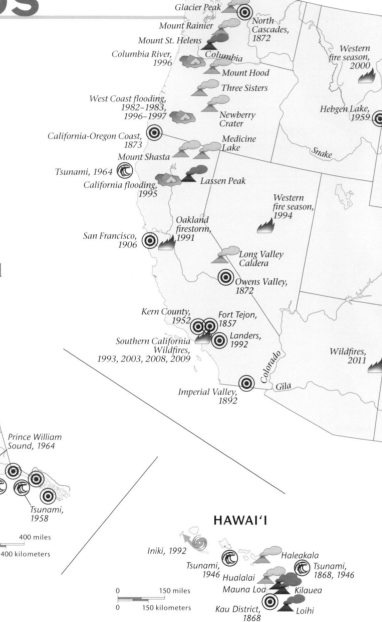

Mount Baker
Glacier Peak
Mount Rainier
North Cascades, 1872
Mount St. Helens
Columbia River, 1996
Columbia
Western fire season, 2000
Mount Hood
Three Sisters
West Coast flooding, 1982–1983, 1996–1997
Newberry Crater
Hebgen Lake, 1959
California-Oregon Coast, 1873
Medicine Lake
Snake
Mount Shasta
Tsunami, 1964
California flooding, 1995
Lassen Peak
Western fire season, 1994
Oakland firestorm, 1991
San Francisco, 1906
Long Valley Caldera
Owens Valley, 1872
Kern County, 1952
Fort Tejon, 1857
Landers, 1992
Southern California Wildfires, 1993, 2003, 2008, 2009
Wildfires, 2011
Imperial Valley, 1892
Colorado
Gila

ALASKA

Alaska has about 80 major volcanic centers.

More earthquakes occur in Alaska than in the other 49 states combined.

Prince William Sound, 1964

Novarupta, 1912
Tsunami, 1964
Tsunami, 1958
Tsunami, 1946, 1957

0   400 miles
0   400 kilometers

HAWAI'I

Iniki, 1992
Haleakala
Tsunami, 1946
Tsunami, 1868, 1946
Hualalai
Mauna Loa
Kilauea
Kau District, 1868
Loihi

0   150 miles
0   150 kilometers

NATURAL HAZARDS

BLIZZARD. Severe storm with bitter cold temperatures and wind-whipped snow and ice particles that reduce visibility to less than 650 feet (198 m), paralyzing transportation systems

FLOOD. Inundation of buildings or roadways caused by overflow of a river or stream swollen by heavy rainfall or rapid snowmelt; may involve displacement of people

DROUGHT. Long and continuous period of abnormally low precipitation, resulting in water shortages that negatively impact people, animals, and plant life; may result in crop loss

HURRICANE. Tropical storm in the Atlantic, Caribbean, Gulf of Mexico, or eastern Pacific with a minimum sustained wind speed of 74 miles per hour (119 kmph)

ICE STORM. Damaging accumulations of ice associated with freezing rain; may pull down trees or utility lines, causing extensive damage and creating dangerous travel conditions

NATURAL HAZARDS

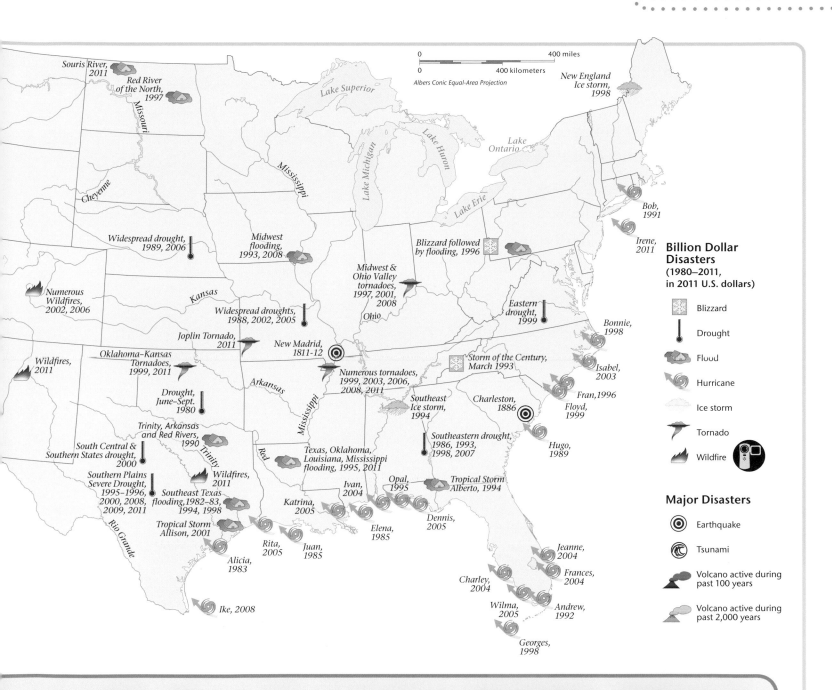

Souris River, 2011

Red River of the North, 1997

Missouri

New England Ice storm, 1998

Lake Superior

Lake Michigan

Lake Huron

Lake Ontario

Lake Erie

Bob, 1991

Irene, 2011

Cheyenne

Widespread drought, 1989, 2006

Midwest flooding, 1993, 2008

Blizzard followed by flooding, 1996

Numerous Wildfires, 2002, 2006

Kansas

Midwest & Ohio Valley tornadoes, 1997, 2001, 2008

Ohio

Eastern drought, 1999

Bonnie, 1998

Widespread droughts, 1988, 2002, 2005

Joplin Tornado, 2011

New Madrid, 1811-12

Storm of the Century, March 1993

Isabel, 2003

Wildfires, 2011

Oklahoma–Kansas Tornadoes, 1999, 2011

Arkansas

Numerous tornadoes, 1999, 2003, 2006, 2008, 2011

Fran, 1996

Floyd, 1999

Drought, June–Sept. 1980

Mississippi

Southeast Ice storm, 1994

Charleston, 1886

Charleston, 1886

Hugo, 1989

Trinity, Arkansas and Red Rivers, 1990

Red

Texas, Oklahoma, Louisiana, Mississippi flooding, 1995, 2011

Southeastern drought, 1986, 1993, 1998, 2007

South Central & Southern States drought, 2000

Trinity

Southern Plains Severe Drought, 1995–1996, 2000, 2008, 2009, 2011

Southeast Texas flooding, 1982–83, 1994, 1998

Wildfires, 2011

Opal, 1995

Tropical Storm Alberto, 1994

Ivan, 2004

Tropical Storm Allison, 2001

Rio Grande

Katrina, 2005

Elena, 1985

Dennis, 2005

Rita, 2005

Juan, 1985

Alicia, 1983

Jeanne, 2004

Frances, 2004

Charley, 2004

Ike, 2008

Wilma, 2005

Andrew, 1992

Georges, 1998

Scale: 0 — 400 miles / 0 — 400 kilometers
Albers Conic Equal-Area Projection

Billion Dollar Disasters
(1980–2011, in 2011 U.S. dollars)

- Blizzard
- Drought
- Flood
- Hurricane
- Ice storm
- Tornado
- Wildfire

Major Disasters

- Earthquake
- Tsunami
- Volcano active during past 100 years
- Volcano active during past 2,000 years

TORNADO. Violently rotating column of air that, when it reaches the ground, is the most damaging of all atmospheric phenomena; most common in the central U.S.

WILDFIRE. Free-burning, uncontained fire in a forest or grassland; may result from lightning strikes or accidental or deliberate human activity in areas where conditions are dry

EARTHQUAKE. Shaking or vibration created by the energy released by movement of Earth's crust along plate boundaries; can cause structural damage and loss of life

TSUNAMI. Series of unusually large ocean waves caused by an underwater earthquake, landslide, or volcanic eruption; very destructive in coastal areas

VOLCANO. Vent or opening in Earth's surface through which molten rock called lava, ash, and gases are released; often associated with tectonic plate boundaries

THE POLITICAL UNITED STATES

Like a giant patchwork quilt, the United States is made up of 50 states, each uniquely different but together making a national fabric held together by a Constitution and a federal government. State boundaries, outlined in various colors on the map, set apart internal political units within the country. The national capital—Washington, D.C.—is marked by a star in a double circle on the map. The capital of each state is marked by a star in a single circle.

⇧ TIME ZONES. Earth is divided into 24 time zones, each about 15 degrees of longitude wide, reflecting the distance Earth turns from west to east each hour. The U.S. is divided into six time zones, indicated by red dotted lines on the maps. When it is noon in Boston, what is the time in Seattle?

11:00 AM | **12:00 PM**
CENTRAL TIME | EASTERN TIME

0 ——————— 300 miles
0 ——————— 300 kilometers
Albers Conic Equal-Area Projection

Minot
Grand Forks
International Falls
Lake of the Woods
Isle Royale
Lake Superior
MAINE
Bangor
NORTH DAKOTA
Bismarck Fargo
Duluth
Superior
Marquette
MICHIGAN
Burlington
VT.
Augusta
Aberdeen
MINNESOTA
N.H.
Portland
Lake Champlain
Montpelier
Concord
SOUTH DAKOTA
Pierre
WISCONSIN
Green Bay
Lake Michigan
Grand Rapids
Lansing
Lake Ontario
Rochester
Syracuse Albany
Hartford
MASS.
Boston
Cape Cod
Providence
Rapid City
Minneapolis
St. Paul
Madison
Milwaukee
Detroit
Lake Erie
Erie
Buffalo
NEW YORK
CONN. RHODE ISLAND
Long Island
Sioux Falls
Mississippi
Missouri
IOWA
Cedar Rapids
Rockford
Chicago
Gary
Fort Wayne
Toledo Cleveland
Newark
New York
Trenton
NEBRASKA
Omaha
Des Moines
Davenport
Peoria
OHIO
Columbus
PENNSYLVANIA
Pittsburgh
Harrisburg
NEW JERSEY
Philadelphia
Grand Island
Platte
Lincoln
ILLINOIS
INDIANA
Indianapolis
Dayton
Cincinnati
Baltimore
Dover
DELAWARE
S. Platte
Springfield
WEST VIRGINIA
Washington D.C.
Annapolis
MARYLAND
Chesapeake Bay
Kansas City
Jefferson City
St. Louis
Louisville
Frankfort
Lexington
Charleston
Richmond
Topeka
Ohio
Evansville
Roanoke
Norfolk
Virginia Beach
KANSAS
Wichita
MISSOURI
Springfield
KENTUCKY
Greensboro
VIRGINIA
Dodge City
Arkansas
Paducah
Knoxville
Raleigh
Cape Hatteras
Tulsa
Nashville
NORTH CAROLINA
Charlotte
OKLAHOMA
Oklahoma City
Fort Smith
Memphis
Chattanooga
Greenville
Amarillo
ARKANSAS
Little Rock
Huntsville
Columbia
SOUTH CAROLINA
Lawton
Red
Wichita Falls
Birmingham
Atlanta
Charleston
Lubbock
Fort Worth
Shreveport
Jackson
MISSISSIPPI
ALABAMA
Montgomery
GEORGIA
Macon
Columbus
Savannah
Midland
Abilene
Dallas
Brazos
Waco
LOUISIANA
Red
Natchez
Jacksonville
Odessa
TEXAS
Austin
Beaumont
Lafayette
Baton Rouge
Mobile
Biloxi
Mobile Bay
Tallahassee
FLORIDA
Gainesville
Orlando
Cape Canaveral
Houston
San Antonio
New Orleans
Mississippi River Delta
Apalachee Bay
Tampa
St. Petersburg
Lake Okeechobee
Laredo
Corpus Christi
Rio Grande
Fort Lauderdale
The Everglades
Miami
Brownsville
Florida Keys

Red River basin ceded by Great Britain, 1818
Ceded by Great Britain, 1842
Ceded by Great Britain, 1842
Oregon Country ceded by Great Britain, 1846
Louisiana Purchase from France, 1803
United States, 1783
Ceded by Mexico, 1848
Western boundary of original 13 colonies, 1775
Texas annexed by U.S., 1845
Alaska purchased from Russia, 1867
Gadsden Purchase from Mexico, 1853
Florida ceded by Spain, 1819
Hawai'i annexed in 1898

⟵ **WESTWARD EXPANSION.** The United States had its origins in 13 British colonies established along the Atlantic coast. After gaining independence in 1783, the young country began adding new territories—some by treaty, others by purchase or by war. The map traces the country's expansion and shows the date each territory was acquired.

POPULATION

More than 312 million and growing! The population of the United States topped the 300 million mark in 2006, and it continues to grow by more than 600,000 people each year. Before the arrival of European settlers, the population consisted of Native Americans living in tribal groups scattered across the country. In the 16th and 17th centuries, Europeans, some with slaves from Africa, settled first along the eastern seaboard and later moved westward. In 1790 the U.S. population was not quite 4 million people. Today, New York City alone has a population more than double that number. The country's population is unevenly distributed. The map shows the number of people per square mile for each county in every state. Greatest densities are in the East and along the West Coast, especially around major cities. The most rapid growth is occurring in the South and the West—an area referred to as the Sunbelt—as well as in suburban areas around cities.

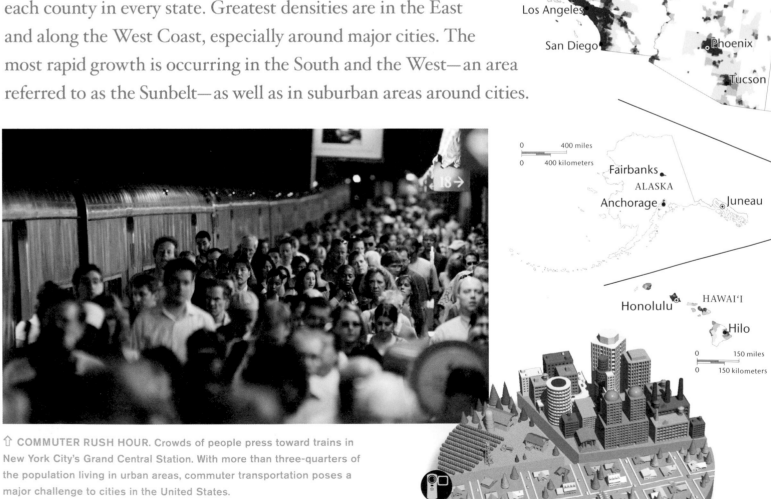

⇧ COMMUTER RUSH HOUR. Crowds of people press toward trains in New York City's Grand Central Station. With more than three-quarters of the population living in urban areas, commuter transportation poses a major challenge to cities in the United States.

⇨ WHERE WE LIVE. The first U.S. census in 1790 revealed that only 5 percent of people lived in towns. As industry has grown and agriculture has become increasingly mechanized, people have left farms (green), moving to urban places (blue) and their surrounding suburbs (orange).

0 | 400 miles
0 | 400 kilometers
Albers Conic Equal-Area Projection

Population Density
(Number of people
per square mile)

Less than 10
10–24
25–49
50–99
100–249
250 or more

⊛ National capital
⊙ State capital

HOW OLD ARE WE?

Population pyramids show the distribution of population by sex and age groups, called cohorts. In 1960 the largest cohorts, born after World War II and known as Baby Boomers, were under 15 years of age. By 2000 Baby Boomers had become middle-age. By 2040 they will reach the top of the pyramid.

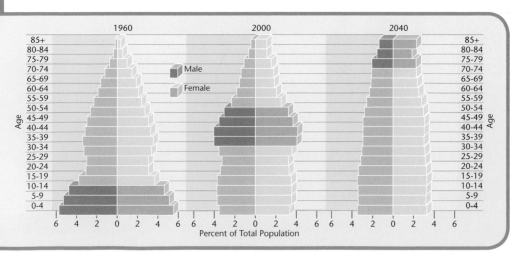

Percent of Total Population

PEOPLE ON THE MOVE

From earliest human history, the land of the United States has been a focus of migration. Native peoples arrived thousands of years ago. The first European settlers came in the 16th and 17th centuries, and slave ships brought people from Africa. Today, people are still on the move. Since the mid-20th century, most international migrants have come from Latin America—especially Mexico and countries of Central America and the Caribbean—and Asia, particularly China, the Philippines, and India. While most of the population is still of European descent, certain regions have large minority concentrations, as shown on the map, that influence local cultural landscapes.

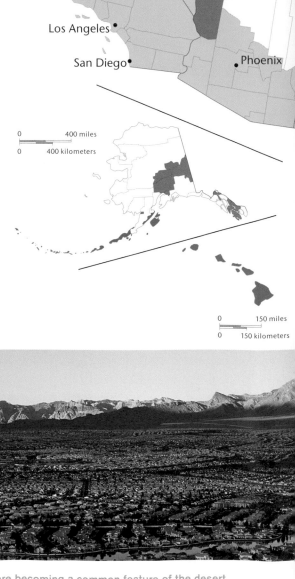

⇧ BRIDGE OF HOPE. Many Mexicans enter the U.S. (foreground) by bridges across the Rio Grande, such as this one between Nuevo Laredo, Mexico, and Laredo, Texas.

⇧ IMMIGRANT INFLUENCE. With Hispanics making up over 16 percent of the population, signs in Spanish are popping up everywhere—even at voting areas.

⇧ SUNBELT SPRAWL. Spreading suburbs are becoming a common feature of the desert Southwest as people flock to the Sunbelt.

PEOPLE ON THE MOVE

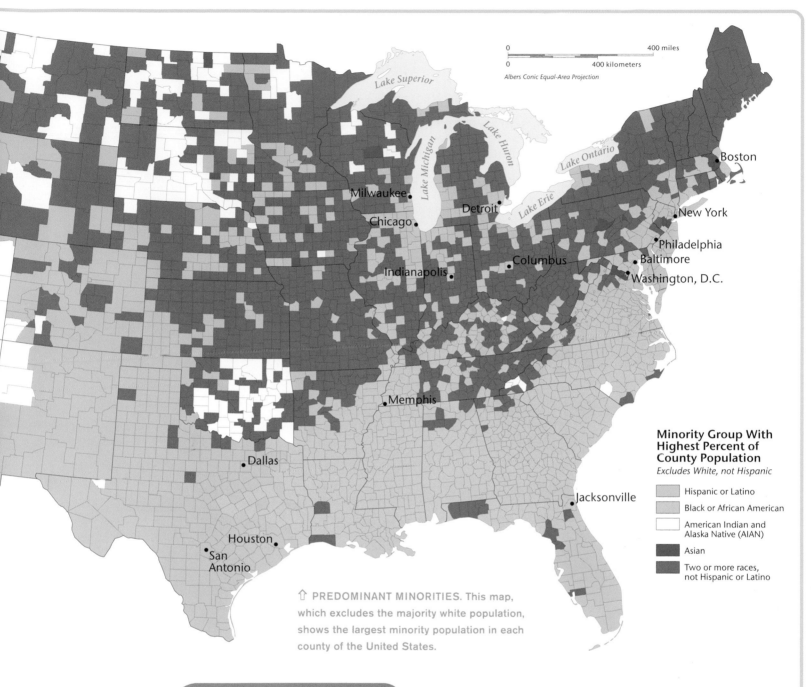

Lake Superior

Lake Michigan

Lake Huron

Lake Ontario

Lake Erie

Boston

Milwaukee

Detroit

New York

Chicago

Philadelphia

Columbus

Baltimore

Indianapolis

Washington, D.C.

Memphis

Minority Group With Highest Percent of County Population
Excludes White, not Hispanic

Dallas

Hispanic or Latino

Jacksonville

Black or African American

American Indian and Alaska Native (AIAN)

Houston

Asian

San Antonio

Two or more races, not Hispanic or Latino

⇧ PREDOMINANT MINORITIES. This map, which excludes the majority white population, shows the largest minority population in each county of the United States.

POPULATION SHIFT

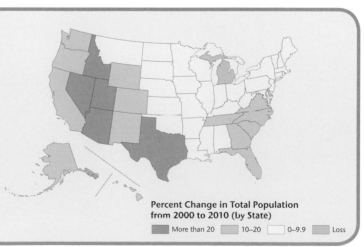

In the last half century, people have begun moving from the historical industrial and agricultural regions of the Northeast and Midwest toward the South and West, attracted by the promise of jobs, generally lower living costs, and a more relaxed way of life. This trend can be seen in the population growth patterns shown in the map at right.

Percent Change in Total Population from 2000 to 2010 (by State)

More than 20   10–20   0–9.9   Loss

GETTING GREEN

Every day the media are filled with stories about global warming, pollution, and dwindling resources. Headlines warn of environmental risks that may threaten our way of life. The United States is the source of a quarter of the world's greenhouse gas emissions, and Americans generate more than 250 million tons of trash each year. The average American also uses 32 times more resources than a person in the African country of Kenya. But there's a bright side to these grim statistics: We can make a positive difference to the environment by making simple lifestyle changes. Scientists and engineers have developed energy-efficient appliances, cars that run on alternative fuels, and products made from recycled paper and plastics. But it is up to each of us to make changes that take advantage of these environment-friendly developments.

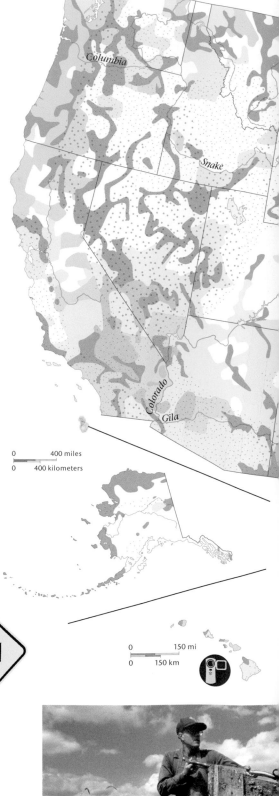

| 0 | 400 miles |
| 0 | 400 kilometers |

| 0 | 150 mi |
| 0 | 150 km |

THINGS YOU CAN DO

Each year the average American household generates more than 80 tons of carbon dioxide gases, uses 102,000 gallons (386,111 l) of water, and creates 3.3 tons of landfill waste. Improving the health of our environment begins with you. You can make a difference if you practice the 3 R's of "getting green."

- REDUCE resource consumption by turning off lights, the TV, computers, and other electronic devices when you leave the room. Close the faucet when you are not using the water. Avoid buying things you do not need.

- REUSE items whenever possible, rather than throwing things away. Consider whether a container can be used again or a pair of shoes repaired.

- RECYCLE paper, plastic, glass, and aluminum cans. Recycling makes for less landfill trash, plus it preserves resources by reusing old products to make new ones.

Visit the library or go online to learn what your community is doing to protect the environment.

Share the Road

⇧ GREEN STREETS. Biking to work or school reduces use of gasoline, a source of greenhouse gases, and it is healthy, too.

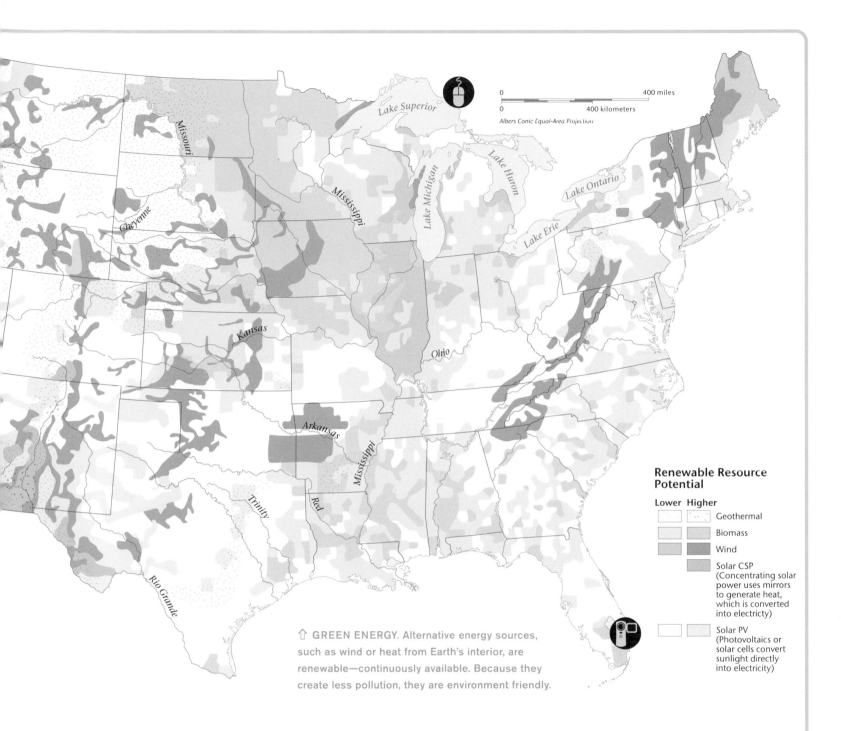

⇧ GREEN ENERGY. Alternative energy sources, such as wind or heat from Earth's interior, are renewable—continuously available. Because they create less pollution, they are environment friendly.

Renewable Resource Potential

Lower Higher

Geothermal

Biomass

Wind

Solar CSP (Concentrating solar power uses mirrors to generate heat, which is converted into electricty)

Solar PV (Photovoltaics or solar cells convert sunlight directly into electricity)

⇦ GREEN GARDENING. An organic farmer turns a compost pile with a pitchfork. Compost is a natural fertilizer made from decayed plant material. It is good for the environment because it reuses natural materials and avoids the use of chemicals that can pollute soil and water.

⇦ RECYCLE. Bright blue trash collectors overflow with plastic containers waiting to go to a recycling center. Citizen participation is an important step toward reducing landfill waste and restoring the health of the environment.

THE NATIONAL CAPITAL

THE BASICS

STATS

Area
68 sq mi (177 sq km)

Population
601,723

Ethnic/racial groups
50.7% African American; 38.5% white; 3.5% Asian; .3% Native American. Hispanic (any race) 9.1%

Industry
Government, services, tourism

Founded
1790–91

GEO WHIZ

License plates in the District of Columbia bear the slogan "Taxation Without Representation," reflecting the fact that residents of the District have no voting representative in either house of the U.S. Congress.

The flag of the District of Columbia, with its three red stars and two red stripes, is based on the shield in George Washington's family coat of arms.

In 1790 Benjamin Banneker, a free black, helped survey the land that would become the capital city. The 40 stones that were placed at one-mile intervals to mark the boundaries were set according to his celestial measurements.

WOOD THRUSH

AMERICAN BEAUTY ROSE

Chosen as a compromise location between Northern and Southern interests and built on land ceded by Virginia and Maryland in the late 1700s, Washington, D.C., sits on a bank of the Potomac River. It is the seat of U.S. government and symbol of the country's history. Pierre L'Enfant, a French architect, was appointed by President George Washington to design the city, which is distinguished by a grid pattern cut by diagonal avenues. At the city's core is the National Mall, a broad park lined by monuments, museums, and stately government buildings.

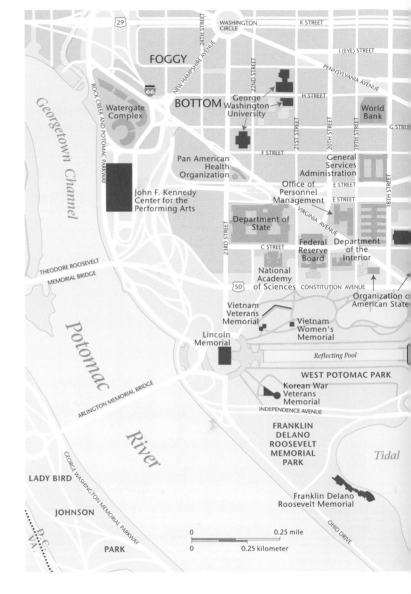

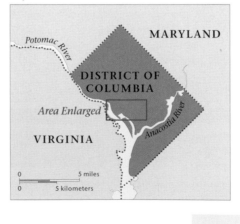

⇐ DISTRICT OF COLUMBIA. Originally on both sides of the Potomac River, the city returned land to Virginia in 1846.

⇐ GREAT LEADER. Abraham Lincoln, who was president during the Civil War and a strong opponent of slavery, is remembered in a monument that houses this seated statue at the west end of the National Mall.

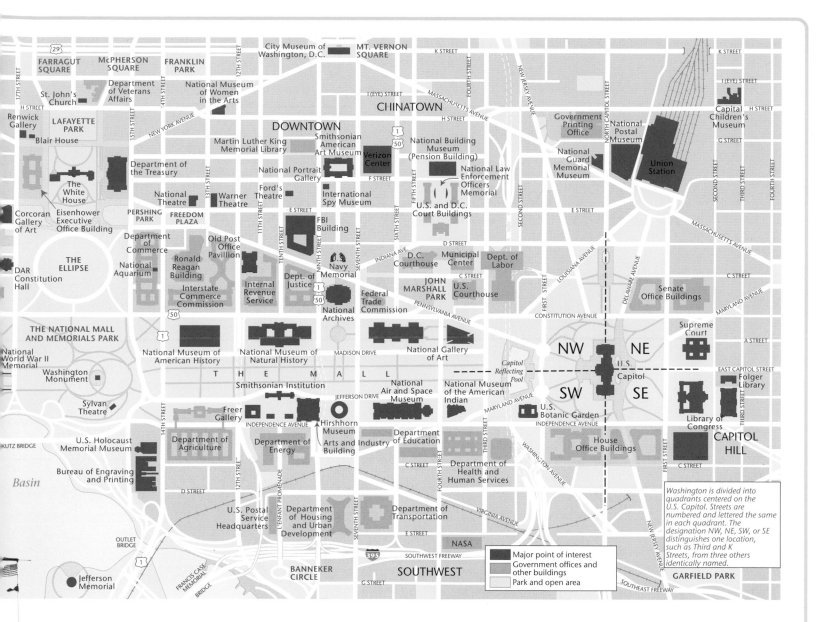

Washington is divided into quadrants centered on the U.S. Capitol. Streets are numbered and lettered the same in each quadrant. The designation NW, NE, SW, or SE distinguishes one location, such as Third and K Streets, from three others identically named.

Major point of interest
Government offices and other buildings
Park and open area

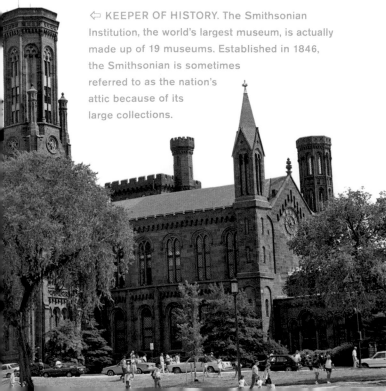

⇐ KEEPER OF HISTORY. The Smithsonian Institution, the world's largest museum, is actually made up of 19 museums. Established in 1846, the Smithsonian is sometimes referred to as the nation's attic because of its large collections.

⇑ NATIONAL ICON. The gleaming dome of the U.S. Capitol, home to the Senate and House of Representatives, is a familiar symbol of Washington's main business—the running of the country's government.

THE REGION

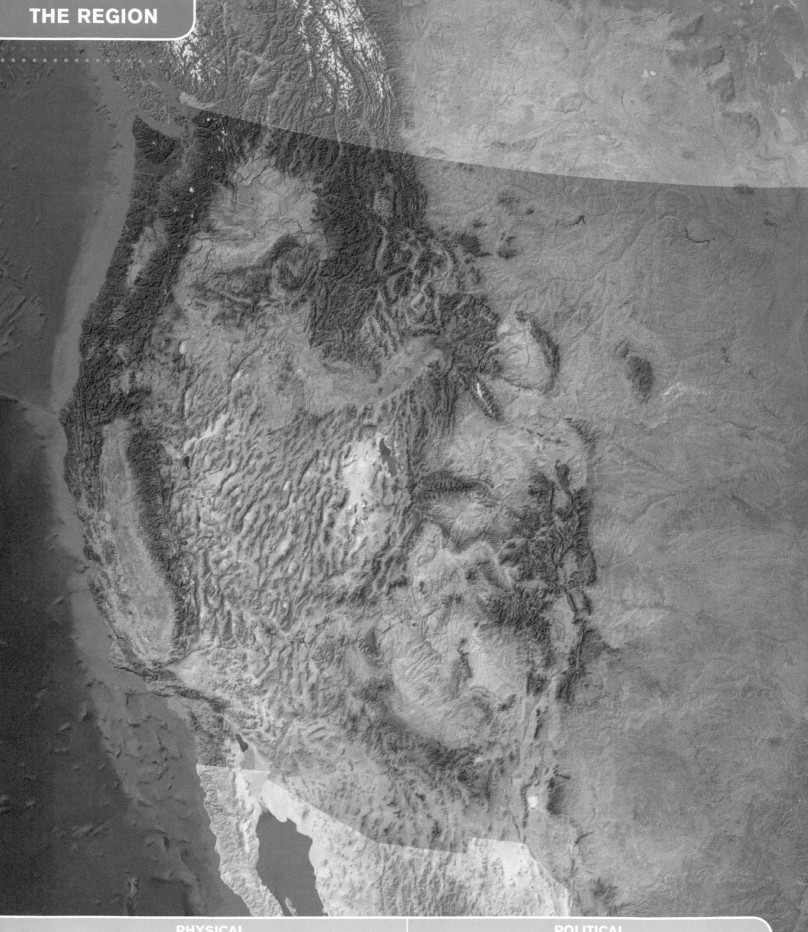

PHYSICAL

Total area
196,220 sq mi
(508,209 sq km)

Highest point
Mount Washington, NH
6,288 ft (1,917 m)

Lowest point
Sea level, shores of the
Atlantic Ocean

Longest rivers
St. Lawrence, Susquehanna,
Connecticut, Hudson

Largest lakes
Erie, Ontario, Champlain

Vegetation
Needleleaf, broadleaf, and
mixed forest

Climate
Continental to mild, with cool
to warm summers, cold winters,
and moderate precipitation
throughout the year

POLITICAL

Total population
61,988,726

States (11):
Connecticut, Delaware, Maine, Maryland,
Massachusetts, New Hampshire,
New Jersey, New York, Pennsylvania,
Rhode Island, Vermont

Largest state
New York: 54,556 sq mi (141,300 sq km)

Smallest state
Rhode Island: 1,545 sq mi (4,002 sq km)

Most populous state
New York: 19,378,102

Least populous state
Vermont: 625,741

Largest city proper
New York, NY: 8,175,133

The Northeast

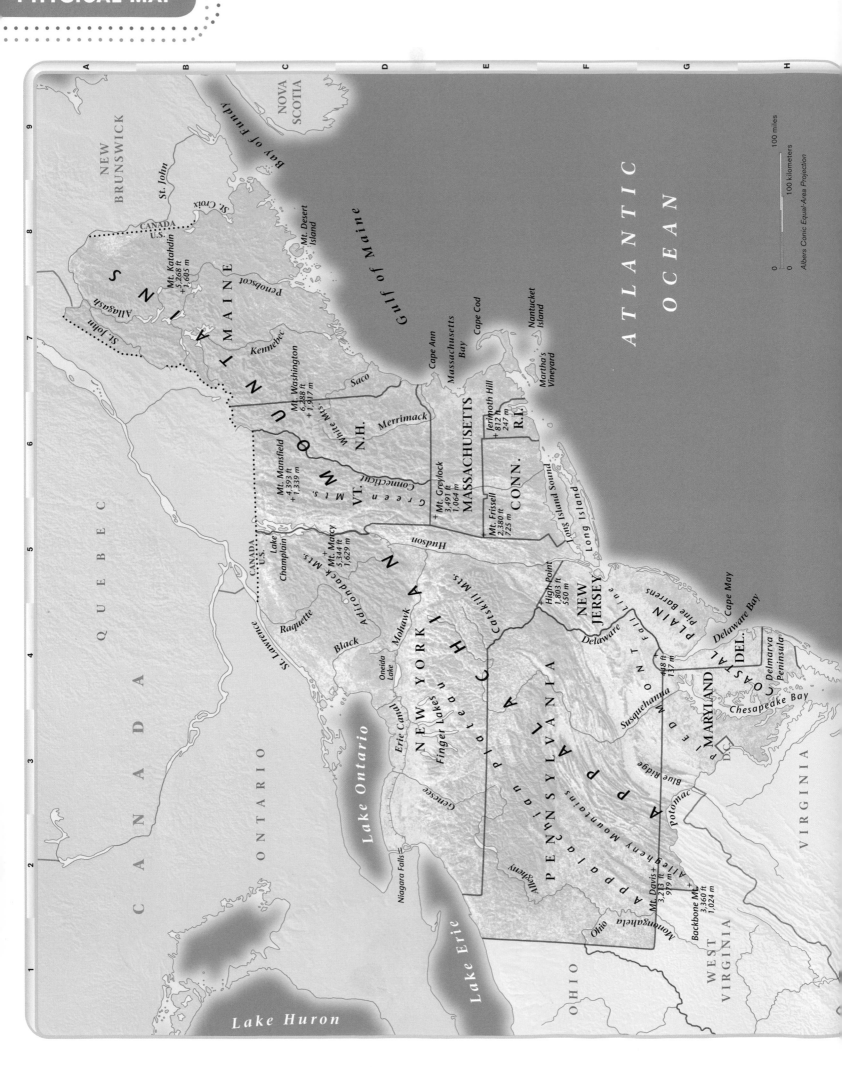

NEW BRUNSWICK

NOVA SCOTIA

QUEBEC

CANADA

St. John

St. Croix

Bay of Fundy

CANADA
U.S.

Mt. Katahdin
+5,268 ft
1,605 m

Allagash

St. John

M A I N E

Penobscot

Mt. Desert Island

Gulf of Maine

Kennebec

Saco

Mt. Washington
6,288 ft
1,917 m

White Mts.

N.H.

Merrimack

Cape Ann

Massachusetts Bay

Cape Cod

Nantucket Island

Martha's Vineyard

M O U N T A I N S

Green Mts.

Connecticut

Mt. Mansfield
4,393 ft
+1,339 m

VT.

Mt. Greylock
3,491 ft
1,064 m

MASSACHUSETTS

Jerimoth Hill
+812 ft
247 m

R.I.

CONN.

Mt. Frissell
2,380 ft
725 m

Long Island Sound

Long Island

CANADA
U.S.

Lake Champlain

Adirondack Mts.

Mt. Marcy
5,344 ft
1,629 m

Hudson

High Point
1,803 ft
550 m

NEW JERSEY

St. Lawrence

Raquette

Black

N E W   Y O R K

Mohawk

Catskill Mts.

Delaware

Fall Line

COASTAL

Pine Barrens

Cape May

Delaware Bay

DEL.

Delmarva Peninsula

Oneida Lake

A P P A L A C H I A N

Erie Canal

Finger Lakes

Allegheny Plateau

PENNSYLVANIA

48 ft
13 m

Susquehanna

PLAIN

MARYLAND

Chesapeake Bay

Lake Ontario

ONTARIO

CANADA

Genesee

Niagara Falls

Allegheny

Blue Ridge

Allegheny Mountains

Potomac

Monongahela

Mt. Davis +
3,213 ft
979 m

Backbone Mt. +
3,360 ft
1,024 m

D.C.

FED.

VIRGINIA

WEST VIRGINIA

Ohio

OHIO

Lake Erie

Lake Huron

ATLANTIC   OCEAN

100 miles

100 kilometers

0

Albers Conic Equal-Area Projection

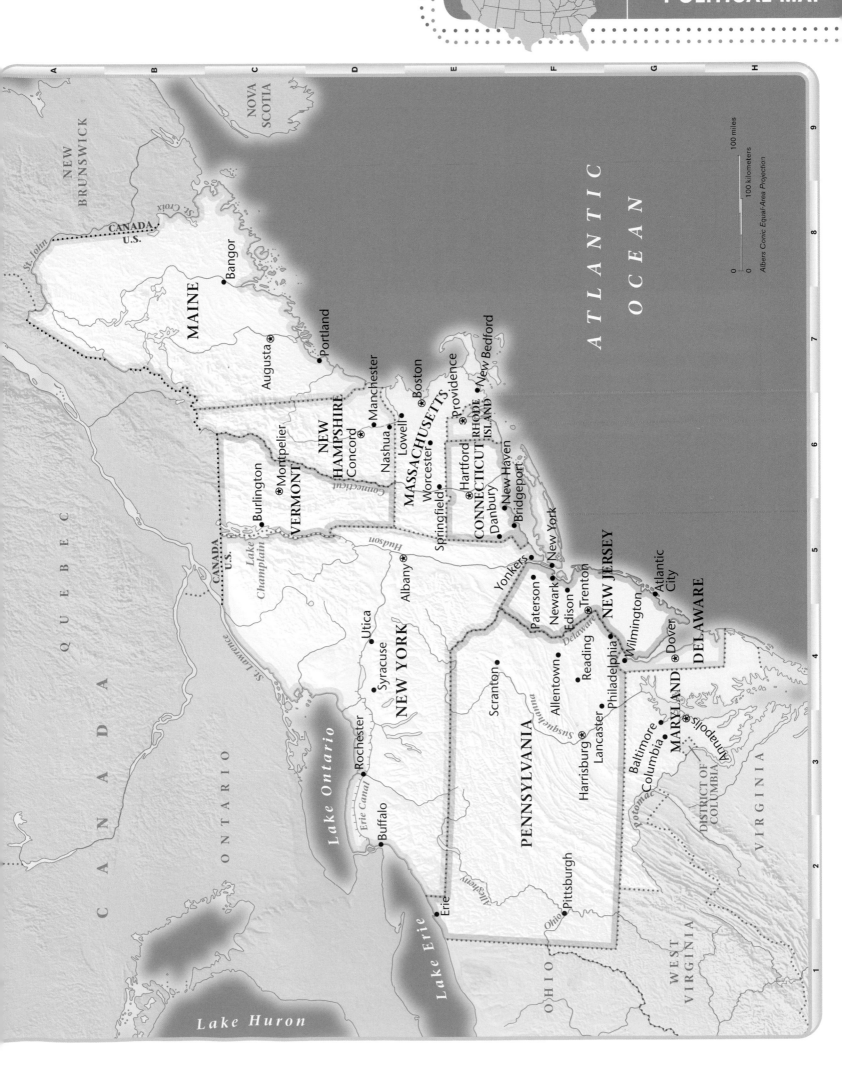

CANADA
U.S.

NEW BRUNSWICK

NOVA SCOTIA

St. John

St. Croix

MAINE

Bangor

Portland

Augusta

QUEBEC

CANADA
U.S.

Burlington

Montpelier

VERMONT

Lake Champlain

NEW HAMPSHIRE

Concord

Manchester

Nashua

Lowell

Connecticut

MASSACHUSETTS

Worcester

Springfield

Boston

Providence

RHODE ISLAND

New Bedford

CONNECTICUT

Hartford

New Haven

Danbury

Bridgeport

Yonkers

New York

ATLANTIC OCEAN

100 miles

100 kilometers

Albers Conic Equal-Area Projection

CANADA

ONTARIO

Lake Ontario

St. Lawrence

Rochester

Erie Canal

Buffalo

Utica

Syracuse

Albany

Hudson

NEW YORK

Scranton

PENNSYLVANIA

Susquehanna

Allentown

Reading

Harrisburg

Lancaster

Pittsburgh

Allegheny

Ohio

Erie

Lake Erie

Lake Huron

OHIO

Paterson

Newark

Edison

Trenton

NEW JERSEY

Atlantic City

Delaware

Philadelphia

Wilmington

Dover

DELAWARE

Baltimore

Columbia

MARYLAND

Annapolis

Potomac

DISTRICT OF COLUMBIA

VIRGINIA

WEST VIRGINIA

⇨ DINNER DELICACY. Lobsters, a favorite food for many people, turn bright red when cooked. These crustaceans live in the cold waters of the Atlantic Ocean and are caught using baited traps.

The Northeast
BIRTHPLACE OF A NATION

The United States had its beginnings in the Northeast region. Early European traders and settlers were quickly followed by immigrants from around the globe, making the region's population the most diverse in the country. The region includes the country's financial center, New York City, and its political capital, Washington, D.C. While the region boasts tranquil mountains, lakes, and rivers, its teeming cities have always been the heart of the Northeast.

⇩ MELTING POT. From colonial times, the Northeast has been a gateway for immigration. These young girls, dressed in traditional saris and performing in an India Cultural Festival in New Jersey, reflect the rich diversity of the region.

⇨ DEFENDER OF FREEDOM. Rising 548 feet (167 m) above Penn Square, Philadelphia's City Hall, with its statue of William Penn, is the country's largest municipal building. Penn was founder of the Pennsylvania colony and defender of equal rights for men and women.

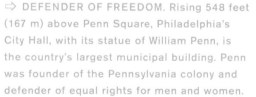

⇧ DAWN'S EARLY LIGHT. The lights of New York City's skyline sparkle against the early morning sky. The tall buildings of Lower Manhattan, reflected in the dark waters of the East River, are home to companies whose influence reaches around the world.

⇧ STILL WATERS. A father and son enjoy a quiet day of fishing on the smooth-as-glass waters of Lake Chocurua in New Hampshire's White Mountains. Deciduous trees turning red and gold will soon shed their leaves, and the hillsides will turn white with winter's snow, attracting skiers to the valley.

WHERE THE PICTURES ARE

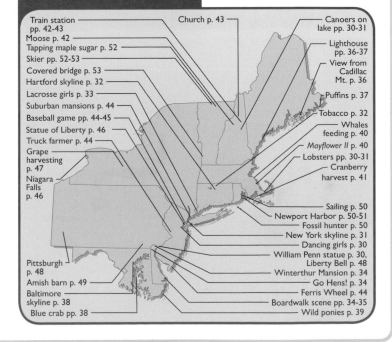

Train station pp. 42-43
Moose p. 42
Tapping maple sugar p. 52
Skier pp. 52-53
Covered bridge p. 53
Hartford skyline p. 32
Lacrosse girls p. 33
Suburban mansions p. 44
Baseball game pp. 44-45
Statue of Liberty p. 46
Truck farmer p. 44
Grape harvesting p. 47
Niagara Falls p. 46

Church p. 43

Canoers on lake pp. 30-31
Lighthouse pp. 36-37
View from Cadillac Mt. p. 36
Puffins p. 37
Tobacco p. 32
Whales feeding p. 40
Mayflower II p. 40
Lobsters pp. 30-31
Cranberry harvest p. 41

Sailing p. 50
Newport Harbor p. 50-51
Fossil hunter p. 50
New York skyline p. 31
Dancing girls p. 30
William Penn statue p. 30, Liberty Bell p. 48
Winterthur Mansion p. 34
Go Hens! p. 34
Ferris Wheel p. 44
Boardwalk scene pp. 34-35
Wild ponies p. 39

Pittsburgh p. 48
Amish barn p. 49
Baltimore skyline p. 38
Blue crab pp. 38

CONNECTICUT

As early as 1614, Dutch explorers founded trading posts along the coast of Connecticut, but the first permanent European settlements were established in 1635 by English Puritans from nearby Massachusetts. The Connecticut Fundamental Orders, which in 1639 established a democratic system of government in the colony, were an important model for the writing of the U.S. Constitution in 1787. This earned the state its nickname—Constitution State. Even in colonial times, Connecticut was an important industrial center, producing goods that competed with factories in England. During the Revolutionary War, Connecticut produced military goods for the colonial army. Today, Connecticut industries produce jet aircraft engines, helicopters, and nuclear submarines. Connecticut is home to many international corporations, but it is best known as the "insurance state." Following independence, businessmen offered to insure ship cargoes in exchange for a share of the profits. Soon after, other types of insurance were offered. Today, Connecticut is home to more than 100 insurance companies.

⇧ LEAFY HARVEST. The Connecticut River Valley is a major source of world-class premium cigar tobacco in the United States. Most of the harvest is used for cigar wrappers.

THE BASICS
STATS

Area
5,543 sq mi (14,357 sq km)

Population
3,574,097

Capital
Hartford
Population 124,775

Largest city
Bridgeport
Population 144,229

Ethnic/racial groups
77.6% white; 10.1% African American; 3.8% Asian; .3% Native American. Hispanic (any race) 13.4%.

Industry
Transportation equipment, metal products, machinery, electrical equipment, printing and publishing, scientific instruments, insurance

Agriculture
Nursery stock, dairy products, poultry, eggs, shellfish

Statehood
January 9, 1788; 5th state

GEO WHIZ

The sperm whale, Connecticut's state animal, is known for its massive head. Its brain is larger than that of any other creature known to have lived on Earth.

The first hamburgers in U.S. history were served by Louis Lassen at his New Haven lunch wagon in 1895. He didn't like to waste the excess beef left after the daily noon rush, so he ground it up, grilled it, and served it between two slices of bread.

The nuclear-powered U.S.S. *Virginia*, the first of a class of technologically advanced submarines, was built at Groton, home of the U.S. Naval Submarine Base.

ROBIN
MOUNTAIN LAUREL

⇦ BRIGHT CITY LIGHTS. Established as a fort in the early 1600s, Hartford was one of the earliest cities of colonial America. Today, this modern state capital is a center of economic growth and cultural diversity.

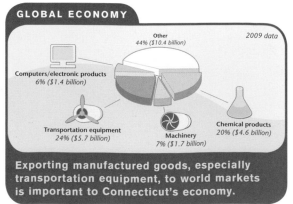

GLOBAL ECONOMY

2009 data

Other
44% ($10.4 billion)

Computers/electronic products
6% ($1.4 billion)

Transportation equipment
24% ($5.7 billion)

Machinery
7% ($1.7 billion)

Chemical products
20% ($4.6 billion)

Exporting manufactured goods, especially transportation equipment, to world markets is important to Connecticut's economy.

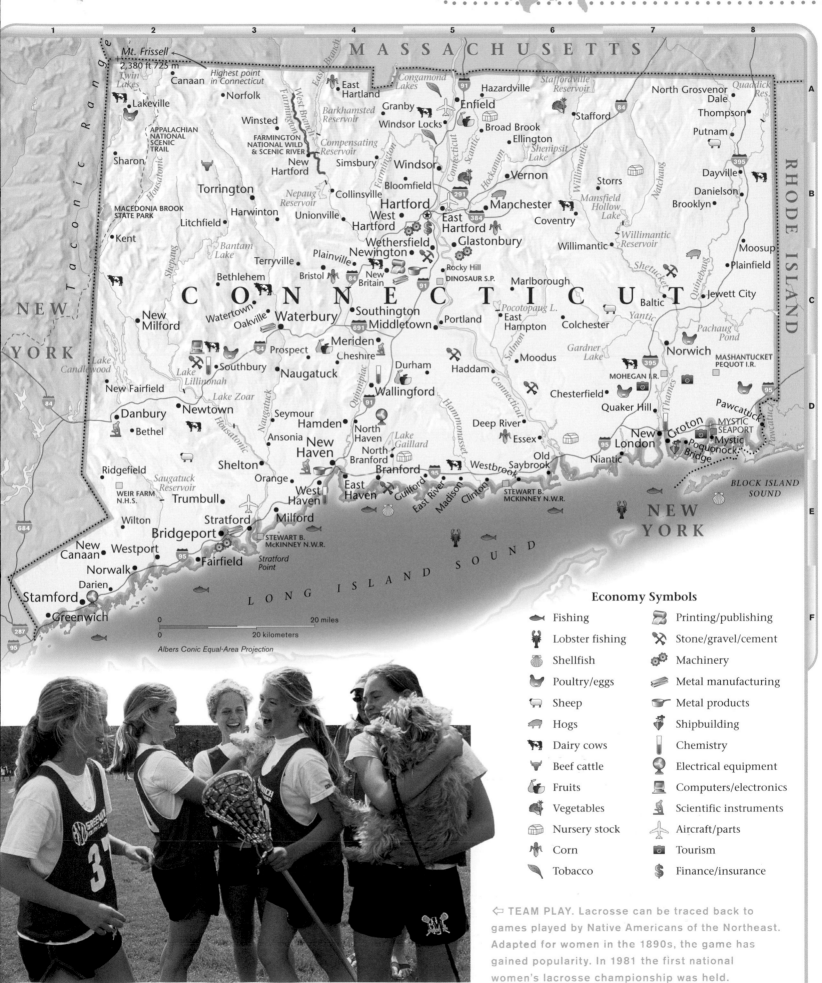

M A S S A C H U S E T T S

NEW YORK

RHODE ISLAND

Mt. Frissell ←
2,380 ft 725 m
Highest point
in Connecticut

Twin
Lakes
Canaan
Lakeville
Norfolk
East
Hartland
Congamond
Lakes
Hazardville
Staffordville
Reservoir
North Grosvenor
Dale
Quaddick
Res.
Thompson
Putnam
Winsted
Granby
Enfield
Stafford
Appalachian
National
Scenic
Trail
Barkhamsted
Reservoir
Windsor Locks
Broad Brook
Ellington
Dayville
Sharon
Farmington
National Wild
& Scenic River
Compensating
Reservoir
Simsbury
Windsor
Shenipsit
Lake
Vernon
Storrs
Danielson
New
Hartford
Bloomfield
Manchester
Mansfield
Hollow
Lake
Brooklyn
Torrington
Nepaug
Reservoir
Collinsville
Hartford
Coventry
Willimantic
Reservoir
Moosup
Harwinton
Unionville
West
Hartford
East
Hartford
Glastonbury
Willimantic
Plainfield
Litchfield
Wethersfield
Newington
Jewett City
Kent
Bantam
Lake
Terryville
Plainville
Rocky Hill
Marlborough
Baltic
CONNECTICUT
Bethlehem
Bristol
New
Britain
Dinosaur S.P.
Pocotopaug L.
Shetucket
New
Milford
Watertown
Waterbury
Southington
Middletown
Portland
East
Hampton
Colchester
Norwich
Oakville
Moodus
Gardner
Lake
Mashantucket
Pequot I.R.
Meriden
Cheshire
Durham
Haddam
Mohegan I.R.
New Fairfield
Prospect
Salmon
Chesterfield
Lake
Candlewood
Southbury
Naugatuck
Wallingford
Quaker Hill
Pawcatuck
Lake
Lillinonah
Danbury
Newtown
Seymour
Hamden
North
Haven
Lake
Gaillard
Deep River
New
London
Groton
Mystic
Seaport
Bethel
Ansonia
New
Haven
North
Branford
Essex
Niantic
Mystic
Poquonock
Bridge
Ridgefield
Saugatuck
Reservoir
Shelton
Orange
Branford
Saybrook
Old
Westbrook
Block Island
Sound
Weir Farm
N.H.S.
Trumbull
West
Haven
East
Haven
Guilford
Madison
Clinton
Stewart B.
McKinney N.W.R.
Wilton
Stratford
Milford
Stewart B.
McKinney N.W.R.
NEW YORK
New
Canaan
Westport
Fairfield
Stratford
Point
Norwalk
Darien
Stamford
Greenwich
L O N G   I S L A N D   S O U N D

0   20 miles
0   20 kilometers

Albers Conic Equal-Area Projection

Economy Symbols

🐟	Fishing	📰	Printing/publishing
🦞	Lobster fishing	⚒	Stone/gravel/cement
🐚	Shellfish	⚙	Machinery
🐔	Poultry/eggs		Metal manufacturing
🐑	Sheep	🍳	Metal products
🐖	Hogs		Shipbuilding
🐄	Dairy cows		Chemistry
🐂	Beef cattle	🌐	Electrical equipment
🍒	Fruits	💻	Computers/electronics
🥬	Vegetables	🔬	Scientific instruments
	Nursery stock	✈	Aircraft/parts
🌽	Corn	📷	Tourism
🍃	Tobacco	$	Finance/insurance

← TEAM PLAY. Lacrosse can be traced back to
games played by Native Americans of the Northeast.
Adapted for women in the 1890s, the game has
gained popularity. In 1981 the first national
women's lacrosse championship was held.

THE FIRST STATE:
DELAWARE

DECEMBER 7, 1787

THE BASICS

STATS

Area
2,489 sq mi (6,447 sq km)

Population
897,934

Capital
Dover
Population 36,047

Largest city
Wilmington
Population 70,851

Ethnic/racial groups
68.9% white; 21.4% African American; 3.2% Asian; .5% Native American. Hispanic (any race) 8.2%.

Industry
Food processing, chemicals, rubber and plastic products, scientific instruments, printing and publishing, financial services

Agriculture
Poultry, soybeans, nursery stock, corn, vegetables, dairy products

Statehood
December 7, 1787; 1st state

GEO WHIZ

Each year contestants bring their pumpkins and launching machines to the Punkin Chunkin World Championship in Bridgeville to see who can catapult their big, orange squash the farthest.

The Delaware Estuary is one of the four most important shorebird migration sites in the world and has the second highest concentration of shorebirds in North America. The estuary also provides wintering and migratory habitat to many species of songbirds and raptors.

The first steam railroad to provide regular service began operations in New Castle in 1831.

BLUE HEN CHICKEN
PEACH BLOSSOM

DELAWARE

Second smallest among the states in area, Delaware has played a big role in the history of the U.S. Explored at various times by the Spanish, Portuguese, and Dutch, it was Swedes who established the first permanent European settlement in 1638 in the Delaware River Valley. In 1655 the colony fell under Dutch authority, but in 1682 the land was annexed by William Penn and the Pennsylvania colony. In 1787 Delaware was the first state to ratify the new U.S. Constitution. Delaware's Atlantic coast beaches are popular with tourists. Its fertile farmland, mainly in the south, produces soybeans, corn, dairy products, and poultry. But the state's real economic power is located in the north, around Wilmington, where factories employ thousands of workers to process food products and produce machinery and chemicals. Industry has been a source of wealth, but it also poses a danger to the environment. Protecting the environment is a high priority for Delaware.

⬇ TEAM SPIRIT. Enthusiastic fans and the University of Delaware band support the "Fightin' Blue Hens." Located in Newark, the university was founded in 1743.

⬆ PAST GRANDEUR. Built in 1837 in the fashion of a British country house, Winterthur was expanded from 12 to 196 rooms by the du Ponts, chemical industry tycoons. In 1951 the house was opened to the public as a museum for the family's extensive collection of antiques and Americana.

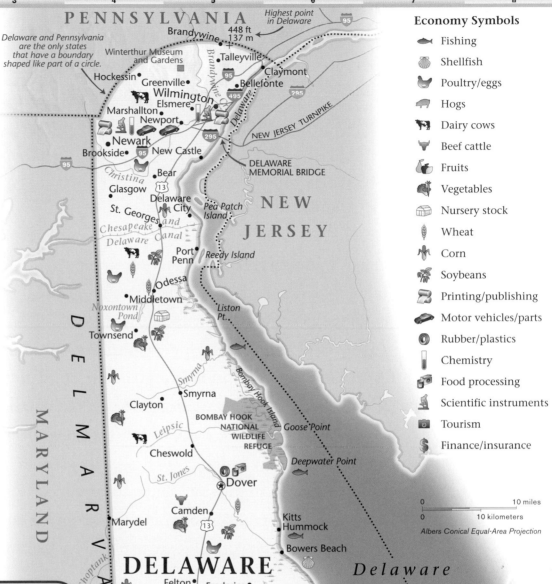

PENNSYLVANIA

Delaware and Pennsylvania are the only states that have a boundary shaped like part of a circle.

Highest point in Delaware — 448 ft / 137 m

Brandywine
Winterthur Museum and Gardens
Talleyville
Hockessin
Greenville
Claymont
Bellefonte
Wilmington
Elsmere
Marshallton
Newport
Newark
Brookside
New Castle
Bear
Glasgow
Delaware City
St. Georges
Chesapeake and Delaware Canal
Pea Patch Island
Port Penn
Reedy Island
Odessa
Middletown
Noxontown Pond
Townsend
Smyrna
Smyrna
Clayton
BOMBAY HOOK NATIONAL WILDLIFE REFUGE
Bombay Hook Island
Goose Point
Leipsic
Cheswold
Deepwater Point
St. Jones
Dover
Camden
Kitts Hummock
Marydel
Bowers Beach
DELAWARE
Felton
Frederica
Delaware Bay
Houston
Milford
Harrington
Lincoln
Slaughter Beach
PRIME HOOK NATIONAL WILDLIFE REFUGE
Greenwood
Ellendale
Broadkill Beach
Bridgeville
Milton
Cape Henlopen
Lewes
Lewes & Rehoboth Canal
Harbeson
Midway
ATLANTIC
Rehoboth Beach
Seaford
Blades
Georgetown
Dewey Beach
Rehoboth Bay
OCEAN
Laurel
Millsboro
Oak Orchard
Indian River Bay
Indian River Inlet
Dagsboro
Ocean View
Assawoman Canal
Bethany Beach
Frankford
Cypress Swamp
Delmar
Selbyville
Fenwick Island

NEW JERSEY
NEW JERSEY TURNPIKE
DELAWARE MEMORIAL BRIDGE
Liston Pt.

MARYLAND

Christina
Brandywine
Delaware

D E L M A R V A   P E N I N S U L A

Choptank
Marshyhope Creek
Nanticoke

Economy Symbols

- Fishing
- Shellfish
- Poultry/eggs
- Hogs
- Dairy cows
- Beef cattle
- Fruits
- Vegetables
- Nursery stock
- Wheat
- Corn
- Soybeans
- Printing/publishing
- Motor vehicles/parts
- Rubber/plastics
- Chemistry
- Food processing
- Scientific instruments
- Tourism
- Finance/insurance

0 — 10 miles
0 — 10 kilometers
Albers Conical Equal-Area Projection

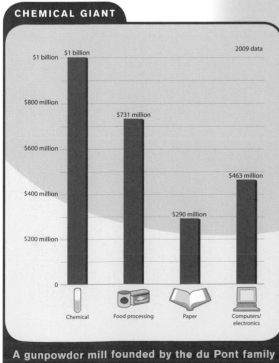

⇧ SEASIDE RETREAT. Originally established in 1873 as a church campground, Rehoboth Beach is still a popular getaway destination on Delaware's Atlantic coastline. A concrete dolphin overlooks the town's boardwalk, a popular promenade that separates shops and restaurants from the beach. The boardwalk has been destroyed on several occasions by storms.

CHEMICAL GIANT

2009 data

Chemical	$1 billion
Food processing	$731 million
Paper	$290 million
Computers/electronics	$463 million

$1 billion
$800 million
$600 million
$400 million
$200 million
0

A gunpowder mill founded by the du Pont family in 1802 gave rise to a chemical industry that is now the state's leading industry and employer.

THE BASICS
STATS

Area
35,385 sq mi (91,646 sq km)

Population
1,328,361

Capital
Augusta
Population 19,136

Largest city
Portland
Population 66,194

Ethnic/racial groups
95.2% white; 1.2% African American;
1.0% Asian; .6% Native American.
Hispanic (any race) 1.3%.

Industry
Health services, tourism, forest products,
leather products, electrical equipment,
food processing, textiles

Agriculture
Seafood, potatoes, dairy products,
poultry and eggs, livestock, apples,
blueberries, vegetables

Statehood
March 15, 1820; 23rd state

GEO WHIZ

With world shark populations declining,
some conservation-minded deep-sea
fishermen in Maine have turned the
idea of a shark tournament upside-
down. They still compete to see
who can catch the biggest fish, but
then they tag and release the sharks.

Eartha, a scale model of our planet,
holds the Guinness World Record as
the World's Largest Revolving/Rotating
Globe. It is on display in a three-story
glass building in Yarmouth.

Forests cover nearly 90 percent of
Maine. No wonder it is called the
Pine Tree State.

Until the last ice age, Maine's coast
was relatively straight. Glaciers
carved hundreds of bays and
inlets out of its shoreline
and created some 2,000
islands off the coast.

CHICKADEE

WHITE PINE
CONE AND
TASSEL

MAINE

Maine's story begins long before the arrival of European settlers in the 1600s. Evidence of native people dates back to at least 3000 B.C., and Leif Erikson and his Viking sailors may have explored Maine's coastline 500 years before Columbus crossed the Atlantic. English settlements were established along the southern coast in the 1620s, and in 1677 the territory of Maine came under control of Massachusetts. Following the Revolutionary War, the people of Maine pressed for separation from Massachusetts, and in 1820 Maine entered the Union as a non-slave state under the terms of the Missouri Compromise. Most of Maine's population is concentrated in towns along the coast. Famous for its rugged beauty, it is the focus of the tourist industry. Cold offshore waters contribute to a lively fishing industry, while timber from the state's mountainous interior supports wood product and paper businesses. Maine, a leader in environmental awareness, seeks a balance between economic growth and environmental protection.

⇓ACADIA NATIONAL PARK, established in 1929, attracts thousands of tourists each year. The park includes Cadillac Mountain, the highest point along the North Atlantic coast and the site from which the earliest sunrises in the United States can be viewed from October 7 through March 6.

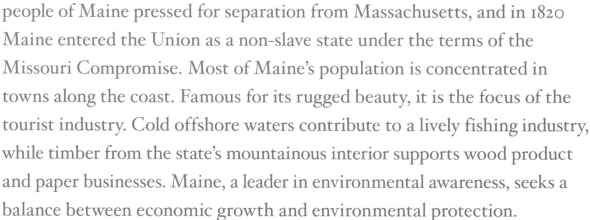

BLUEBERRY LEADER

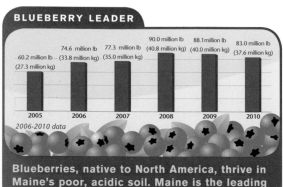

60.2 million lb
(27.3 million kg) **2005**

74.6 million lb
(33.8 million kg) **2006**

77.3 million lb
(35.0 million kg) **2007**

90.0 million lb
(40.8 million kg) **2008**

88.1 million lb
(40.0 million kg) **2009**

83.0 million lb
(37.6 million kg) **2010**

2006-2010 data

Blueberries, native to North America, thrive in
Maine's poor, acidic soil. Maine is the leading
harvester of wild blueberries in the U.S.

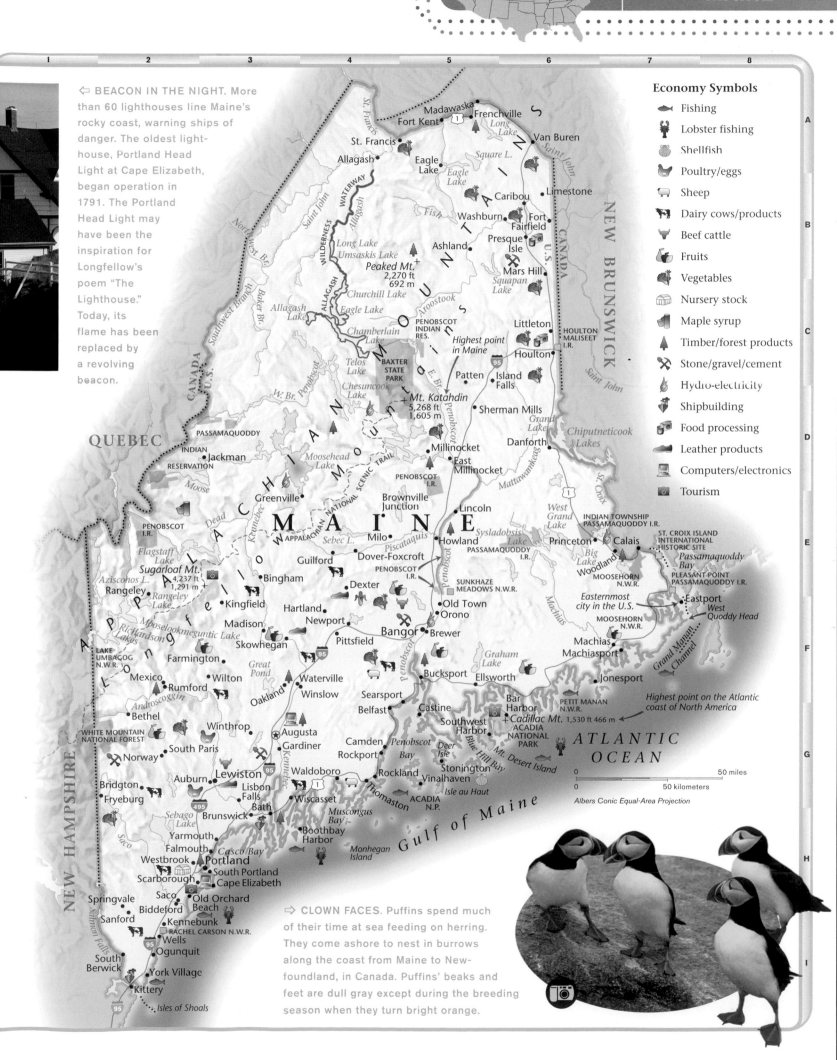

⇦ BEACON IN THE NIGHT. More than 60 lighthouses line Maine's rocky coast, warning ships of danger. The oldest light-house, Portland Head Light at Cape Elizabeth, began operation in 1791. The Portland Head Light may have been the inspiration for Longfellow's poem "The Lighthouse." Today, its flame has been replaced by a revolving beacon.

Economy Symbols

- Fishing
- Lobster fishing
- Shellfish
- Poultry/eggs
- Sheep
- Dairy cows/products
- Beef cattle
- Fruits
- Vegetables
- Nursery stock
- Maple syrup
- Timber/forest products
- Stone/gravel/cement
- Hydro-electricity
- Shipbuilding
- Food processing
- Leather products
- Computers/electronics
- Tourism

QUEBEC

NEW BRUNSWICK

NEW HAMPSHIRE

CANADA
U.S.

M A I N E

APPALACHIAN MOUNTAINS

Madawaska
Fort Kent
Frenchville
Van Buren
St. Francis
Allagash
Eagle Lake
Caribou
Limestone
Washburn
Fort Fairfield
Ashland
Presque Isle
Mars Hill
Peaked Mt. 2,270 ft 692 m
Churchill Lake
Eagle Lake
Littleton
HOULTON MALISEET I.R.
Houlton
Chamberlain Lake
PENOBSCOT INDIAN RES.
Patten
Island Falls
Telos Lake
BAXTER STATE PARK
Highest point in Maine
Chesuncook Lake
Mt. Katahdin 5,268 ft 1,605 m
Sherman Mills
PASSAMAQUODDY
INDIAN RESERVATION
Jackman
Millinocket
East Millinocket
Danforth
Greenville
Brownville Junction
Lincoln
Milo
Howland
Princeton
Calais
PENOBSCOT I.R.
Dover-Foxcroft
PENOBSCOT I.R.
Eastport
West Quoddy Head
Sugarloaf Mt. 4,237 ft 1,291 m
Rangeley
Bingham
Dexter
SUNKHAZE MEADOWS N.W.R.
Old Town
Orono
Easternmost city in the U.S.
Kingfield
Hartland
Newport
Bangor
Brewer
Machias
Machiasport
Madison
Pittsfield
Jonesport
Skowhegan
Farmington
Mexico
Rumford
Wilton
Waterville
Winslow
Searsport
Bucksport
Ellsworth
Bethel
Oakland
Belfast
Castine
Bar Harbor
PETIT MANAN N.W.R.
Winthrop
Augusta
Gardiner
Camden
Southwest Harbor
Cadillac Mt. 1,530 ft 466 m
Highest point on the Atlantic coast of North America
South Paris
Norway
Rockport
ACADIA NATIONAL PARK
ATLANTIC OCEAN
Auburn
Lewiston
Waldoboro
Rockland
Vinalhaven
Stonington
Bridgton
Fryeburg
Lisbon Falls
Bath
Wiscasset
Isle au Haut
Brunswick
Boothbay Harbor
Monhegan Island
Yarmouth
Falmouth
Westbrook
Portland
South Portland
Cape Elizabeth
Scarborough
Saco
Old Orchard Beach
Springvale
Biddeford
Sanford
Kennebunk
RACHEL CARSON N.W.R.
Wells
Ogunquit
South Berwick
York Village
Kittery
Isles of Shoals

Gulf of Maine

⇨ CLOWN FACES. Puffins spend much of their time at sea feeding on herring. They come ashore to nest in burrows along the coast from Maine to New-foundland, in Canada. Puffins' beaks and feet are dull gray except during the breeding season when they turn bright orange.

0   50 miles
0   50 kilometers
Albers Conic Equal-Area Projection

THE BASICS

STATS

Area
12,407 sq mi (32,133 sq km)

Population
5,773,552

Capital
Annapolis
Population 38,394

Largest city
Baltimore
Population 620,961

Ethnic/racial groups
58.2% white; 29.4% African American;
5.5% Asian; .4% Native American.
Hispanic (any race) 8.2%.

Industry
Real estate, federal government, health
services, business services, engineering services, electrical and gas services,
communications, banking, insurance

Agriculture
Poultry and eggs, dairy products,
nursery stock, soybeans, corn, seafood,
cattle, vegetables

Statehood
April 28, 1788; 7th state

GEO WHIZ

The Captain John Smith Chesapeake
National Historic Water Trail, which
traces some 3,000 miles (4,800 km)
of Smith's 1607–1608 explorations
of the bay, is the first national
water trail in the United States.

The Naval Support Facility Thurmont,
better known as Camp David, the
mountain retreat of American presidents, is part of Catoctin Mountain
Park in north-central Maryland.

Residents on Smith Island, in the lower
Chesapeake Bay, are being robbed of
their land by rising sea levels and of
their traditional livelihood by dwindling
blue crab harvests. They fear a major
Atlantic hurricane could wipe out their
island home.

The name of Baltimore's professional
football team—the Ravens—may
have been inspired by the title
of a poem written by noted
American author Edgar Allan
Poe, who lived in Baltimore
in the mid-1800s and whose
grave is in that city.

NORTHERN
(BALTIMORE)
ORIOLE

BLACK-EYED
SUSAN

MARYLAND

Native Americans, who raised crops and harvested oysters from the nearby waters of Chesapeake Bay, lived on the land that would become Maryland long before early European settlers arrived. In 1608 Captain John Smith explored the waters of the bay, and in 1634 English settlers established the colony of Maryland. In 1788 Maryland became the 7th state to ratify the new U.S. Constitution. Chesapeake Bay, the largest estuary in the U.S., almost splits Maryland into two parts. East of the bay lies the flat coastal plain, while to the west the land rises through the hilly piedmont and mountainous panhandle. Chesapeake Bay, the state's economic and environmental focal point, supports a busy seafood industry. It is also a major transportation artery, linking Baltimore and other Maryland ports to the Atlantic Ocean. Most of the people of Maryland live in an urban corridor between Baltimore and Washington, D.C., where jobs in government, research, and high-tech businesses provide employment.

⇧ GATEWAY CITY. Since the early 1700s, Baltimore, near the upper Chesapeake Bay, has been a major seaport and focus of trade, industry, and immigration. Today, the Inner Harbor is not only a modern working port, but also the city's vibrant cultural center.

⇦ COLORFUL CRUSTACEAN. Blue crabs, found in Maryland's Chesapeake Bay waters, were a staple in the diet of Native Americans. They have been harvested commercially since the mid-1800s, and the tasty meat is a popular menu item—especially crab cakes—in seafood restaurants throughout the area.

Map labels

PENNSYLVANIA

Hancock
Williamsport
Hagerstown
Thurmont
CATOCTIN MOUNTAIN PARK
Taneytown
Manchester
Boonsboro
Westminster
Sharpsburg
ANTIETAM NAT. BATTLEFIELD
Walkersville
Reisterstown
Cockeysville
Bel Air
Havre de Grace
Elkton
Aberdeen
Mason-Dixon Line
Frederick
U.S. center of population in 1800
HAMPTON N.H.S.
Towson
Perry Hall
Edgewood
Brunswick
MONOCACY NAT. BATTLEFIELD
Baltimore
Parkville
Essex
Catonsville
Dundalk
Chestertown
Montgomery Village
Ellicott City
FT. McHENRY NAT. MON. & HISTORIC SHRINE
Germantown
Columbia
Glen Burnie
Gaithersburg
WILLIAM PRESTON LANE JR. MEMORIAL BRIDGE (CHESAPEAKE BAY BRIDGE)
Rockville
MARYLAND
Silver Spring
PATUXENT N.W.R.
Severna Park
EASTERN NECK N.W.R.
Potomac N.H.P.
GREENBELT PARK
Bowie
Grasonville
CLARA BARTON N.H.S.
Hyattsville
Annapolis
Kent Island
Denton
Bethesda
D.C.
Suitland
Eastern Bay
St. Michaels
Easton
OXON COVE PARK & OXON HILL FARM
Deale
FT. FOOTE PARK
FT. WASHINGTON PARK
Chesapeake Beach
Federalsburg
DELAWARE
PISCATAWAY PARK
Waldorf
Hurlock
Indian Head
St. Charles
Cambridge
THOMAS STONE N.H.S.
La Plata
Prince Frederick
Bucktown
Golden Beach
BLACKWATER NATIONAL WILDLIFE REFUGE
Ocean Pines
Salisbury
Ocean City
Solomons
Fruitland
Berlin
Lexington Park
Fishing Bay
St. Marys City
Bloodsworth Island
Snow Hill
ASSATEAGUE ISLAND NATIONAL SEASHORE
Pocomoke City
Assateague Island
Point Lookout
Smith Island
Crisfield
Pocomoke Sound
VIRGINIA
ATLANTIC OCEAN

Chesapeake Bay
Potomac
Patuxent
Choptank
Nanticoke
Pocomoke
Tangier Sound
Chincoteague Bay
Susquehanna
Sassafras
Chester
Chesapeake and Delaware Canal
Monocacy
DELMARVA PENINSULA

APPALACHIAN MOUNTAINS
APPALACHIAN NATIONAL SCENIC TRAIL
CHESAPEAKE & OHIO CANAL
PIEDMONT

NEW JERSEY

Named after its surveyors, the Maryland-Pennsylvania boundary became the traditional division between North and South.

Economy Symbols

- Fishing
- Shellfish
- Poultry/eggs
- Sheep
- Hogs
- Dairy cows/products
- Beef cattle
- Fruits
- Vegetables
- Vegetable oil
- Nursery stock
- Wheat
- Corn
- Soybeans
- Tobacco
- Printing/publishing
- Stone/gravel/cement
- Coal
- Oil/gas
- Machinery
- Metal manufacturing
- Motor vehicles/parts
- Chemistry
- Food processing
- Clothing/textiles
- Electrical equipment
- Computers/electronics
- Scientific instruments
- Tourism
- Finance/insurance

CHESAPEAKE HARVEST

Thousands of bushels, 1985-2010

Year	Value
1985	1,500
1990	411
1995	199
2000	348
2005	154
2010	124

Maryland's oyster harvest has been reduced from millions of pounds to a few thousand by overharvesting, pollution, and disease.

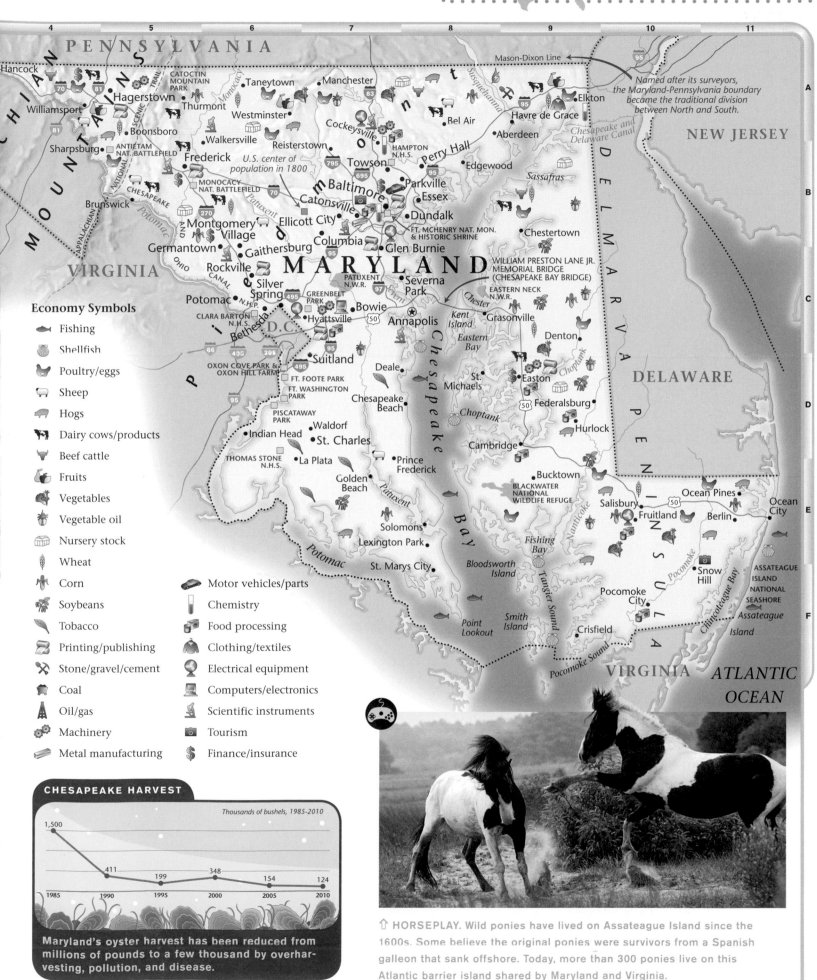

⇧ HORSEPLAY. Wild ponies have lived on Assateague Island since the 1600s. Some believe the original ponies were survivors from a Spanish galleon that sank offshore. Today, more than 300 ponies live on this Atlantic barrier island shared by Maryland and Virginia.

THE BASICS

STATS

Area
10,555 sq mi (27,336 sq km)

Population
6,547,629

Capital
Boston
Population 617,594

Largest city
Boston
Population 617,594

Major ethnic/racial groups
80.4% white; 6.6% African American; 5.3% Asian; .3% Native American. Hispanic (any race) 9.6%.

Industry
Electrical equipment, machinery, metal products, scientific instruments, printing and publishing, tourism

Agriculture
Fruits, nuts, berries, nursery stock, dairy products

Statehood
February 6, 1788; 6th state

GEO WHIZ

In 1717 the pirate ship *Whydah*, under the command of Captain Samuel Bellamy (also known as Black Sam), went down in a storm off Cape Cod. Treasure and artifacts recovered from the ship are on display at the Whydah Museum, in Provincetown, and are also part of a National Geographic traveling exhibit.

Massachusetts is the birthplace of several famous inventors, including Eli Whitney, Samuel Morse, and Benjamin Franklin.

The country's first lighthouse was built on Little Brewster Island in Boston Harbor in 1716. It is the last manned lighthouse in the United States. Use the online link to see what it's like to be a lighthouse keeper for Boston Light.

Cape Cod is considered one of the world's best spots for whale watching, thanks to Stellwagen Bank, a protected area at the mouth of Massachusetts Bay.

CHICKADEE
MAYFLOWER

⇨ LEVIATHANS OF THE DEEP. In the 19th century, Massachusetts was an important center for the whaling industry, with more than 300 registered whaling ships. Today, humpback whales swim in the protected waters of a marine sanctuary in Massachusetts Bay.

MASSACHUSETTS

Earliest human inhabitants of Massachusetts were Native Americans who arrived more than 10,000 years ago. The first Europeans to visit Massachusetts may have been Norsemen around A.D. 1000, and later fishermen from France and Spain. But the first permanent European settlement was established in 1620 when people aboard the sailing ship *Mayflower* landed near Plymouth on the coast of Massachusetts. The Puritans arrived soon after, and by 1630 they had established settlements at Salem and Boston. By 1640 more than 16,000 people, most seeking religious freedom, had settled in Massachusetts. In the early days, the economy of Massachusetts was based on shipping, fishing, and whaling. By the 19th century, industry, taking advantage of abundant water power, had a firm foothold. Factory jobs attracted thousands of immigrants, mainly from Europe. In the late 20th century, Massachusetts experienced a boom in high-tech jobs, drawing on the state's skilled labor force and its more than 80 colleges and universities.

⇧ REMINDER OF TIMES PAST. Shrouded in morning mist, this replica of the *Mayflower* docked in Plymouth Harbor is a reminder of Massachusetts's early history.

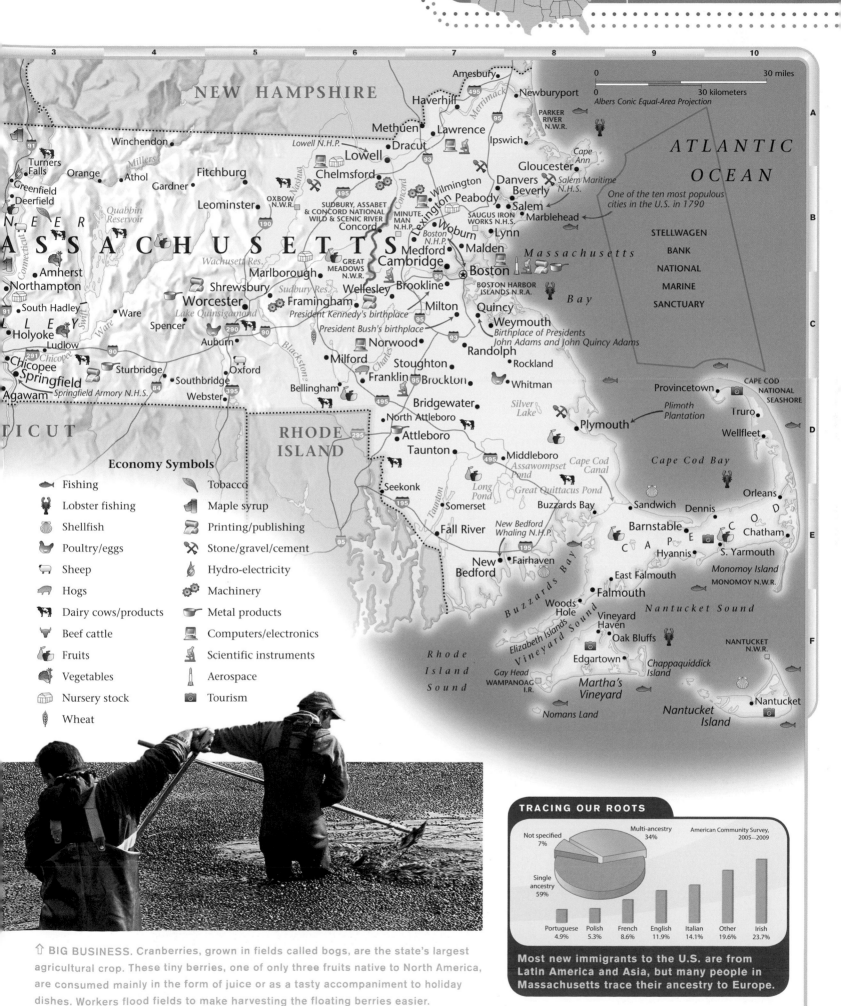

NEW HAMPSHIRE

ATLANTIC OCEAN

Massachusetts Bay

One of the ten most populous cities in the U.S. in 1790

STELLWAGEN BANK NATIONAL MARINE SANCTUARY

Amesbury
Newburyport
PARKER RIVER N.W.R.
Haverhill
Methuen
Lawrence
Ipswich
Dracut
Lowell N.H.P.
Lowell
Chelmsford
Winchendon
Turners Falls
Orange
Athol
Gardner
Fitchburg
Leominster
Quabbin Reservoir
OXBOW N.W.R.
SUDBURY, ASSABET & CONCORD NATIONAL WILD & SCENIC RIVER
Wilmington
Peabody
Danvers
Beverly
Gloucester
Cape Ann
Salem Maritime N.H.S.
Salem
Marblehead
MINUTE MAN N.H.P.
Concord
Lexington
Woburn
SAUGUS IRON WORKS N.H.S.
Lynn
Boston N.H.P.
Medford
Malden
Wachusett Res.
GREAT MEADOWS N.W.R.
Cambridge
Boston
BOSTON HARBOR ISLANDS N.R.A.
Marlborough
Shrewsbury
Sudbury Res.
Wellesley
Brookline
Worcester
Framingham
Milton
Quincy
Lake Quinsigamond
President Kennedy's birthplace
Weymouth
Birthplace of Presidents John Adams and John Quincy Adams
Amherst
Northampton
South Hadley
Holyoke
Ludlow
Spencer
Auburn
290
Norwood
Randolph
Rockland
Chicopee
Springfield
Agawam
Springfield Armory N.H.S.
Sturbridge
Southbridge
Webster
Oxford
Milford
Stoughton
Whitman
CONNECTICUT
RHODE ISLAND
Bellingham
Franklin
Brockton
Bridgewater
North Attleboro
Attleboro
Taunton
Seekonk
Somerset
Fall River
Middleboro
Assawompset Pond
Long Pond
Great Quittacus Pond
Silver Lake
Plymouth
Plimoth Plantation
Provincetown
CAPE COD NATIONAL SEASHORE
Truro
Wellfleet
Cape Cod Bay
Cape Cod Canal
Buzzards Bay
Sandwich
Dennis
Orleans
Chatham
Barnstable
Hyannis
S. Yarmouth
Monomoy Island
MONOMOY N.W.R.
New Bedford
New Bedford Whaling N.H.P.
Fairhaven
East Falmouth
Falmouth
Woods Hole
Nantucket Sound
Vineyard Haven
Oak Bluffs
NANTUCKET N.W.R.
Elizabeth Islands
Edgartown
Chappaquiddick Island
Rhode Island Sound
Gay Head WAMPANOAG I.R.
Martha's Vineyard
Nomans Land
Nantucket
Nantucket Island

Economy Symbols

Fishing	Tobacco
Lobster fishing	Maple syrup
Shellfish	Printing/publishing
Poultry/eggs	Stone/gravel/cement
Sheep	Hydro-electricity
Hogs	Machinery
Dairy cows/products	Metal products
Beef cattle	Computers/electronics
Fruits	Scientific instruments
Vegetables	Aerospace
Nursery stock	Tourism
Wheat	

⇧ BIG BUSINESS. Cranberries, grown in fields called bogs, are the state's largest agricultural crop. These tiny berries, one of only three fruits native to North America, are consumed mainly in the form of juice or as a tasty accompaniment to holiday dishes. Workers flood fields to make harvesting the floating berries easier.

TRACING OUR ROOTS

Multi-ancestry 34%

Not specified 7%

Single ancestry 59%

American Community Survey, 2005–2009

| Portuguese 4.9% | Polish 5.3% | French 8.6% | English 11.9% | Italian 14.1% | Other 19.6% | Irish 23.7% |

Most new immigrants to the U.S. are from Latin America and Asia, but many people in Massachusetts trace their ancestry to Europe.

0 — 30 miles
0 — 30 kilometers
Albers Conic Equal-Area Projection

THE GRANITE STATE:
NEW HAMPSHIRE

THE BASICS
STATS

Area
9,350 sq mi (24,216 sq km)

Population
1,316,470

Capital
Concord
Population 42,695

Largest city
Manchester
Population 109,565

Ethnic/racial groups
93.9% white; 2.2% Asian;
1.1% African American; .2% Native
American. Hispanic (any race) 2.8%.

Industry
Machinery, electronics, metal products

Agriculture
Nursery stock, poultry and eggs, fruits
and nuts, vegetables

Statehood
June 21, 1788; 9th state

GEO WHIZ

About ten million tourists visit New
Hampshire each year, nearly ten times the
number of people who live in the state.

The Granite State boasts more than
200 different kinds of rocks and
minerals. Use the icon to play Rock
Stars and test your knowledge.

The first potato grown in the United
States was planted in 1719 in
Londonderry on the Common Field,
now known simply as the Commons.

Ben Kilham's unique ways of
rehabilitating abandoned black
bear cubs he finds in
the New Hampshire
woods has earned him
the nickname Bear Man by
residents of Lyme. He has
been working with orphaned,
sick, and injured cubs for
more than nine years.

PURPLE FINCH
PURPLE LILAC

NEW HAMPSHIRE

The territory that would become the state of New Hampshire, the 9th state to approve the U.S. Constitution in 1788, began as a fishing colony established along the short 18-mile-long coastline (29 km) in 1623. New Hampshire was named a royal colony in 1679, but as the Revolutionary War approached, it was the first colony to declare its independence from English rule.

In the early 19th century, life in New Hampshire followed two very different paths. Near the coast, villages and towns grew up around sawmills, shipyards, and warehouses. But in the forested, mountainous interior, people lived on small, isolated farms, and towns provided only basic services. Today, New Hampshire is one of the fastest growing states in the Northeast. Modern industries, such as computers and electronics, and high-tech companies have brought prosperity to the state. Its natural beauty attracts tourists year-round to hike on forest trails, swim in pristine lakes, and ski on snow-covered mountain slopes.

⇑ LUMBERING GIANT.
Averaging 6 feet (2 m) tall
at the shoulders, moose are
the largest of North America's
deer. Moose are found
throughout New Hampshire.

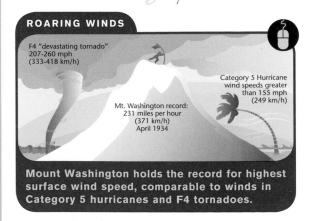

ROARING WINDS

F4 "devastating tornado"
207-260 mph
(333-418 km/h)

Mt. Washington record:
231 miles per hour
(371 km/h)
April 1934

Category 5 Hurricane
wind speeds greater
than 155 mph
(249 km/h)

**Mount Washington holds the record for highest
surface wind speed, comparable to winds in
Category 5 hurricanes and F4 tornadoes.**

⇨ ALL ABOARD. Tourists traveling by train through the White
Mountains enjoy the cool autumn weather and the colorful
fall foliage of deciduous trees that cover the mountains.

↑ AUTUMN PEACE. A white steepled church sits nestled among trees in a village near New Hampshire's White Mountains. Such traditional churches, common in the New England landscape, are a reminder of early settlers' search for religious freedom.

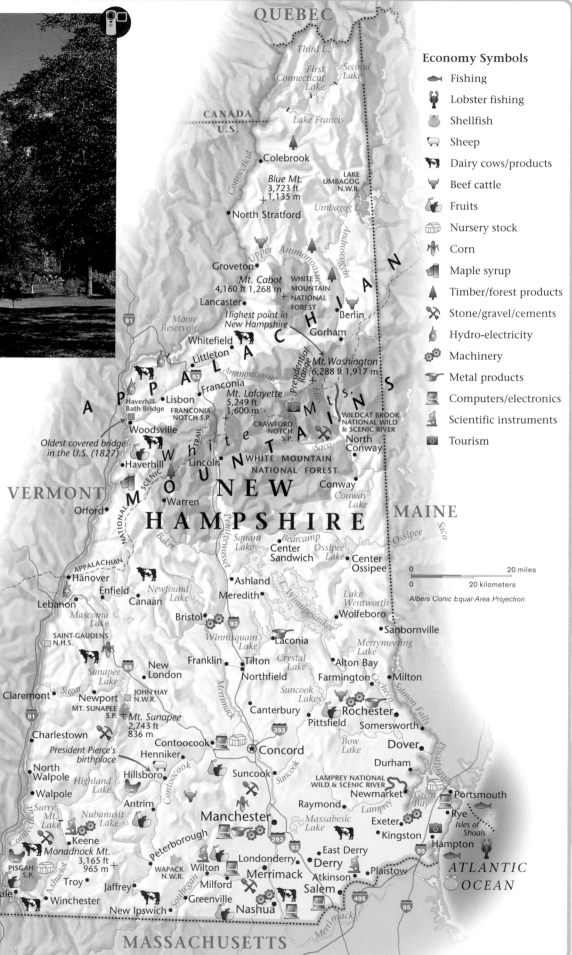

Economy Symbols

- Fishing
- Lobster fishing
- Shellfish
- Sheep
- Dairy cows/products
- Beef cattle
- Fruits
- Nursery stock
- Corn
- Maple syrup
- Timber/forest products
- Stone/gravel/cements
- Hydro-electricity
- Machinery
- Metal products
- Computers/electronics
- Scientific instruments
- Tourism

QUEBEC

Third L.

First Connecticut Lake
Second Lake

CANADA
U.S.

Lake Francis

Colebrook

Blue Mt.
3,723 ft
1,135 m

LAKE
UMBAGOG
N.W.R.

North Stratford

Umbagog L.

Upper Ammonoosuc

Groveton

Mt. Cabot
4,160 ft 1,268 m

WHITE
MOUNTAIN
NATIONAL
FOREST

Lancaster

Berlin

Highest point in
New Hampshire

Gorham

Whitefield

Littleton

Ammonoosuc

Presidential Range

Mt. Washington
6,288 ft 1,917 m

Franconia

Mt. Lafayette
5,249 ft
1,600 m

WILDCAT BROOK
NATIONAL WILD
& SCENIC RIVER

Lisbon

FRANCONIA
NOTCH S.P.

CRAWFORD
NOTCH
S.P.

North
Conway

Haverhill-
Bath Bridge

Woodsville

Saco

Oldest covered bridge
in the U.S. (1827)

Lincoln

WHITE MOUNTAIN
NATIONAL FOREST

Haverhill

VERMONT

Warren

Conway

Conway
Lake

MAINE

Orford

Squam
Lakes

Bearcamp

Ossipee
Lake

Ossipee

Saco

Center
Sandwich

Center
Ossipee

Pemigewasset

Baker

APPALACHIAN

Hanover

Enfield

Newfound
Lake

Meredith

Ashland

Lake
Wentworth

Wolfeboro

Lebanon

Mascoma
Lake

Canaan

Winnipesaukee

Sanbornville

SAINT-GAUDENS
N.H.S.

Bristol

Winnisquam
Lake

Laconia

Merrymeeting
Lake

Claremont

Sunapee
Lake

Sugar

New
London

Franklin

Tilton

Crystal
Lake

Alton Bay

Milton

Newport

JOHN HAY
N.W.R.

Northfield

Farmington

Cochecco

MT. SUNAPEE
S.P.

Mt. Sunapee
2,743 ft
836 m

Canterbury

Suncook
Lakes

Rochester

Somersworth

Charlestown

President Pierce's
birthplace

Contoocook

Henniker

Pittsfield

Bow
Lake

Dover

Concord

Durham

North
Walpole

Hillsboro

Suncook

Suncook

LAMPREY NATIONAL
WILD & SCENIC RIVER

Highland
Lake

Walpole

Antrim

Raymond

Newmarket

Great
Bay

Portsmouth

Surry
Mt.
Lake

Nubanusit
Lake

Manchester

Massabesic
Lake

Lamprey

Rye

Keene

Peterborough

Exeter

Kingston

Isles of
Shoals

Monadnock Mt.
3,165 ft
965 m

WAPACK
N.W.R.

Londonderry

East Derry

Hampton

PISGAH
S.P.

Wilton

Derry

Plaistow

ATLANTIC
OCEAN

Hinsdale

Troy

Jaffrey

Milford

Atkinson

Salem

Winchester

Greenville

Merrimack

New Ipswich

Nashua

MASSACHUSETTS

Moore
Reservoir

Connecticut

Androscoggin

Ellis

White MOUNTAINS

TRAIL

APPALACHIAN

NATIONAL

SCENIC

Winnipesaukee

Merrimack

Contoocook

Ashuelot

Souhegan

Connecticut

Merrimack

Piscataqua

Salmon Falls

Ossipee

NEW JERSEY

Long before Europeans settled in New Jersey, the region was home to hunting and farming communities of Delaware Indians. The Dutch set up a trading post in northern New Jersey in 1618, calling it New Netherland, but yielded the land in 1664 to the English, who named it New Jersey after the English Channel Isle of Jersey. New Jersey saw more than 90 battles during the Revolutionary War. It became the 3rd U.S. state in 1787 and the first to sign the Bill of Rights. In the 19th century southern New Jersey remained largely agricultural, while the northern part of the state rapidly industrialize. Today highways and railroads link the state to urban centers along the Atlantic seaboard. More than 10,000 farms grow fruits and vegetables for nearby urban markets. Industries as well as services and trade are thriving. Beaches along the Atlantic coast attract thousands of tourists each year.

THE BASICS

STATS

Area
8,721 sq mi (22,588 sq km)

Population
8,791,894

Capital
Trenton
Population 84,913

Largest city
Newark
Population 277,140

Ethnic/racial groups
68.6% white; 13.7% African American; 8.3% Asian; .3% Native American. Hispanic (any race) 17.1%.

Industry
Machinery, electronics, metal products, chemicals

Agriculture
Nursery stock, poultry and eggs, fruits and nuts, vegetables

Statehood
December 18, 1787; 3rd state

GEO WHIZ

Site of a one-time trash heap, the Meadowlands, a swampy lowland on either side of the Hackensack River, is now home to a major sports complex, bustling suburban neighborhoods, and congested roadways. Parts of it are isolated enough to allow days of quiet canoeing.

In 1930 New Jerseyite Charles Darrow developed the game Monopoly. He named Boardwalk and other streets in the game after those in Atlantic City.

The first dinosaur skeleton found in North America was excavated at Haddonfield in 1858. It was named *Hadrosaurus* in honor of its discovery site.

AMERICAN GOLDFINCH
VIOLET

⇧ HOLD ON! New Jersey's Atlantic coast is lined with sandy beaches that attract vacationers from near and far. Amusement parks, such as this one in Wildwood, add to the fun.

⇨ HEADED TO MARKET. New Jersey is a leading producer of fresh fruits and vegetables. These organic vegetables are headed for urban markets in the Northeast.

⇦ SUBURBAN SPRAWL. With more than 90 percent of the state's population living in urban areas, housing developments, with close-set, look-alike houses, are a common characteristic of the suburban landscape. Residents commute to jobs in the city.

⇧ PLAY BALL! Fans pack the seats at Newark's Bear and Eagles Riverfront Stadium to watch a minor league baseball game. Built in 1999, the stadium is a part of Newark's plan to revitalize the downtown area, drawing people into the city.

Economy Symbols

🐟	Fishing	🌽	Corn
🐚	Shellfish		Soybeans
🐔	Poultry/eggs		Printing/publishing
🐑	Sheep	⚒	Stone/gravel/cement
🐖	Hogs	⚙	Machinery
🐄	Dairy cows/products		Chemistry
🐂	Beef cattle	📷	Food processing
🍓	Fruits	💻	Computers/electronics
	Vegetables		Aerospace
	Nursery stock	📷	Tourism
🌾	Wheat		

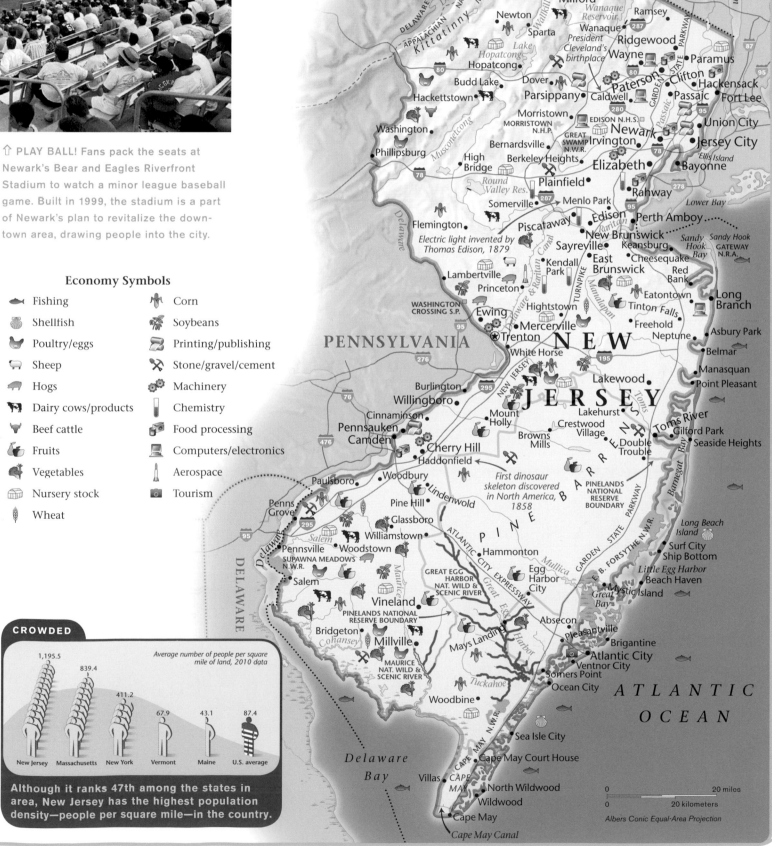

CROWDED

Average number of people per square mile of land, 2010 data

- 1,195.5 — New Jersey
- 839.4 — Massachusetts
- 411.2 — New York
- 67.9 — Vermont
- 43.1 — Maine
- 87.4 — U.S. average

Although it ranks 47th among the states in area, New Jersey has the highest population density—people per square mile—in the country.

THE EMPIRE STATE:
NEW YORK

THE BASICS

STATS

Area
54,556 sq mi (141,300 sq km)

Population
19,378,102

Capital
Albany
Population 97,856

Largest city
New York City
Population 8,175,133

Ethnic/racial groups
65.7% white; 15.9% African American;
7.3% Asian; .6% Native American.
Hispanic (any race) 17.6%.

Industry
Printing and publishing, machinery,
computer products, finance, tourism

Agriculture
Dairy products, cattle and other livestock, vegetables, nursery stock, apples

Statehood
July 26, 1788; 11th state

GEO WHIZ

Each year at Halloween the Headless
Horseman rides again through the countryside of Sleepy Hollow as residents
reenact Washington Irving's *The Legend
of Sleepy Hollow*.

The Erie Canal, built in the 1820s
between Albany and Buffalo, helped
New York City become a worldwide
trading center and opened the Midwest
to development by linking the Hudson
River and the Great Lakes.

Cooperstown, New York, home of the
National Baseball Hall of
Fame, takes its name
from a town estab-
lished in the late 1700s
by the father of James
Fenimore Cooper, author of
such American classics as
The Last of the Mohicans and
The Deerslayer.

EASTERN
BLUEBIRD

ROSE

NEW YORK

1   2   3

When Englishman Henry Hudson explored New York's
Hudson River Valley in 1609, the territory was already
inhabited by large tribes of Native Americans, including
the powerful Iroquois. In 1624 a Dutch trading company
established the New Netherland colony, but after just
40 years the colony was taken over by the English and
renamed for England's Duke of York. In 1788 New
York became the 11th state. The state can be
divided into two parts. The powerful
port city of New York, center of
trade and commerce and gateway to immigrants, is the
largest city in the U.S. Its
metropolitan area has
more than 18 million
people. Everything
north of the city
is simply referred
to as "Upstate."
Cities such as Buffalo
and Rochester are industrial centers, while
Ithaca and Syracuse boast major universities. Agriculture is also
important in New York. With almost 5 million acres in cropland,
the state is a major producer of dairy products, fruits, and vegetables.

⇧ **LADY LIBERTY.**
Standing in New York
Harbor, the Statue of
Liberty, a gift from the
people of France, is
a symbol of freedom
and democracy.

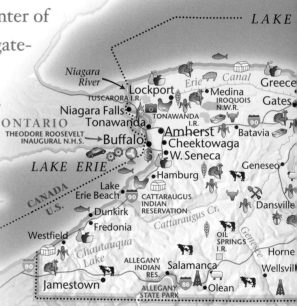

⇦ **NATURAL WONDER.**
As many as 12 million
tourists annually visit
Niagara Falls on the
U.S.-Canada border.
Visitors in rain slickers
trek through the mists
below Bridal Veil Falls
on the American side.

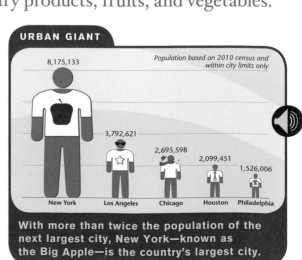

URBAN GIANT

*Population based on 2010 census and
within city limits only*

8,175,133

3,792,621

2,695,598

2,099,451

1,526,006

New York   Los Angeles   Chicago   Houston   Philadelphia

With more than twice the population of the
next largest city, New York—known as
the Big Apple—is the country's largest city.

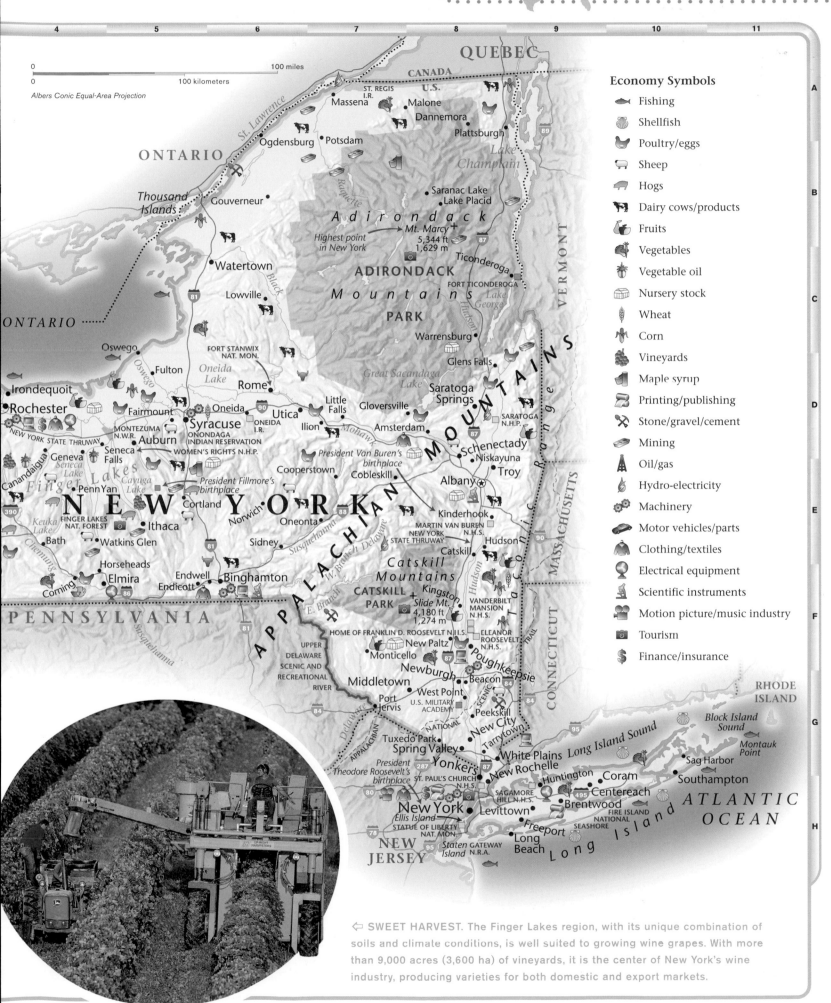

Economy Symbols

- Fishing
- Shellfish
- Poultry/eggs
- Sheep
- Hogs
- Dairy cows/products
- Fruits
- Vegetables
- Vegetable oil
- Nursery stock
- Wheat
- Corn
- Vineyards
- Maple syrup
- Printing/publishing
- Stone/gravel/cement
- Mining
- Oil/gas
- Hydro-electricity
- Machinery
- Motor vehicles/parts
- Clothing/textiles
- Electrical equipment
- Scientific instruments
- Motion picture/music industry
- Tourism
- $ Finance/insurance

0 ___ 100 miles
0 ___ 100 kilometers
Albers Conic Equal-Area Projection

QUEBEC
CANADA
U.S.
ONTARIO
VERMONT
MASSACHUSETTS
CONNECTICUT
RHODE ISLAND
PENNSYLVANIA
NEW JERSEY
ATLANTIC OCEAN

N E W   Y O R K

ADIRONDACK Mountains PARK
Adirondack
Mt. Marcy
Highest point in New York
5,344 ft
1,629 m
CATSKILL PARK
Catskill Mountains
Slide Mt.
4,180 ft
1,274 m
APPALACHIAN MOUNTAINS
FINGER LAKES NAT. FOREST
Finger Lakes
Thousand Islands

Massena, Malone, Dannemora, Plattsburgh, Ogdensburg, Potsdam, ST. REGIS I.R., Saranac Lake, Lake Placid, Gouverneur, Watertown, Lowville, Ticonderoga, FORT TICONDEROGA, Warrensburg, Glens Falls, Oswego, Fulton, Rome, FORT STANWIX NAT. MON., Little Falls, Gloversville, Saratoga Springs, SARATOGA N.H.P., Irondequoit, Rochester, Fairmount, Oneida, Utica, Ilion, Amsterdam, Schenectady, Niskayuna, Troy, Geneva, Syracuse, Auburn, ONONDAGA INDIAN RESERVATION, WOMEN'S RIGHTS N.H.P., President Van Buren's birthplace, Albany, Seneca Falls, Cooperstown, Cobleskill, Kinderhook, Penn Yan, Cortland, Norwich, Oneonta, MARTIN VAN BUREN N.H.S., Ithaca, Sidney, NEW YORK STATE THRUWAY, Hudson, Catskill, Bath, Watkins Glen, Horseheads, Elmira, Endwell, Binghamton, Kingston, VANDERBILT MANSION N.H.S., Corning, Endicott, HOME OF FRANKLIN D. ROOSEVELT N.H.S., ELEANOR ROOSEVELT N.H.S., UPPER DELAWARE SCENIC AND RECREATIONAL RIVER, New Paltz, Monticello, Poughkeepsie, Middletown, Newburgh, Beacon, Port Jervis, West Point, U.S. MILITARY ACADEMY, Peekskill, President Theodore Roosevelt's birthplace, Tuxedo Park, Spring Valley, New City, Tarrytown, White Plains, New Rochelle, ST. PAUL'S CHURCH N.H.S., Yonkers, SAGAMORE HILL N.H.S., Huntington, Coram, Centereach, Brentwood, New York, Levittown, Freeport, Long Beach, Ellis Island, STATUE OF LIBERTY NAT. MON., Staten Island, GATEWAY N.R.A., Sag Harbor, Southampton, Montauk Point, Block Island Sound, Long Island Sound, FIRE ISLAND NATIONAL SEASHORE, MONTEZUMA N.W.R.

President Fillmore's birthplace

Seneca Lake, Cayuga Lake, Keuka Lake, Canandaigua, Oneida Lake, Lake Champlain, Lake George, Great Sacandaga Lake, St. Lawrence, Raquette, Black, Oswego, Mohawk, Hudson, Susquehanna, Delaware, W. Branch Delaware, E. Branch, Chemung, Taconic Range

APPALACHIAN NATIONAL SCENIC TRAIL

SWEET HARVEST
The Finger Lakes region, with its unique combination of soils and climate conditions, is well suited to growing wine grapes. With more than 9,000 acres (3,600 ha) of vineyards, it is the center of New York's wine industry, producing varieties for both domestic and export markets.

THE KEYSTONE STATE:
PENNSYLVANIA

PENNSYLVANIA

1   2

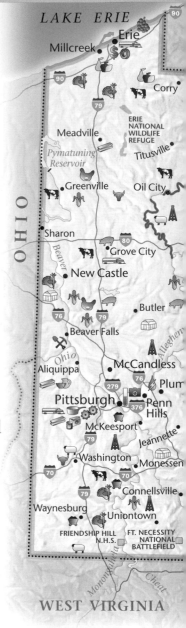

Pennsylvania, the 12th of England's 13 American colonies, was established in 1682 by Quaker William Penn and 360 settlers seeking religious freedom and fair government. The colony enjoyed abundant natural resources—dense woodlands, fertile soils, industrial minerals, and water power—that soon attracted Germans, Scotch-Irish, and other immigrants. Pennsylvania played a central role in the move for independence from Britain, and Philadelphia served as the new country's capital from 1790 to 1800. In the 19th century Philadelphia, in the east, and Pittsburgh, in the west, became booming centers of industrial growth. Philadelphia produced ships, locomotives, and textiles, while the iron and steel industry fueled Pittsburgh's growth. Jobs in industry as well as agriculture attracted immigrants from around the world. Today, Pennsylvania's economy has shifted toward information technology, health care, financial services, and tourism, but the state remains a leader in coal and steel production.

⇧ LET FREEDOM RING. The Liberty Bell, cast in 1753 by Pennsylvania craftsmen, hangs silent in Philadelphia. Because of a crack, it is no longer rung.

THE BASICS

STATS

Area
46,055 sq mi (119,283 sq km)

Population
12,702,379

Capital
Harrisburg
Population 49,528

Largest city
Philadelphia
Population 1,526,006

Ethnic/racial groups
81.9% white; 10.8% African American; 2.7% Asian; .2% Native American. Hispanic (any race) 5.7%.

Industry
Machinery, printing and publishing, forest products, metal products

Agriculture
Dairy products, poultry and eggs, mushrooms, cattle, hogs, grains

Statehood
December 12, 1787; 2nd state

GEO WHIZ

If you are into guitars or other acoustic instruments, you will want to put the Martin Guitar Company, in Nazareth, on your list of places to visit. It has been handcrafting these instruments for musicians all over the world for more than 150 years.

For more than a century, the streets of Philadelphia have been transformed on New Year's Day as some 15,000 revelers dressed in sequined and feathered costumes "strut their stuff" to the sound of string-band music in the Mummers Parade past millions of onlookers.

RUFFED GROUSE
MOUNTAIN LAUREL

⇨ RIVER TOWN. Pittsburgh, one of the largest inland ports in the U.S., was established in 1758 where the Monongahela and Allegheny Rivers meet to form the Ohio River. Once a booming steel town, Pittsburgh is now a center of finance, medicine, and education.

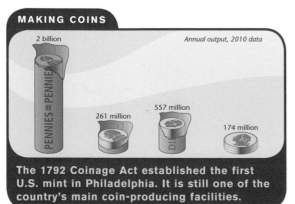

MAKING COINS

Annual output, 2010 data

2 billion

PENNIES = PENNIE[S]

261 million

557 million

174 million

The 1792 Coinage Act established the first U.S. mint in Philadelphia. It is still one of the country's main coin-producing facilities.

3 4 5 6 7 8 9 10

NEW YORK

50 miles
50 kilometers
Albers Conic Equal-Area Projection

Allegheny Reservoir
Warren · Bradford
ALLEGHENY NATIONAL WILD & SCENIC RIVER
ALLEGHENY NATIONAL FOREST
Coudersport
Mansfield
Wellsboro
Sayre
Towanda
Chemung
Tioga
Susquehanna
Carbondale
Archbald
UPPER DELAWARE SCENIC & RECREATIONAL RIVER
Emporium
St. Marys
Ridgway
Pine Creek Gorge
Scranton · Dunmore
STEAMTOWN N.H.S.
Lake Wallenpaupack
Clarion
CLARION NATIONAL WILD & SCENIC RIVER
Du Bois
Clearfield
Jersey Shore
Williamsport
Lock Haven
Kingston
Wilkes-Barre
Pocono Mts.
DELAWARE WATER GAP NATIONAL RECREATION AREA
West Branch Susquehanna
Punxsutawney
Lewisburg
Bloomsburg
Hazleton
Stroudsburg
Delaware Water Gap
PENNSYLVANIA
MOUNTAINS
Selinsgrove
Sunbury
Mt. Carmel
Tamaqua
Bangor
Kittanning
State College
Shamokin
Pottsville
Nazareth
Easton
Indiana
Tyrone
Lewistown
Juniata
Pottsville
Bethlehem
Allentown
NEW JERSEY
ALLEGHENY PORTAGE RAILROAD N.H.S.
Altoona
Huntingdon
APPALACHIAN NATIONAL SCENIC TRAIL
Blue
Quakertown
JOHNSTOWN FLOOD NAT. MEM.
Hollidaysburg
Mountain
Reading
Doylestown
Conemaugh
Raystown Lake
Harrisburg
Lebanon
Pottstown
Greensburg
Mechanicsburg
Hershey
HOPEWELL FURNACE N.H.S.
Johnstown
Carlisle
PENNSYLVANIA TURNPIKE
Norristown
Levittown
Windber
Three Mile Island
Ephrata
VALLEY FORGE N.H.P.
PENNSYLVANIA TURNPIKE
President Buchanan's birthplace
Shippensburg
Elizabethtown
Lancaster
Coatesville
Upper Darby
Somerset
Bedford
Columbia
York
Red Lion
West Chester
Kennett Square
Philadelphia
Mt. Davis 3,213 ft 979 m
Highest point in Pennsylvania
Chambersburg
Gettysburg
EISENHOWER N.H.S.
GETTYSBURG N.M.P.
Hanover
JOHN HEINZ N.W.R.
Chester
Mercersburg
Waynesboro
Mason-Dixon Line
DEL.
MARYLAND
W.VA.
Named after its surveyors, the Pennsylvania-Maryland boundary became the traditional division between North and South.

Busiest freshwater port in the U.S., Independence N.H.P. (includes Independence Hall, Liberty Bell, Christ Church, Franklin Court), Betsy Ross House, Edgar Allan Poe N.H.S., Deshler-Morris House, Gloria Dei Church N.H.S.

Economy Symbols

- Poultry/eggs
- Sheep
- Hogs
- Dairy cows/products
- Beef cattle
- Fruits
- Vegetables
- Nursery stock
- Corn
- Soybeans
- Tobacco
- Vineyards
- Timber/forest products
- Printing/publishing
- Stone/gravel/cement
- Mining
- Coal
- Oil/gas
- Hydro-electricity
- Machinery
- Metal manufacturing
- Railroad equipment
- Motor vehicles/parts
- Rubber/plastics
- Chemistry
- Food processing
- Glass/clay products
- Computers/electronics
- Tourism
- Finance/insurance

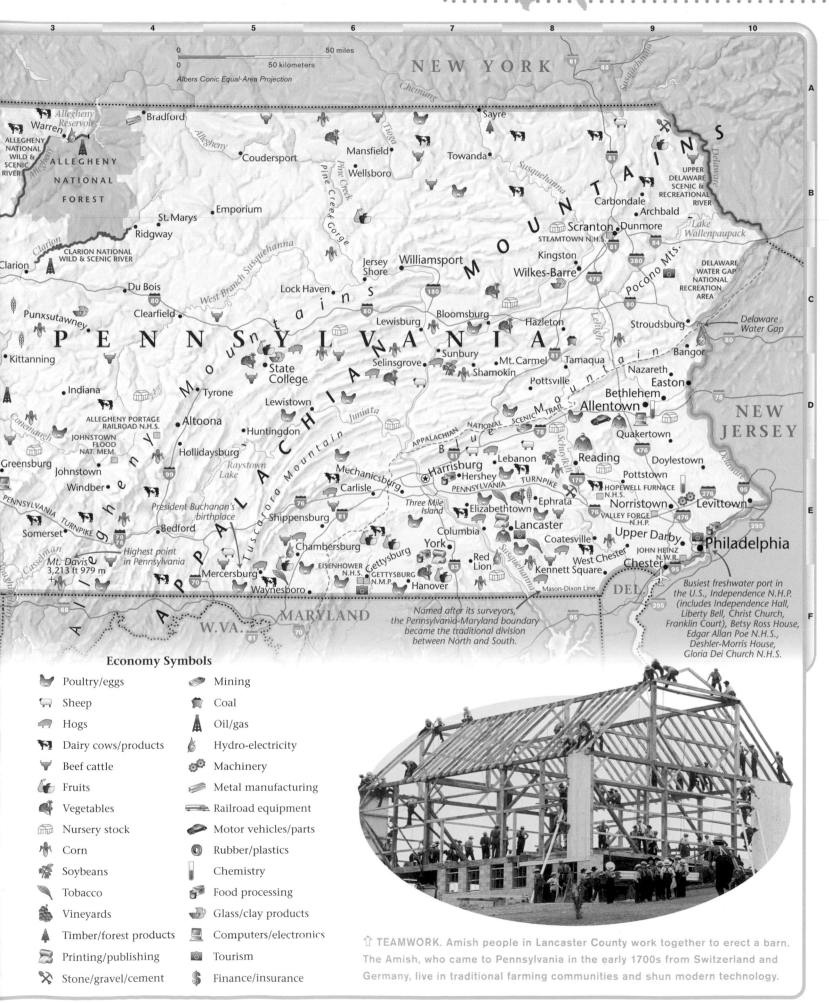

⇧ TEAMWORK. Amish people in Lancaster County work together to erect a barn. The Amish, who came to Pennsylvania in the early 1700s from Switzerland and Germany, live in traditional farming communities and shun modern technology.

RHODE ISLAND

In 1524 Italian navigator Giovanni Verrazzano was the first European explorer to visit Rhode Island, but place-names such as Quonochontaug and Narragansett tell of an earlier Native American population. In 1636 Roger Williams, seeking greater religious freedom, left Massachusetts and established the first European settlement in what was to become the colony of Rhode Island. In the years following the Revolutionary War, Rhode Island pressed for fairness in trade, taxes, and representation in Congress, as well as greater freedom of worship, before becoming the 13th state. By the 19th century, Rhode Island had become an important center of trade and textile factories, attracting many immigrants from Europe. In addition to commercial activities, Rhode Island's coastline became a popular vacation retreat for the wealthy. Today, Rhode Island, like many other states, has seen its economy shift toward high-tech jobs and service industries. It is also promoting its coastline and bays, as well as its rich history, to attract tourists.

⇧ CLUES TO THE PAST. Fossils embedded in rocks left behind 10,000 years ago by retreating glaciers tell of Block Island's past.

THE BASICS

STATS

Area
1,545 sq mi (4,002 sq km)

Population
1,052,567

Capital
Providence
Population 178,042

Largest city
Providence
Population 178,042

Ethnic/racial groups
81.4% white; 5.7% African American; 2.9% Asian; .6% Native American. Hispanic (any race) 12.4%.

Industry
Health services, business services, silver and jewelry products, metal products

Agriculture
Nursery stock, vegetables, dairy products, eggs

Statehood
May 29, 1790; 13th state

GEO WHIZ

Pawtucket is one of several communities in Rhode Island that have become home to a growing number of people from Cape Verde. Drought has forced people from this African country to find a new place to live. Massachusetts and North Dakota are the only other states with measurable Cape Verdean populations.

Wild coyotes are living and thriving on islands in Narragansett Bay. Researchers have outfitted some of the animals with radio collars so that their numbers and whereabouts can be tracked online—even by schoolkids.

RHODE ISLAND RED
VIOLET

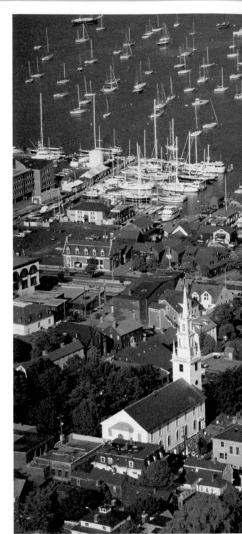

⇦ SETTING SAIL. Newport Harbor invites sailors of all ages. From 1930 to 1983, the prestigious America's Cup Yacht Race took place in the waters off Newport. Today, the town provides 900 moorings for boats of all types.

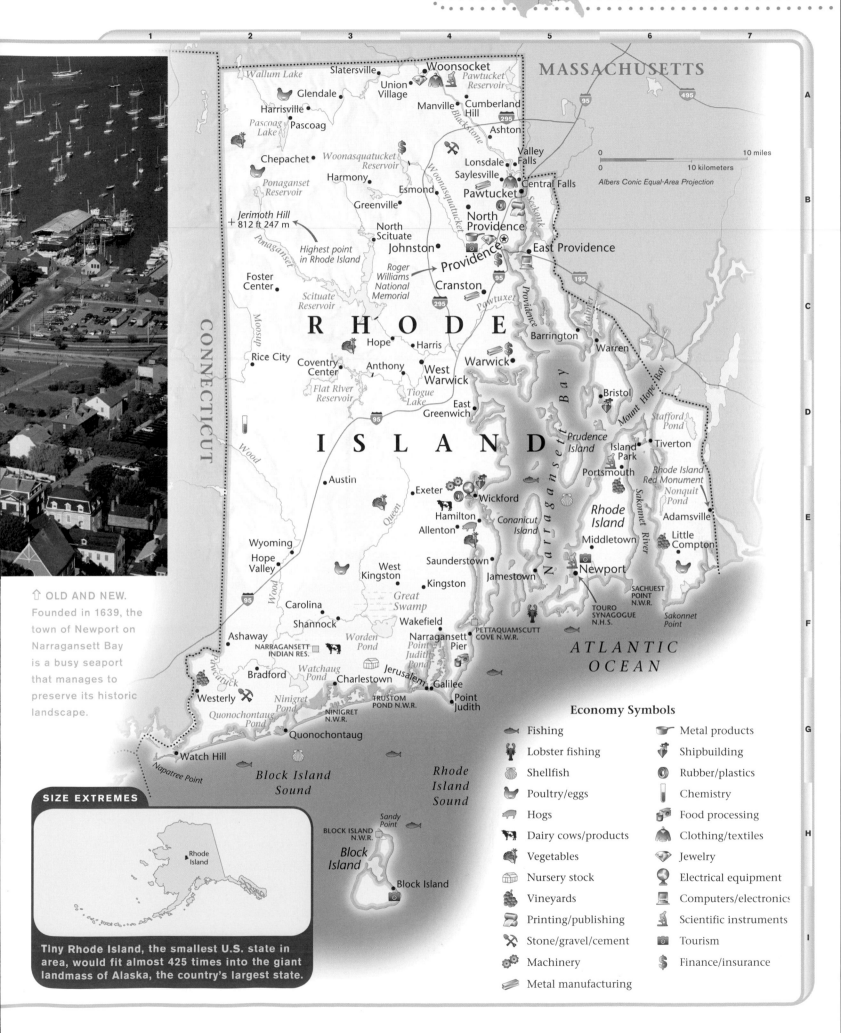

1 2 3 4 5 6 7

MASSACHUSETTS

Wallum Lake   Slatersville   **Woonsocket**
Glendale   Union   *Pawtucket*
Village   *Reservoir*
Harrisville   Manville   Cumberland
Pascoag   Pascoag   Hill
Lake   Ashton
Chepachet   *Woonasquatucket*   Valley
Reservoir   Falls
Harmony   Lonsdale
Esmond   Saylesville   Central Falls
Greenville   **Pawtucket**
North   North
+ Jerimoth Hill   Scituate   Providence
812 ft 247 m   Johnston   East Providence
Highest point   Roger
in Rhode Island   Williams   Providence
National   Cranston
Foster   Memorial
Center

R H O D E

Scituate   Barrington
Reservoir   Hope   Harris   Warren
Rice City   Coventry   Warwick
Center   Anthony   West
Flat River   Warwick   Bristol
Reservoir   *Tiogue*
Lake   East   Prudence   Island   Tiverton
Greenwich   Island   Park
Portsmouth   *Stafford*
Pond
I S L A N D   *Rhode Island*
Red Monument
Austin   *Rhode*   *Nonquit*
Island   *Pond*
Exeter   Wickford   Middletown   Adamsville
Conanicut   Little
Hamilton   *Island*   Compton
Wyoming   Allenton
Hope   Saunderstown   Newport
Valley   West   *Sachuest*
Kingston   Jamestown   *Point*
Carolina   Kingston   TOURO   *N.W.R.*
SYNAGOGUE   *Sakonnet*
Great   N.H.S.   *Point*
Shannock   *Swamp*   Wakefield
Ashaway   Narragansett   *ATLANTIC*
NARRAGANSETT   *Worden*   Point   Pier   PETTAQUAMSCUTT   *OCEAN*
INDIAN RES.   *Pond*   *Judith*   COVE N.W.R.
Pond
Bradford   *Watchaug*   Jerusalem
Pond   Charlestown   Galilee
Westerly   *Ninigret*   Point
Pond   TRUSTOM   Judith
Quonochontaug   NINIGRET   POND N.W.R.
Pond   N.W.R.
Watch Hill   Quonochontaug

CONNECTICUT

Wood   *Moosup*   *Queen*   *Pawtuxet*   *Providence*
Ponaganset   *Woonasquatucket*   *Blackstone*   *Seekonk*   *Palmer*
Narragansett   Bay   *Mount   Hope   Bay*   *Sakonnet   River*

Napatree Point
Block Island   *Rhode*
Sound   *Island*
Sound

0   10 miles
0   10 kilometers
Albers Conic Equal-Area Projection

⬆ OLD AND NEW.
Founded in 1639, the
town of Newport on
Narragansett Bay
is a busy seaport
that manages to
preserve its historic
landscape.

SIZE EXTREMES

▶ Rhode
Island

BLOCK ISLAND   *Sandy*
N.W.R.   *Point*
Block
Island
Block Island

Tiny Rhode Island, the smallest U.S. state in
area, would fit almost 425 times into the giant
landmass of Alaska, the country's largest state.

Economy Symbols

🦐 Fishing   🔧 Metal products
🦞 Lobster fishing 🔨 Shipbuilding
🐚 Shellfish   ◎ Rubber/plastics
🐔 Poultry/eggs   🧪 Chemistry
🐖 Hogs   📷 Food processing
🐄 Dairy cows/products   👚 Clothing/textiles
🥬 Vegetables   💎 Jewelry
🏠 Nursery stock   🌐 Electrical equipment
🍇 Vineyards   💻 Computers/electronics
📰 Printing/publishing   🔬 Scientific instruments
⚒ Stone/gravel/cement   📷 Tourism
⚙ Machinery   💲 Finance/insurance
🛠 Metal manufacturing

THE GREEN MOUNTAIN STATE:
VERMONT

VERMONT

When French explorer Jacques Cartier arrived in Vermont in 1535, Native Americans living in woodland villages had been there for hundreds of years. Settled first by the French in 1666 and then by the English in 1724, the territory of Vermont became an area of conflict between these colonial powers. The French finally withdrew, but conflict continued between New York and New Hampshire, both of which wanted to take over Vermont. The people of Vermont declared their independence in 1777, and Vermont became the 14th U.S. state in 1791. Vermont's name, which means "Green Mountain," comes from the extensive forests that cover much of the state and provide the basis for furniture and pulp industries. Vermont also boasts the world's largest granite quarry and the largest underground marble quarry, both of which produce valuable building materials. Tourism and recreation are also important in Vermont. Lakes, rivers, and mountain trails are popular summer attractions, while snow-covered mountains attract skiers throughout the winter.

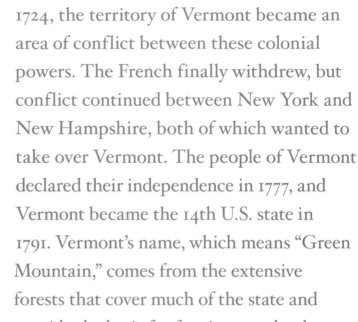

⇧ LIQUID GOLD. In spring, sap from maple trees is collected in buckets by drilling a hole in the tree trunk—called "tapping." The sap is boiled to remove water, then filtered, and finally bottled.

THE BASICS

STATS

Area
9,614 sq mi (24,901 sq km)

Population
625,741

Capital
Montpelier
Population 7,855

Largest city
Burlington
Population 42,417

Ethnic/racial groups
95.3% white; 1.3% Asian; 1.0% African American; .4% Native American. Hispanic (any race) 1.5%.

Industry
Health services, tourism, finance, real estate, computer components, electrical parts, printing and publishing, machine tools

Agriculture
Dairy products, maple products, apples

Statehood
March 4, 1791; 14th state

GEO WHIZ

Barre is famous for producing granite gravestones. The tombstones of President Harry S. Truman, industrialist John D. Rockefeller, Sr., songwriter Stephen Foster, and fast-food-chain founder Col. Harland Sanders are all made of Barre Gray granite, as are the steps of the U.S. Capitol in Washington, D.C.

Burlington is the home of Ben & Jerry's ice cream. The company gives its leftovers to local farmers, who feed it to their hogs. The hogs seem to like every flavor except Mint Oreo.

From 1777 until it became a state in 1791, Vermont was an independent country. It had its own postal and monetary systems.

Vermont, the third-largest state in New England, is the only state in the region that does not border the Atlantic Ocean.

HERMIT THRUSH
RED CLOVER

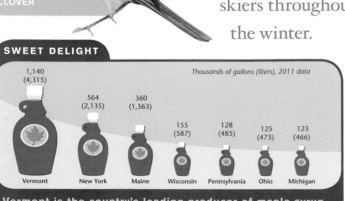

SWEET DELIGHT

Thousands of gallons (liters), 2011 data

Vermont	New York	Maine	Wisconsin	Pennsylvania	Ohio	Michigan
1,140 (4,315)	564 (2,135)	360 (1,363)	155 (587)	128 (485)	125 (473)	123 (466)

Vermont is the country's leading producer of maple syrup. The syrup is all natural, with no added ingredients or preservatives, just boiled sap collected from maple trees.

⇧ WINTER WONDERLAND. One of the snowiest places in the Northeast, Jay Peak averages 355 inches (900 cm) of snow each year. With 76 trails, the mountain, near Vermont's border with Canada, attracts beginner and expert skiers from near and far.

Economy Symbols

- 🐔 Poultry/eggs
- 🐑 Sheep
- 🐄 Dairy cows/products
- 🐂 Beef cattle
- 🍓 Fruits
- 🥦 Vegetables
- 🏛 Nursery stock
- 🌽 Corn
- 🍁 Maple syrup
- 🌲 Timber/forest products
- 🖨 Printing/publishing
- ⚒ Stone/gravel/cement
- 💧 Hydro-electricity
- 🍳 Metal products
- 📷 Food processing
- 💻 Computers/electronics
- 📷 Tourism

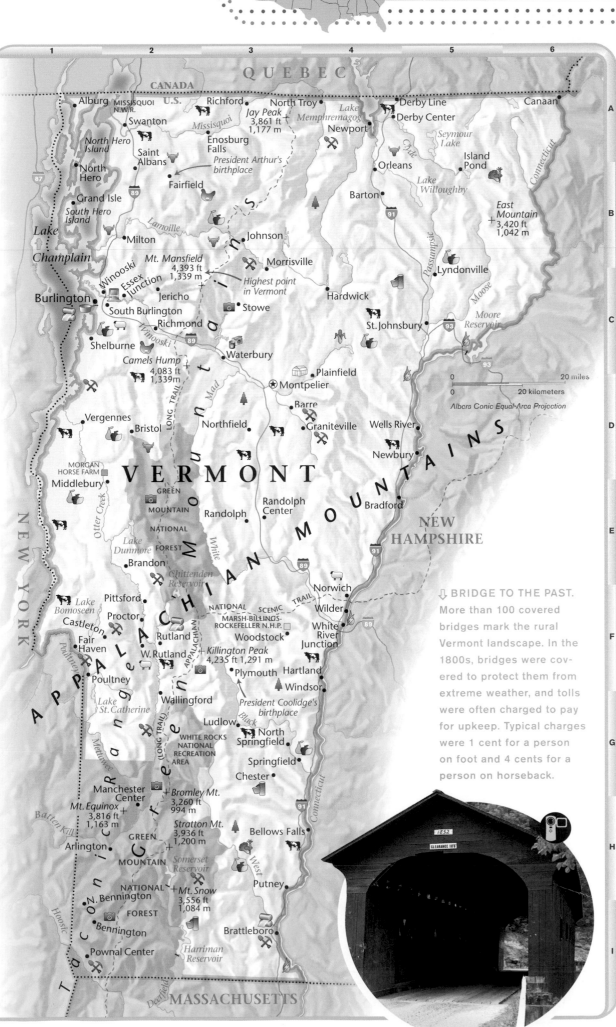

⇩ BRIDGE TO THE PAST.
More than 100 covered
bridges mark the rural
Vermont landscape. In the
1800s, bridges were cov-
ered to protect them from
extreme weather, and tolls
were often charged to pay
for upkeep. Typical charges
were 1 cent for a person
on foot and 4 cents for a
person on horseback.

THE REGION

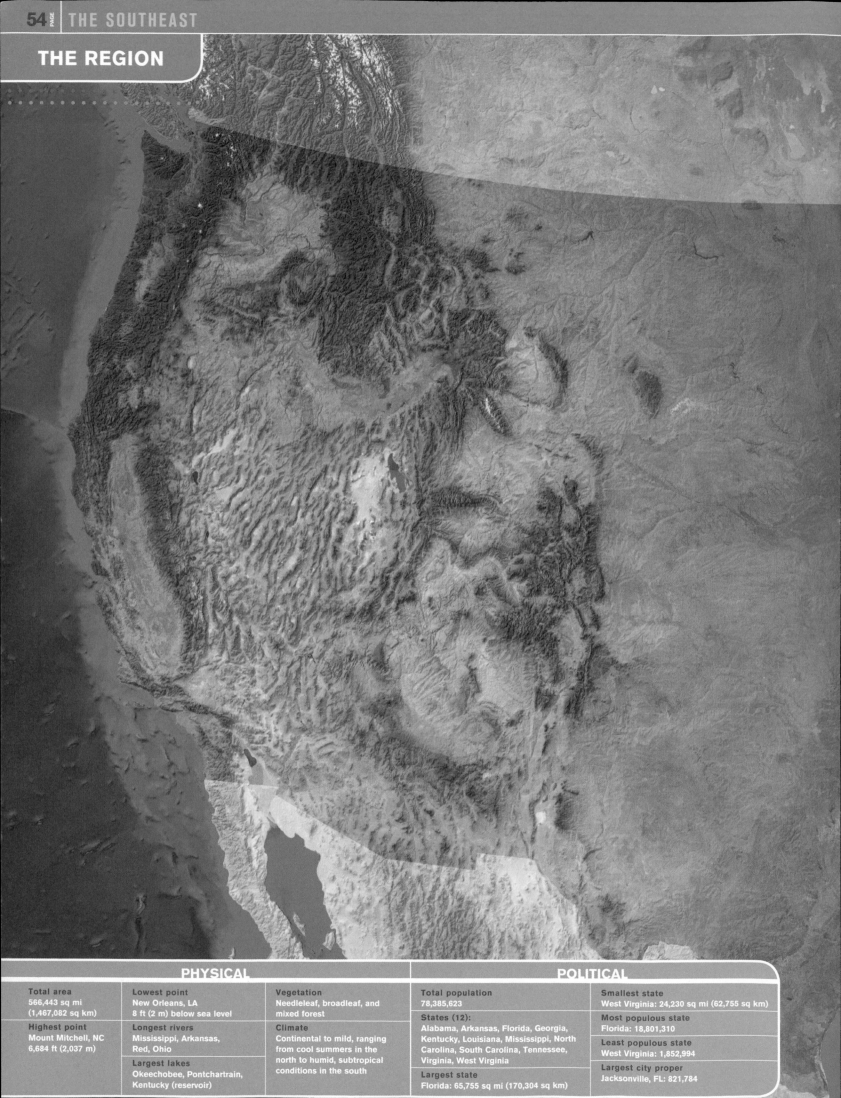

PHYSICAL

Total area
566,443 sq mi
(1,467,082 sq km)

Highest point
Mount Mitchell, NC
6,684 ft (2,037 m)

Lowest point
New Orleans, LA
8 ft (2 m) below sea level

Longest rivers
Mississippi, Arkansas,
Red, Ohio

Largest lakes
Okeechobee, Pontchartrain,
Kentucky (reservoir)

Vegetation
Needleleaf, broadleaf, and
mixed forest

Climate
Continental to mild, ranging
from cool summers in the
north to humid, subtropical
conditions in the south

POLITICAL

Total population
78,385,623

States (12):
Alabama, Arkansas, Florida, Georgia,
Kentucky, Louisiana, Mississippi, North
Carolina, South Carolina, Tennessee,
Virginia, West Virginia

Largest state
Florida: 65,755 sq mi (170,304 sq km)

Smallest state
West Virginia: 24,230 sq mi (62,755 sq km)

Most populous state
Florida: 18,801,310

Least populous state
West Virginia: 1,852,994

Largest city proper
Jacksonville, FL: 821,784

The Southeast

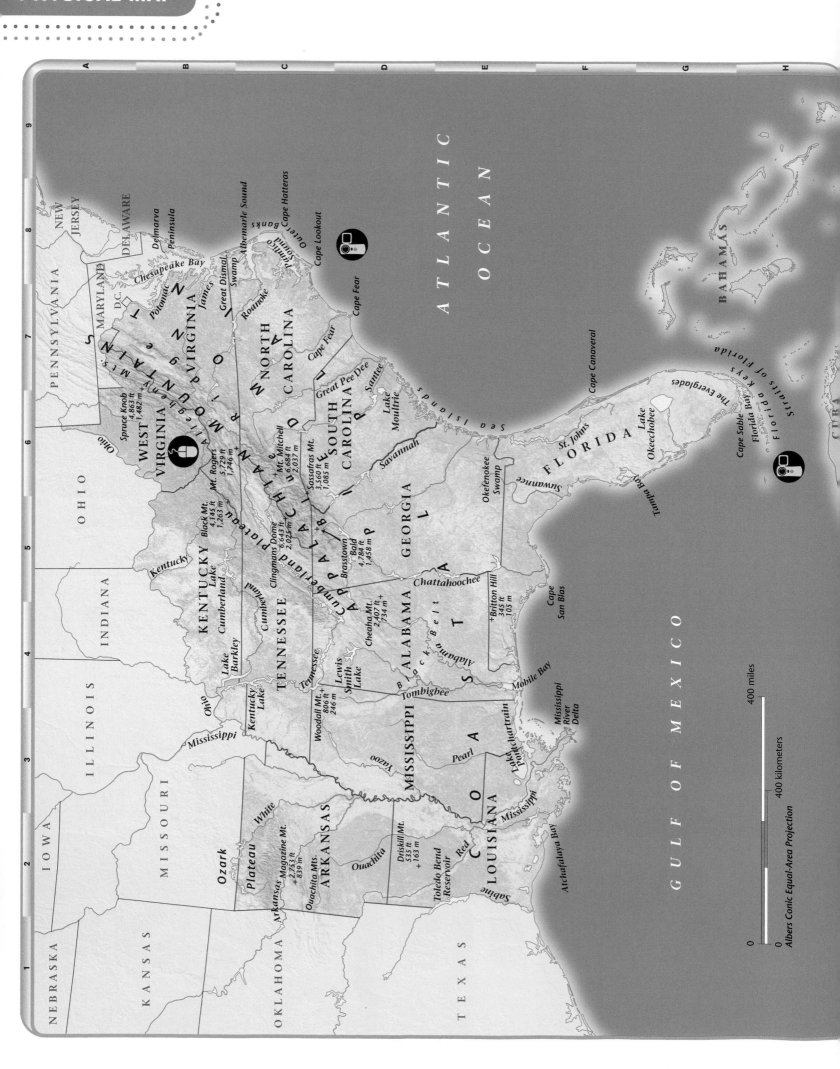

A B C D E F G H

9 8 7 6 5 4 3 2 1

NEW JERSEY
DELAWARE
PENNSYLVANIA
MARYLAND
D.C.
Delmarva Peninsula
Chesapeake Bay
Potomac
VIRGINIA
WEST VIRGINIA
James
Great Dismal Swamp
Albemarle Sound
Pamlico Sound
Outer Banks
Cape Hatteras
Cape Lookout

ATLANTIC OCEAN

Spruce Knob 4,863 ft 1,482 m +
Ohio
Roanoke
NORTH CAROLINA
Cape Fear
Cape Fear

Blue Ridge Mts.
Allegheny Mountains
Mt. Rogers 5,729 ft 1,746 m
Black Mt. 4,145 ft 1,263 m
+ Mt. Mitchell 6,684 ft 2,037 m
Sassafras Mt. 3,560 ft 1,085 m +
Great Pee Dee
Santee
SOUTH CAROLINA
Lake Moultrie
Savannah
Sea Islands

OHIO
KENTUCKY
Kentucky Lake
Clingmans Dome 6,643 ft 2,025 m +
Cumberland Plateau
APPALACHIAN MOUNTAINS
Brasstown Bald 4,784 ft 1,458 m +
GEORGIA
Chattahoochee

FLORIDA
St. Johns
Cape Canaveral
BAHAMAS
Straits of Florida
Florida Keys
The Everglades
Cape Sable
Florida Bay
Lake Okeechobee
Okefenokee Swamp
Suwannee

INDIANA
Lake Cumberland
TENNESSEE
Tennessee
Cumberland
Lewis Smith Lake
Cheaha Mt. 2,407 ft 734 m +
ALABAMA
Black Belt
Alabama
+ Britton Hill 345 ft 105 m
Cape San Blas
Mobile Bay
Tombigbee

ILLINOIS
Lake Barkley
Kentucky Lake
Woodall Mt. 806 ft 246 m +
MISSISSIPPI
Tombigbee
Pearl
Lake Pontchartrain
Mississippi River Delta

MISSOURI
Ohio
Mississippi
Yazoo
COASTAL PLAIN
LOUISIANA
Mississippi
Atchafalaya Bay

IOWA
NEBRASKA
KANSAS
Ozark Plateau
White
Magazine Mt. 2,753 ft 839 m +
Arkansas
Ouachita Mts.
ARKANSAS
Ouachita
Driskill Mt. 535 ft 163 m +
Toledo Bend Reservoir
Red
Sabine

OKLAHOMA
TEXAS

GULF OF MEXICO

Tampa Bay

400 miles
400 kilometers
Albers Conic Equal-Area Projection
0

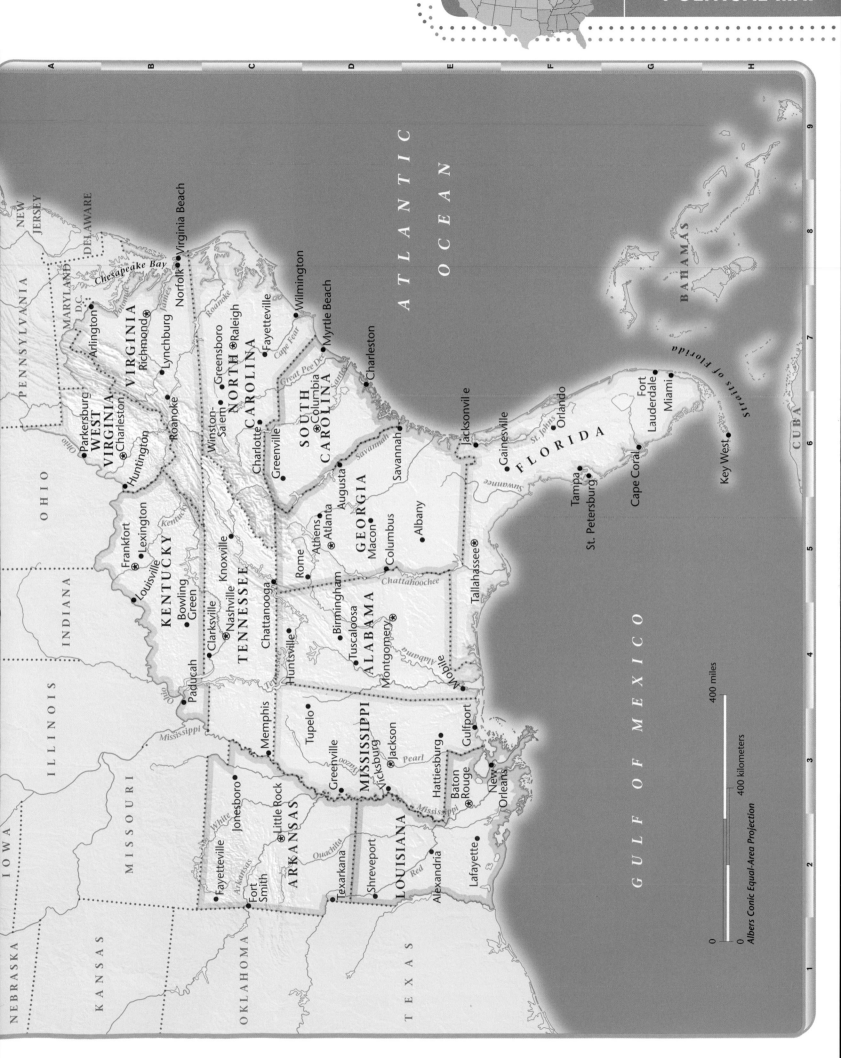

THE SOUTHEAST

ATLANTIC OCEAN

GULF OF MEXICO

States and features labeled on map:

NEW JERSEY
PENNSYLVANIA
DELAWARE
MARYLAND
D.C.
Arlington
Parkersburg
WEST VIRGINIA
Charleston
Huntington
Chesapeake Bay
Potomac
VIRGINIA
Richmond
Lynchburg
James
Norfolk
Virginia Beach
Roanoke
Roanoke
OHIO
Frankfort
Lexington
Kentucky
Louisville
KENTUCKY
Bowling Green
Clarksville
Nashville
Knoxville
TENNESSEE
Chattanooga
Paducah
Memphis
Greensboro
Winston-Salem
NORTH CAROLINA
Raleigh
Fayetteville
Charlotte
Greenville
Cape Fear
Wilmington
Great Pee Dee
SOUTH CAROLINA
Columbia
Santee
Myrtle Beach
Charleston
Savannah
Savannah
GEORGIA
Augusta
Athens
Atlanta
Rome
Macon
Columbus
Albany
Chattahoochee
Huntsville
Birmingham
Tuscaloosa
ALABAMA
Montgomery
Alabama
Mobile
Tallahassee
Suwannee
FLORIDA
Jacksonville
Gainesville
St. Johns
Orlando
Tampa
St. Petersburg
Cape Coral
Fort Lauderdale
Miami
Key West
Straits of Florida
CUBA
BAHAMAS
Tupelo
MISSISSIPPI
Greenville
Vicksburg
Jackson
Yazoo
Pearl
Hattiesburg
Gulfport
Mississippi
Baton Rouge
New Orleans
LOUISIANA
Shreveport
Alexandria
Lafayette
Red
Texarkana
ARKANSAS
Little Rock
Jonesboro
Fayetteville
Fort Smith
White
Arkansas
Ouachita
Ohio
Tennessee
Mississippi
ILLINOIS
INDIANA
MISSOURI
KANSAS
NEBRASKA
IOWA
OKLAHOMA
TEXAS

400 miles
400 kilometers
0
0
Albers Conic Equal-Area Projection

⇨ OPEN WIDE. An American alligator in Florida's Big Cypress Swamp shows off sharp teeth. These large reptiles live mainly in fresh-water swamps and marshes in coastal areas of the Southeast. Adult males average 14 feet (4 m) in length.

The Southeast

TRADITION MEETS TECHNOLOGY

From deeply weathered mountains in West Virginia to warm, humid wetlands in south Florida and the Mississippi River's sprawling delta in southern Louisiana, the Southeast is marked by great physical diversity. The region's historical roots are in agriculture—especially cotton and tobacco. The Civil War brought economic and political upheaval in the mid-19th century, but today the Southeast is part of the Sunbelt, where 6 of the top 20 metropolitan areas of the U.S. are found and where high-tech industries are redefining the way people earn a living and the way the region is connected to the global economy.

⇨ ENCHANTED KINGDOM. Fireworks light up the night sky above Cinderella's Castle at Walt Disney World near Orlando, Florida. The park, which accounts for 6 percent of all jobs in central Florida, attracts millions of tourists from around the world each year.

⇧ SOCIAL CONSCIENCE. Members of the Big Nine Social Aid and Pleasure Club of New Orleans's Lower Ninth Ward march in a parade through a neighborhood devastated by Hurricane Katrina. Such clubs, which date back to late-19th-century benevolent societies, bring support and hope to communities in need.

WHERE THE PICTURES ARE

Banjo playing p. 69
Horse race p. 68
Black bear family p. 78
Motorboats p. 79
Grand Ole Opry p. 79
Indian
Woman p. 75
Space camp p. 60
Race car
p. 59
Rockclimber
p. 62
Bird-
watchers
p. 62

River rafting
p. 83

Coal miner p. 82
Cyclists on outcrop
pp. 58-59
Harpers
Ferry p. 82
Luray Caverns p. 80
Cyclists
pp. 80-81
Dice p. 80

Wright
Brothers
Memorial
p. 74
Blackbeard's
cannon p. 59
Boys playing
basketball p. 74
Beach scene p. 76
Wild turkey p. 77
Historic
Charleston pp. 76-77
Aerial of
Sea Islands p. 66
Shuttle launch
pp. 64-65
Alligator p. 58

Diamond
hunter p. 63
Paddleboat
p. 72
Blues
guitarist p. 72
Catfish p. 73
Oak Alley
Plantation p. 70
Katrina parade p. 58
Shrimp fisherman p. 70

Atlanta p. 66
Oil rig p. 60
Peanuts p. 66
Manatee p. 64
Cinderella's Castle p. 58,
Girl in parade p. 64

⇧ VIEW FROM ABOVE. Cyclists look out from a rocky ledge across West Virginia's Germany Valley. The area took its name from German immigrants who moved there in the mid-1700s from North Carolina and Pennsylvania and established farming villages.

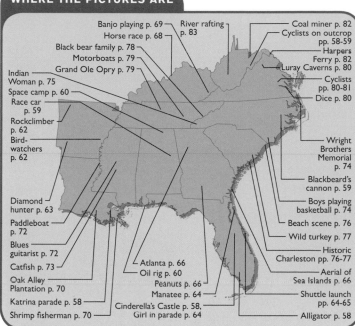

⇨ CAR STARS. For more than 50 years, auto racing has been a leading sport in the U.S., especially in the Southeast. The International Motorsports Hall of Fame, located adjacent to the Talledega Superspeedway in Alabama, features racing cars, motorcycles, and vintage cars.

⇦ PIRATE'S DEFENSE. This 4.5-foot (1.4-m) cast-iron cannon was recovered from the wreck of the *Queen Anne's Revenge* off North Carolina's coast. The vessel, which probably belonged to the notorious pirate Blackbeard, grounded on a sandbar and sank in 1718 near Cape Lookout.

THE BASICS

STATS

Area
52,419 sq mi (135,765 sq km)

Population
4,779,736

Capital
Montgomery
Population 205,764

Largest city
Birmingham
Population 212,237

Ethnic/racial groups
68.5% white; 26.2% African American;
1.1% Asian; .6% Native American.
Hispanic (any race) 3.9%.

Industry
Retail and wholesale trade, services,
government, finance, insurance, real
estate, transportation, construction,
communication

Agriculture
Fruits and vegetables, dairy products,
cattle, forest products, commercial
fishing

Statehood
December 14, 1819; 22nd state

GEO WHIZ

Condoleezza Rice, the first African-American woman to serve as U.S. Secretary of State, and Rosa Parks, whose refusal to give up her seat on a Montgomery bus earned her the title "mother of the modern-day civil rights movement," were both born in Alabama: Rice in Birmingham and Parks in Tuskegee.

Russell Cave, near Bridgeport, was home to prehistoric peoples for more than 10,000 years. In 1961 a national monument was established on land donated by the National Geographic Society. Today, visitors can take guided tours of the cave and see the kinds of tools and weapons its early inhabitants used.

In 2004 Hurricane Ivan, one of the worst storms to batter Alabama's gulf coast since 1900, struck Orange Beach.

NORTHERN
FLICKER
CAMELLIA

ALABAMA

Alabama has a colorful story. The French established the first permanent European settlement at Mobile Bay in 1702, but different groups—British, Native Americans, and U.S. settlers—struggled over control of the land for more than 100 years. In 1819 Alabama became the 22nd state, but in 1861 it joined the Confederacy. During the Civil War, Montgomery was the capital of the secessionist South for a time. After the war Alabama struggled to rebuild its agriculture-based economy. By 1900 the state was producing more than one million bales of cotton annually. In the mid-20th century, Alabama was at the center of the civil rights movement, which pressed for equal rights for all people regardless of race or social status. Key players included Martin Luther King, Jr., and Rosa Parks. Modern industries, including the NASA space program, have given the state's economy a big boost. In 2002 assembly plants built by automakers from Asia created thousands of new jobs.

⇧ UNDERWATER RESOURCE. A massive drill descends from an offshore oil rig to tap petroleum deposits beneath the water of the Gulf of Mexico off Alabama's shore.

ON THE ROAD

Alabama car and light-truck production, 2002–2010

Year	Production
2002	196,291
2004	253,200
2006	698,086
2008	672,000
2010	711,000

Since the first vehicles rolled off the assembly line in 1993, Alabama has risen to number 5 in national car and light-truck production.

⇧ ROCKET POWER. Students inspect giant booster rockets during Space Camp at Marshall Space Flight Center, in Huntsville, Alabama. The center is one of NASA's largest installations, providing support to space shuttle missions and the International Space Station.

Economy Symbols

- Fishing
- Shellfish
- Poultry/eggs
- Hogs
- Dairy cows/products
- Beef cattle
- Fruits
- Vegetables
- Vegetable oil
- Peanuts
- Nursery stock
- Wheat
- Corn
- Soybeans
- Cotton
- Timber/forest products
- Printing/publishing
- Stone/gravel/cement
- Mining
- Coal
- Oil/gas
- Hydro-electricity
- Metal manufacturing
- Metal products
- Shipbuilding
- Motor vehicles/parts
- Rubber/plastics
- Chemistry
- Food processing
- Clothing/textiles
- Glass/clay products
- Electrical equipment
- Computers/electronics
- Aircraft/parts
- Aerospace
- Tourism
- Finance/insurance

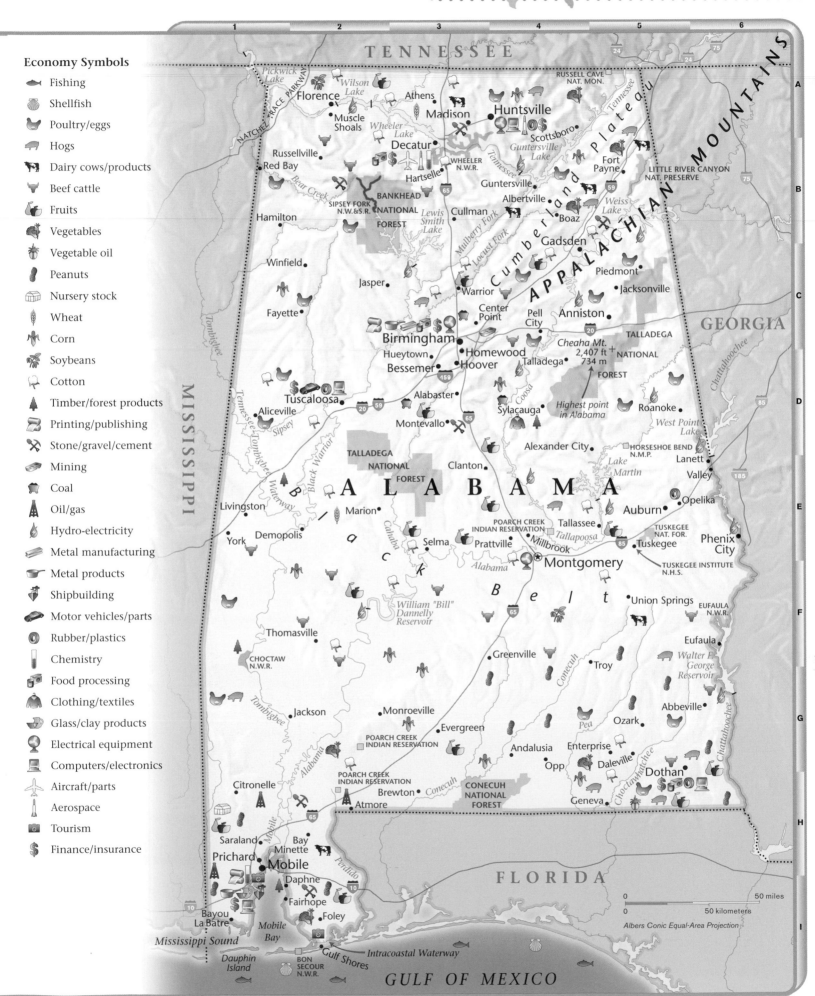

TENNESSEE

GEORGIA

MISSISSIPPI

ALABAMA

FLORIDA

GULF OF MEXICO

Appalachian Mountains

Cumberland Plateau

Florence • Athens • Madison • Huntsville • Scottsboro
Muscle Shoals • Decatur • Hartselle
Russellville • Red Bay
Hamilton • Winfield • Jasper • Warrior • Cullman
Fayette • Center Point • Pell City • Anniston • Jacksonville • Piedmont
Gadsden • Fort Payne • Guntersville • Albertville • Boaz
Bankhead National Forest
Sipsey Fork N.W.&S.R.
Lewis Smith Lake
Wheeler N.W.R.
Little River Canyon Nat. Preserve
Weiss Lake
Guntersville Lake
Wilson Lake
Wheeler Lake
Pickwick Lake

Birmingham • Hueytown • Bessemer • Homewood • Hoover
Tuscaloosa • Aliceville
Alabaster • Montevallo
Talladega • Sylacauga • Roanoke
Cheaha Mt. 2,407 ft 734 m
Highest point in Alabama
Talladega National Forest
Alexander City • Clanton
Horseshoe Bend N.M.P.
Lanett • Valley
West Point Lake
Lake Martin

Livingston • Marion • Auburn • Opelika
York • Demopolis • Selma • Tallassee • Tuskegee • Phenix City
Poorch Creek Indian Reservation
Prattville • Millbrook
Montgomery • Tuskegee Nat. For.
Tuskegee Institute N.H.S.

Thomasville • Union Springs • Eufaula
Greenville • Troy • Eufaula
Monroeville • Ozark • Abbeville
Jackson • Evergreen • Andalusia • Enterprise • Daleville • Dothan
Opp • Geneva
Choctaw N.W.R.
Poorch Creek Indian Reservation
Conecuh National Forest
Brewton • Atmore
Eufaula N.W.R.
Walter F. George Reservoir

Citronelle • Saraland • Bay Minette
Prichard • Mobile • Daphne • Fairhope • Foley
Bayou La Batre • Gulf Shores
Mobile Bay
Dauphin Island
Bon Secour N.W.R.
Mississippi Sound
Intracoastal Waterway

Natchez Trace Parkway
Tombigbee
Tennessee-Tombigbee Waterway
Black Warrior
Cahaba
Alabama
Tallapoosa
Coosa
Conecuh
Pea
Choctawhatchee
Chattahoochee
Sipsey
Bear Creek
Mulberry Fork
Locust Fork
William "Bill" Dannelly Reservoir
Perdido

0 ———— 50 miles
0 ———— 50 kilometers
Albers Conic Equal-Area Projection

THE BASICS

STATS

Area
53,179 sq mi (137,732 sq km)

Population
2,915,918

Capital
Little Rock
Population 193,524

Largest city
Little Rock
Population 193,524

Ethnic/racial groups
77.0% white; 15.4% African American;
1.2% Asian; .8% Native American.
Hispanic (any race) 6.4%.

Industry
Services, food processing, paper
products, transportation, metal
products, machinery, electronics

Agriculture
Poultry and eggs, rice, soybeans,
cotton, wheat

Statehood
June 15, 1836; 25th state

GEO WHIZ

In 1924 Arkansas's Crater of Diamonds
State Park yielded the largest natural
diamond ever found in the United
States—a 40.23-carat whopper
named "Uncle Sam." A 13-year-old
girl from Missouri found a 2.93-carat
diamond there in 2007.

Since 1936 Stuttgart has been the site
of the annual World Championship
Duck Calling Contest. The first winner
took home a grand total of $6.60.
Today, the prize package is worth
more than $15,000.

The city of Texarkana is
divided by the Arkansas-
Texas border. It has two
governments, one for
each state.

MOCKINGBIRD
APPLE BLOSSOM

ARKANSAS

The land that is Arkansas was explored by the Spanish in 1541 and later by the French, but it came under U.S. control with the Louisiana Purchase in 1803. As settlers arrived, Native Americans were pushed out, and cotton fields spread across the fertile valleys of the Arkansas and Mississippi Rivers. Arkansas became the 25th state in 1836, but joined the Confederacy in 1861. Following the war, Arkansas faced hard times, and many people moved away in search of jobs. Today, agriculture remains an important part of the economy. Rice has replaced cotton as the state's main crop, and poultry and grain production are also important. Natural gas, in the northwestern part of the state, and petroleum, along the southern border with Louisiana, are key mining products in Arkansas. The state is headquarters for Wal-Mart, the world's largest retail chain, and tourism is growing as visitors are attracted to the natural beauty of the Ozark and Ouachita Mountains.

⇧ HOLD ON! A rock climber clings to a sandstone cliff in northwest Arkansas, where the Ozark and Ouachita Mountains make up the Interior Highlands of the United States. The Ouachita are folded mountains, but the Ozarks are really a deeply eroded plateau.

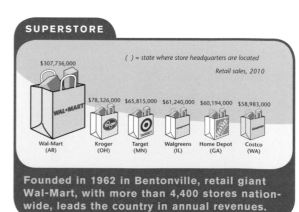

SUPERSTORE

( ) = state where store headquarters are located

Retail sales, 2010

$307,736,000

$78,326,000 $65,815,000 $61,240,000 $60,194,000 $58,983,000

Wal-Mart (AR) Kroger (OH) Target (MN) Walgreens (IL) Home Depot (GA) Costco (WA)

Founded in 1962 in Bentonville, retail giant Wal-Mart, with more than 4,400 stores nation-wide, leads the country in annual revenues.

⇦ BIRDWATCHERS. Biologists and volunteers scan the treetops for a rare ivory-billed woodpecker in the White River National Wildlife Refuge. Established in 1935 along the White River near where it joins the Mississippi, the refuge provides a protected habitat for migratory birds.

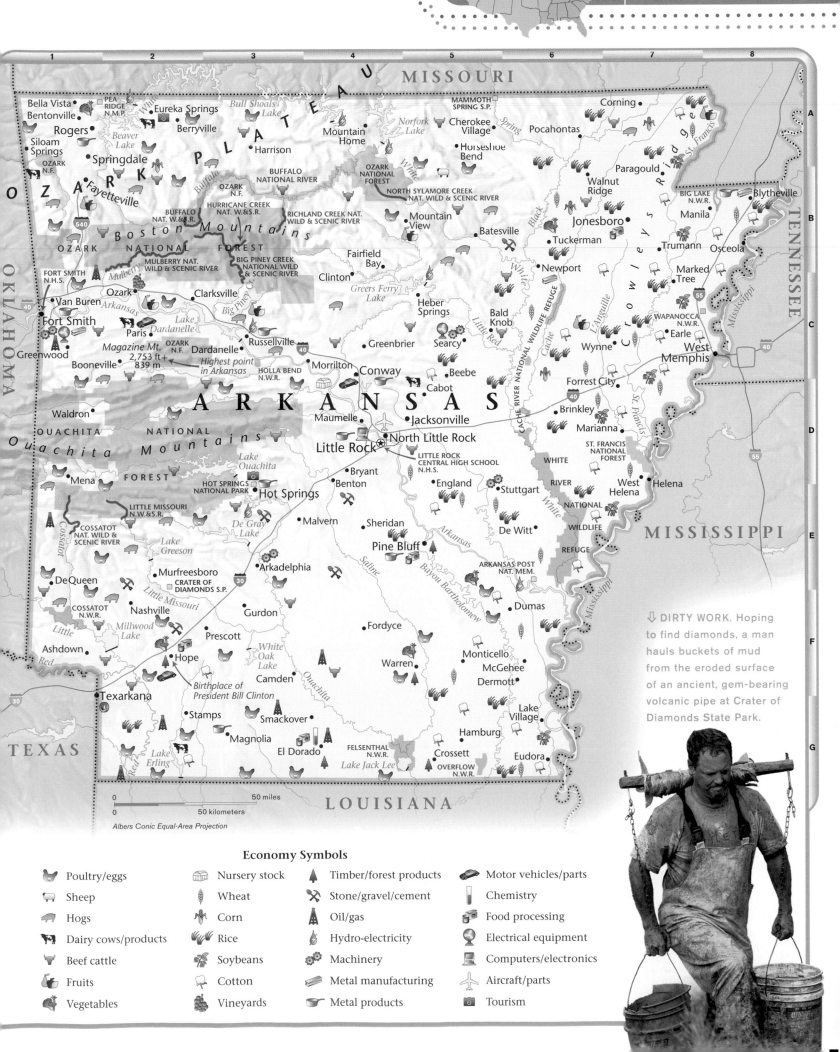

MISSOURI

OZARK PLATEAU

Bella Vista
Bentonville
Rogers
Siloam Springs
Springdale
OZARK N.F.
Fayetteville
540

Beaver Lake
PEA RIDGE N.M.P.
Eureka Springs
Berryville
Bull Shoals Lake

Buffalo
OZARK N.F.
HURRICANE CREEK NAT. W.&S.R.
BUFFALO NAT. W.&S.R.
Boston Mountains
OZARK NATIONAL FOREST
MULBERRY NAT. WILD & SCENIC RIVER
BIG PINEY CREEK NATIONAL WILD & SCENIC RIVER
Mulberry

Mountain Home
Harrison
BUFFALO NATIONAL RIVER
Norfork Lake

OZARK NATIONAL FOREST
NORTH SYLAMORE CREEK NAT. WILD & SCENIC RIVER
RICHLAND CREEK NAT. WILD & SCENIC RIVER
Mountain View

FORT SMITH N.H.S.
Van Buren
Fort Smith
Greenwood
40

Ozark
Paris
Clarksville
Arkansas
Lake Dardanelle
Big Piney
Russellville
Dardanelle
OZARK N.F.
Magazine Mt. 2,753 ft+ 839 m ← Highest point in Arkansas
Booneville

White
Spring

MAMMOTH SPRING S.P.
Cherokee Village
Horseshoe Bend
Corning
Pocahontas

Paragould
Walnut Ridge
BIG LAKE N.W.R.
Blytheville
Manila

White
Black
Batesville
Tuckerman
Jonesboro
Trumann
Osceola
Marked Tree
55

Fairfield Bay
Clinton
Greers Ferry Lake
Heber Springs
Bald Knob
Newport
Little Red
WAPANOCCA N.W.R.
Earle
West Memphis
40

Greenbrier
Searcy
Beebe
Cabot
Conway
Morrilton
HOLLA BEND N.W.R.
ARKANSAS
Maumelle

Wynne
Forrest City
Brinkley
Marianna
St. Francis
ST. FRANCIS NATIONAL FOREST

CACHE RIVER NATIONAL WILDLIFE REFUGE
Cache

OKLAHOMA

Waldron
OUACHITA
Mena
NATIONAL
Ouachita
FOREST
Mountains

Jacksonville
Little Rock
North Little Rock
LITTLE ROCK CENTRAL HIGH SCHOOL N.H.S.
Bryant
Benton
HOT SPRINGS NATIONAL PARK
Hot Springs
LITTLE MISSOURI N.W.&S.R.
Lake Ouachita

England
Stuttgart
De Witt

WHITE
RIVER
NATIONAL
WILDLIFE
REFUGE
West Helena
Helena

MISSISSIPPI

Cossatot
COSSATOT NAT. WILD & SCENIC RIVER
DeQueen
COSSATOT N.W.R.
Nashville
Little Missouri
Millwood Lake
Ashdown
Little
Red
Hope
Birthplace of President Bill Clinton
Texarkana
Stamps
30

Lake Greeson
Murfreesboro
CRATER OF DIAMONDS S.P.
Arkadelphia
Malvern
De Gray Lake
Gurdon
Prescott
30
White Oak Lake
Camden
Ouachita
Magnolia
Lake Erling
El Dorado
Smackover

Sheridan
Pine Bluff
Arkansas
Bayou Bartholomew
Saline
Fordyce
Warren
Monticello
McGehee
Dermott
Dumas
ARKANSAS POST NAT. MEM.
Lake Village
Mississippi

Hamburg
FELSENTHAL N.W.R.
Lake Jack Lee
Crossett
OVERFLOW N.W.R.
Eudora

TEXAS

0 — 50 miles
0 — 50 kilometers
Albers Conic Equal-Area Projection

LOUISIANA

TENNESSEE

DIRTY WORK. Hoping to find diamonds, a man hauls buckets of mud from the eroded surface of an ancient, gem-bearing volcanic pipe at Crater of Diamonds State Park.

Economy Symbols

- Poultry/eggs
- Sheep
- Hogs
- Dairy cows/products
- Beef cattle
- Fruits
- Vegetables

- Nursery stock
- Wheat
- Corn
- Rice
- Soybeans
- Cotton
- Vineyards

- Timber/forest products
- Stone/gravel/cement
- Oil/gas
- Hydro-electricity
- Machinery
- Metal manufacturing
- Metal products

- Motor vehicles/parts
- Chemistry
- Food processing
- Electrical equipment
- Computers/electronics
- Aircraft/parts
- Tourism

THE BASICS

STATS

Area
65,755 sq mi (170,304 sq km)

Population
18,801,310

Capital
Tallahassee
Population 181,376

Largest city
Jacksonville
Population 821,784

Ethnic/racial groups
75.0% white; 16.0% African American; 2.4% Asian; .4% Native American. Hispanic (any race) 22.5%.

Industry
Tourism, health services, business services, communications, banking, electronic equipment, insurance

Agriculture
Citrus fruits, vegetables, field crops, nursery stock, cattle, dairy products

Statehood
March 3, 1845; 27th state

GEO WHIZ

Key West, the southernmost point in the continental U.S., is just 90 miles (145 km) from Cuba.

In 1937 Amelia Earhart and her navigator took off from Miami with the goal of making an around-the-world flight, but disappeared over the Pacific Ocean and were never seen again. You can read all about this famous flying ace in our children's book *Sky Pioneer*, by Corine Szabo.

Everglades National Park, the largest subtropical wilderness in the United States, is home to rare and endangered species such as the American crocodile, Florida panther, and West Indian manatee.

Britton Hill, Florida's highest point, is only 345 feet (105 m) above sea level.

Lightning strikes occur more often in Florida than in any other U.S. state.

MOCKINGBIRD
ORANGE BLOSSOM

FLORIDA

Florida is home to St. Augustine, the country's oldest permanent European settlement, established by the Spanish in 1565. But native peoples had called Florida home long before then. Florida became a U.S. territory in 1821 and a state in 1845. The state's turbulent early history included the Civil War and three wars with Native Americans over control of the land. Railroads opened Florida to migration from the northern states as early as the 1890s. The mild climate and sandy beaches attracted people seeking to escape cold winters in the north. This trend continues today and includes both tourists and retirees. South Florida has a large Hispanic population that has migrated from all over Latin America—especially from nearby Cuba. Florida is working to solve many challenges: competition between city-dwellers and farmers for limited water resources; the annual risk of tropical storms; and the need to preserve its natural environment, including the vast Everglades wetland.

⬆ CULTURAL PRIDE. A young girl marches in Orlando's Puerto Rican Parade, a celebration of the music, dance, and culture of this U.S. island territory.

⇨ LIFTOFF! A NASA rocket rises amid clouds of steam from Cape Canaveral Space Center on Florida's Atlantic coast. The center has been the launch site for many U.S. space exploration projects.

ALABAMA

POORCH CREEK I.R.
Highest point in Florida → Britton Hill 345 ft 105 m
Perdido
Crestview
Niceville
Pensacola
Fort Walton Beach
FORT PICKENS
GULF ISLANDS NATIONAL SEASHORE
Choctawhatchee
Intracoastal Waterway

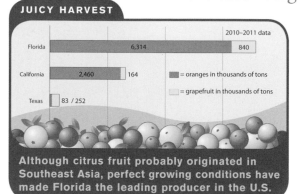

JUICY HARVEST

		2010–2011 data
Florida	6,314	840
California	2,460	164
Texas	83 / 252	

= oranges in thousands of tons
= grapefruit in thousands of tons

Although citrus fruit probably originated in Southeast Asia, perfect growing conditions have made Florida the leading producer in the U.S.

⇨ GENTLE GIANT. The manatee, which is closely related to the elephant, is Florida's state marine mammal. Averaging 10 feet (3 m) in length and 1,000 pounds (453 kg), these endangered animals live on a diet of sea grasses.

GEORGIA

ATLANTIC OCEAN

GULF OF MEXICO

FLORIDA

Economy Symbols

- Fishing
- Lobster fishing
- Shellfish
- Poultry/eggs
- Hogs
- Dairy cows
- Beef cattle
- Fruits
- Vegetables
- Peanuts
- Nursery stock
- Corn
- Rice
- Sugarcane
- Cotton

- Tobacco
- Timber/forest products
- Printing/publishing
- Hydro-electricity
- Metal products
- Shipbuilding
- Chemistry
- Food processing
- Electrical equipment
- Computers/electronics
- Scientific instruments
- Aerospace
- Tourism
- Finance/insurance

Marianna
Lake Seminole
OKEFENOKEE NATIONAL WILDLIFE REFUGE
Panama City
Apalachicola
Ochlockonee
Tallahassee
APALACHICOLA NATIONAL FOREST
ST. MARKS N.W.R.
Perry
Live Oak
Lake City
OSCEOLA NAT. FOREST
Jacksonville
Fernandina Beach
TIMUCUAN ECOLOGICAL AND HISTORIC PRESERVE
FORT CAROLINE NAT. MEM.
Jacksonville Beach
St. Marys
ST. VINCENT N.W.R.
Suwannee
St. Johns
Intracoastal Waterway
CASTILLO DE SAN MARCOS NAT. MON.
St. Augustine
Oldest permanent European settlement on the continent, est. 1565
Gainesville
Palatka
FORT MATANZAS NAT. MON.
Palm Coast
LOWER SUWANNEE NATIONAL WILDLIFE REFUGE
OCALA NATIONAL FOREST
Lake George
Daytona Beach
Ocala
LAKE WOODRUFF N.W.R.
New Smyrna Beach
CEDAR KEYS N.W.R.
CRYSTAL RIVER N.W.R.
De Land
Deltona
CANAVERAL NATIONAL SEASHORE
Homosassa Springs
Leesburg
Sanford
St. Johns
Titusville
CHASSAHOWITZKA N.W.R.
Orlando
MERRITT ISLAND N.W.R.
John F. Kennedy Space Center
Spring Hill
Walt Disney World & EPCOT Center
Cape Canaveral
Bayonet Point
Kissimmee
Merritt Island
Tarpon Springs
Haines City
Melbourne
FLORIDA'S TURNPIKE
Palm Bay
Clearwater
Lakeland
TAMPA I.R.
Winter Haven
PELICAN ISLAND N.W.R.
Tampa
Indian
Vero Beach
St. Petersburg
Tampa Bay
PINELLAS N.W.R.
EGMONT KEY N.W.R.
Sebring
Fort Pierce
FORT PIERCE I.R.
DE SOTO NAT. MEM.
Bradenton
Port St. Lucie
Sarasota
Kissimmee
HOBE SOUND N.W.R.
Arcadia
BRIGHTON SEMINOLE I.R.
St. Lucie Canal
LOXAHATCHEE NAT. WILD & SCENIC RIVER
Venice
Lake Okeechobee
Jupiter
Port Charlotte
Peace
Caloosahatchee
Belle Glade
West Palm Beach
Punta Gorda
Charlotte Harbor
ARTHUR R. MARSHALL LOXAHATCHEE N.W.R.
FLORIDA'S
Cape Coral
Fort Myers
Miami Canal
Delray Beach
J. N. "DING" DARLING N.W.R.
IMMOKALEE I.R.
Boca Raton
Sanibel Island
Immokalee
BIG CYPRESS SEMINOLE I.R.
Coral Springs
COCONUT CREEK I.R.
Fort Lauderdale
Big Cypress Swamp
MICCOSUKEE INDIAN RES.
SEMINOLE I.R.
BIG CYPRESS NATIONAL PRESERVE
Hollywood
Naples
Hialeah
Miami
The Everglades
Kendall
Miami Beach
Ten Thousand Islands
Biscayne Bay
BISCAYNE N.P.
EVERGLADES NATIONAL PARK
Largest subtropical wilderness in the 48 contiguous states
Homestead
Cape Sable
Florida Bay
Key Largo
FLORIDA KEYS NATIONAL MARINE SANCTUARY
NAT. KEY DEER REFUGE
GREAT WHITE HERON N.W.R.
KEY WEST N.W.R.
Marathon
DRY TORTUGAS NATIONAL PARK
Key West
FLORIDA KEYS
STRAITS OF FLORIDA
Southernmost point in the continental United States
STRAITS OF FLORIDA

0   100 miles
0   100 kilometers
Albers Conic Equal-Area Projection

THE EMPIRE STATE OF THE SOUTH:
GEORGIA

THE BASICS

STATS

Area
59,425 sq mi (153,910 sq km)

Population
9,687,653

Capital
Atlanta
Population 420,003

Largest city
Atlanta
Population 420,003

Ethnic/racial groups
59.7% white; 30.5% African American; 3.2% Asian; .3% Native American. Hispanic (any race) 8.8%.

Industry
Textiles and clothing, transportation equipment, food processing, paper products, chemicals, electrical equipment, tourism

Agriculture
Poultry and eggs, cotton, peanuts, vegetables, sweet corn, melons, cattle

Statehood
January 2, 1788; 4th state

GEO WHIZ

The Okefenokee Swamp, the largest swamp in North America, is home to many meat-eating plants, which capture animals for food. The swamp was also the setting for the adventures of Pogo the Possum, Albert the Alligator, and other characters created by cartoonist Walt Kelly.

The Georgia Aquarium in Atlanta, the world's largest, features more than 100,000 animals in more than 8 million gallons (30.3 million liters) of water.

Stone Mountain near Atlanta is famous for its enormous carving of three historic figures from the Confederate States of America: Stonewall Jackson, Robert E. Lee, and Jefferson Davis. It is one of the largest single masses of exposed granite in the world.

BROWN THRASHER
CHEROKEE ROSE

GEORGIA

When Spanish explorers arrived in the mid-1500s in what would become Georgia, they found the land already occupied by Cherokees, Creeks, and other native peoples. Georgia was the frontier separating Spanish Florida and English South Carolina, but in 1733 James Oglethorpe founded a new colony on the site of present-day Savannah. Georgia became the 4th state in 1788 and built an economy based on agriculture and slave labor. The state suffered widespread destruction during the Civil War and endured a long period of poverty in the years that followed. Modern-day Georgia is part of the fast-changing Sunbelt region. Agriculture—especially poultry, cotton, and forest products—remains important. Atlanta has emerged as a regional center of banking, telecommunications, and transportation, and Savannah is a major container port near the Atlantic coast, linking the state to the global economy. Historic sites, sports, and beaches draw thousands of tourists to the state every year.

⇧ CASH CROP. Peanuts are a big moneymaker in Georgia, where almost half the U.S. crop is grown—about half of which is used to make peanut butter.

⇧ LIGHT SHOW. Busy Interstate traffic appears as ribbons of light below Atlanta's nighttime skyline. Atlanta is a center of economic growth, leading all cities in the region with 10 Fortune 500 companies. Its metropolitan area leads the country in population growth, adding almost one million people since 2000.

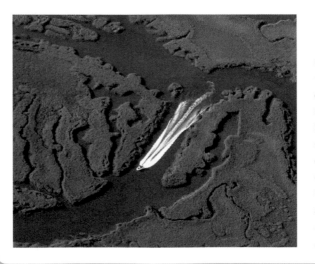

⇦ PAST MEETS PRESENT. Georgia's 100-mile (160-km) coastline is laced with barrier islands, wetlands, and winding streams. In the 19th century plantations grew Sea Island cotton here. Today, tourists are attracted to the area's natural beauty and beaches.

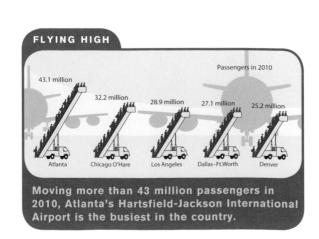

FLYING HIGH

Passengers in 2010

43.1 million — Atlanta
32.2 million — Chicago O'Hare
28.9 million — Los Angeles
27.1 million — Dallas–Ft.Worth
25.2 million — Denver

Moving more than 43 million passengers in 2010, Atlanta's Hartsfield-Jackson International Airport is the busiest in the country.

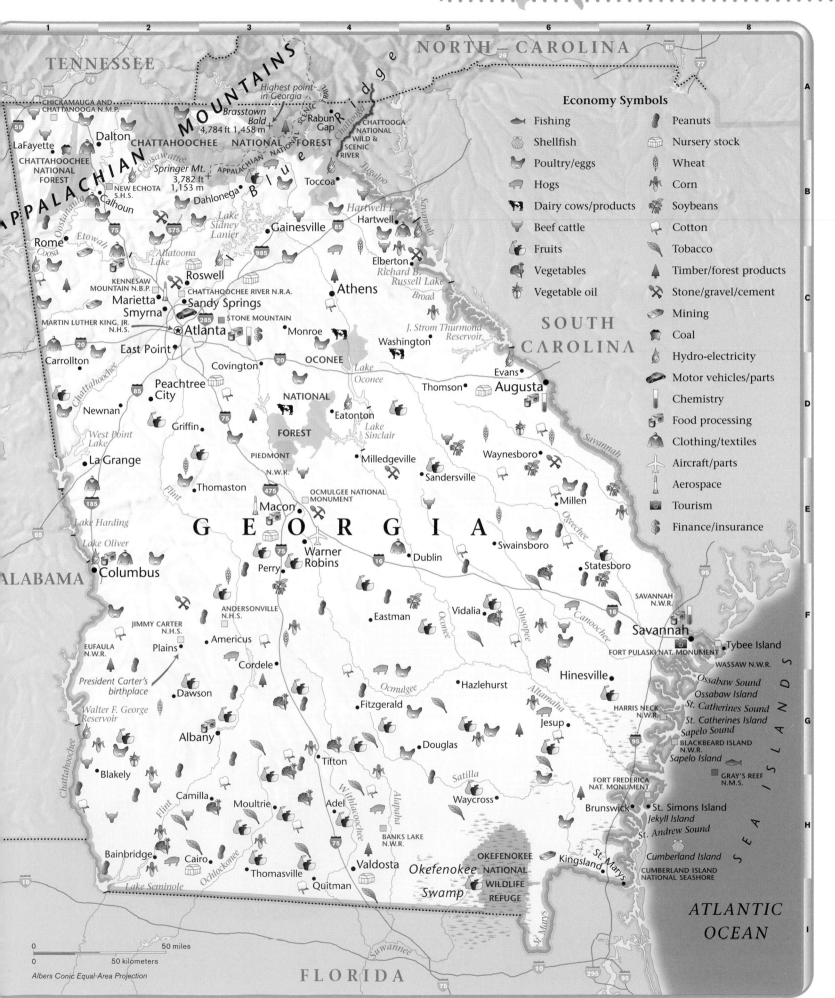

Economy Symbols

- Fishing
- Shellfish
- Poultry/eggs
- Hogs
- Dairy cows/products
- Beef cattle
- Fruits
- Vegetables
- Vegetable oil
- Peanuts
- Nursery stock
- Wheat
- Corn
- Soybeans
- Cotton
- Tobacco
- Timber/forest products
- Stone/gravel/cement
- Mining
- Coal
- Hydro-electricity
- Motor vehicles/parts
- Chemistry
- Food processing
- Clothing/textiles
- Aircraft/parts
- Aerospace
- Tourism
- Finance/insurance

TENNESSEE
NORTH CAROLINA
SOUTH CAROLINA
ALABAMA
FLORIDA
ATLANTIC OCEAN

GEORGIA

APPALACHIAN MOUNTAINS
Blue Ridge
CHATTAHOOCHEE NATIONAL FOREST

Highest point in Georgia
Brasstown Bald
4,784 ft 1,458 m

CHATTOOGA NATIONAL WILD & SCENIC RIVER

Springer Mt.
3,782 ft
1,153 m

CHICKAMAUGA AND CHATTANOOGA N.M.P.
LaFayette
Dalton
CHATTAHOOCHEE NATIONAL FOREST
NEW ECHOTA S.H.S.
Calhoun
Rome
Dahlonega
Toccoa
Rabun Gap
Lake Sidney Lanier
Gainesville
Hartwell L.
Hartwell
Elberton
Roswell
KENNESAW MOUNTAIN N.B.P.
CHATTAHOOCHEE RIVER N.R.A.
Marietta
Smyrna
Sandy Springs
Athens
Richard B. Russell Lake
Broad
MARTIN LUTHER KING, JR. N.H.S.
Atlanta
STONE MOUNTAIN
Monroe
Washington
J. Strom Thurmond Reservoir
East Point
Carrollton
Covington
OCONEE
Lake Oconee
Evans
Thomson
Augusta
Peachtree City
Newnan
Griffin
NATIONAL
Eatonton
Lake Sinclair
FOREST
PIEDMONT N.W.R.
Milledgeville
Waynesboro
La Grange
West Point Lake
Thomaston
Sandersville
Millen
OCMULGEE NATIONAL MONUMENT
Lake Harding
Macon
Lake Oliver
Warner Robins
Perry
Dublin
Swainsboro
Statesboro
Columbus
Vidalia
SAVANNAH N.W.R.
ANDERSONVILLE N.H.S.
Eastman
Savannah
JIMMY CARTER N.H.S.
Americus
FORT PULASKI NAT. MONUMENT
Tybee Island
EUFAULA N.W.R.
Plains
Cordele
Hinesville
WASSAW N.W.R.
President Carter's birthplace
Dawson
Hazlehurst
Ossabaw Sound
Ossabaw Island
Walter F. George Reservoir
Fitzgerald
Jesup
HARRIS NECK N.W.R.
St. Catherines Sound
St. Catherines Island
Albany
Douglas
Sapelo Sound
BLACKBEARD ISLAND N.W.R.
Sapelo Island
Blakely
Tifton
GRAY'S REEF N.M.S.
FORT FREDERICA NAT. MONUMENT
Camilla
Moultrie
Adel
Waycross
Brunswick
St. Simons Island
Jekyll Island
Bainbridge
Cairo
Valdosta
Kingsland
St. Andrew Sound
BANKS LAKE N.W.R.
OKEFENOKEE NATIONAL WILDLIFE REFUGE
Cumberland Island
Thomasville
Quitman
Okefenokee Swamp
St. Marys
CUMBERLAND ISLAND NATIONAL SEASHORE
SEA ISLANDS

Coosawattee
Oostanaula
Etowah
Coosa
Allatoona Lake
Chattahoochee
Flint
Ocmulgee
Oconee
Ogeechee
Canoochee
Ohoopee
Altamaha
Savannah
Tugaloo
Satilla
Alapaha
Withlacoochee
Ochlockonee
Lake Seminole
Suwannee
St. Marys

0   50 miles
0   50 kilometers
Albers Conic Equal-Area Projection

THE BLUEGRASS STATE:
KENTUCKY

THE BASICS
STATS

Area
40,409 sq mi (104,659 sq km)

Population
4,339,367

Capital
Frankfort
Population 25,527

Largest city
Louisville/Jefferson County
Population 597,337

Ethnic/racial groups
87.8% white; 7.8% African American;
1.1% Asian; .2% Native American.
Hispanic (any race) 3.1%.

Industry
Manufacturing, services, government,
finance, insurance, real estate, retail
trade, transportation, wholesale trade,
construction, mining

Agriculture
Horses, tobacco, cattle, corn, dairy
products

Statehood
June 1, 1792; 15th state

GEO WHIZ

A favorite Kentucky dessert is Derby
Pie, a rich chocolate-and-walnut
pastry that was first created by George
Kern, manager of the Melrose Inn, in
Prospect, in the 1950s. It became so
popular that the name was registered
with the U.S. Patent Office and the
Commonwealth of Kentucky.

Pleasant Hill, near Lexington, was
the site of a Shaker religious
community. It is now a National
Historic Site where visitors can
tour the living history museum.

The song "Happy Birthday to You,"
one of the most popular songs in the
English language, was the creation of
two Louisville sisters in 1893.

Post-it notes are manufactured
exclusively in Cynthiana. Millions
of self-stick notes in 27 sizes
and 57 colors are produced
each year.

CARDINAL

GOLDENROD

KENTUCKY

The original inhabitants of the area known today as Kentucky were Native Americans, but a treaty with the Cherokees, signed in 1775, opened the territory to settlers—including the legendary Daniel Boone—from the soon-to-be-independent eastern colonies. In 1776 Kentucky became a western county of the state of Virginia. In 1792 it became the 15th state of the young U.S. Eastern Kentucky is a part of Appalachia, a region rich in soft bituminous coal but burdened with environmental problems that often accompany the mining industry. The region is known for crafts and music that can be traced back to Scotch-Irish immigrants who settled there. In central Kentucky, the Bluegrass region produces some of the finest Thoroughbred horses in the world, and the Kentucky Derby, held in Louisville, is a part of racing's coveted Triple Crown. In western Kentucky, coal found near the surface is strip mined, leaving scars on the landscape, but federal laws now require that the land be restored.

BENEATH THE SURFACE

Mammoth Cave System, KY	367 miles/591 km
Jewel Cave, SD	140 miles/225 km
Wind Cave, SD	125 miles/201 km
Lechuguilla Cave, NM	121 miles/195 km
Fisher Ridge Cave System, KY	110 miles/177 km

Caves, natural openings in Earth's surface
extending beyond the reach of sunlight, are
often created by water dissolving limestone.

⇧ THEY'RE OFF! Riders and horses press for the finish line at Churchill Downs, in Louisville. Kentucky is a major breeder of Thoroughbred race horses, and horses are the leading source of farm income in the state.

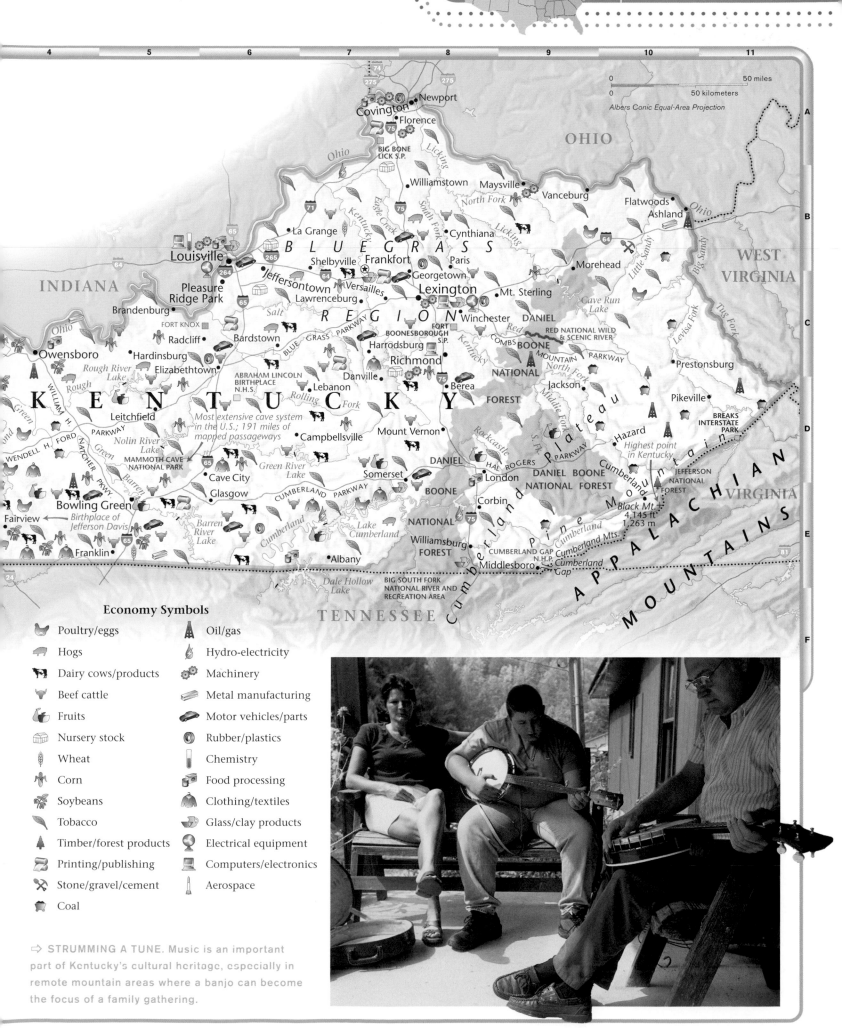

Map Labels

OHIO

WEST VIRGINIA

INDIANA

VIRGINIA

TENNESSEE

BLUEGRASS REGION

KENTUCKY

Newport
Covington
Florence
BIG BONE LICK S.P.
Williamstown
Maysville
Vanceburg
Flatwoods
Ashland
La Grange
Cynthiana
Morehead
Louisville
Shelbyville
Frankfort
Paris
Pleasure Ridge Park
Jeffersontown
Versailles
Georgetown
Lexington
Mt. Sterling
Cave Run Lake
Brandenburg
Lawrenceburg
Winchester
DANIEL
Prestonsburg
FORT KNOX
Radcliff
Bardstown
BOONESBOROUGH S.P.
Harrodsburg
Richmond
BOONE
Pikeville
Owensboro
Hardinsburg
Elizabethtown
Danville
Berea
NATIONAL
Jackson
BREAKS INTERSTATE PARK
Leitchfield
Lebanon
ABRAHAM LINCOLN BIRTHPLACE N.H.S.
Mount Vernon
FOREST
Hazard
Highest point in Kentucky
JEFFERSON NATIONAL FOREST
Campbellsville
Rolling Fork
Most extensive cave system in the U.S.; 191 miles of mapped passageways
MAMMOTH CAVE NATIONAL PARK
Green River Lake
Somerset
DANIEL
DANIEL BOONE NATIONAL FOREST
Cave City
London
Cumberland
Glasgow
BOONE
Black Mt. 4,145 ft 1,263 m
Bowling Green
Corbin
Birthplace of Jefferson Davis
NATIONAL
Barren River Lake
Lake Cumberland
Fairview
Franklin
Williamsburg
CUMBERLAND GAP N.H.P.
Middlesboro
Cumberland Gap
FOREST
Albany
Dale Hollow Lake
BIG SOUTH FORK NATIONAL RIVER AND RECREATION AREA

RED NATIONAL WILD & SCENIC RIVER

APPALACHIAN MOUNTAINS
Cumberland Mountain
Pine Mountain
Cumberland Plateau

RED NATIONAL WILD & SCENIC RIVER

Scale: 0 — 50 miles / 0 — 50 kilometers
Albers Conic Equal-Area Projection

Economy Symbols

- 🐔 Poultry/eggs
- 🐷 Hogs
- 🐄 Dairy cows/products
- 🐂 Beef cattle
- 🍐 Fruits
- Nursery stock
- 🌾 Wheat
- 🌽 Corn
- Soybeans
- Tobacco
- 🌲 Timber/forest products
- Printing/publishing
- ⚒ Stone/gravel/cement
- Coal

- Oil/gas
- Hydro-electricity
- ⚙ Machinery
- Metal manufacturing
- 🚗 Motor vehicles/parts
- Rubber/plastics
- Chemistry
- Food processing
- Clothing/textiles
- ☕ Glass/clay products
- Electrical equipment
- 💻 Computers/electronics
- Aerospace

↪ STRUMMING A TUNE. Music is an important part of Kentucky's cultural heritage, especially in remote mountain areas where a banjo can become the focus of a family gathering.

THE PELICAN STATE:
LOUISIANA

UNION JUSTICE CONFIDENCE

THE BASICS

STATS

Area
51,840 sq mi (134,265 sq km)

Population
4,533,372

Capital
Baton Rouge
Population 229,493

Largest city
New Orleans
Population 343,829

Ethnic/racial groups
62.6% white; 32.0% African American; 1.5% Asian; .7% Native American. Hispanic (any race) 4.2%.

Industry
Chemicals, petroleum products, food processing, health services, tourism, oil and natural gas extraction, paper products

Agriculture
Forest products, poultry, marine fisheries, sugarcane, rice, dairy products, cotton, cattle, aquaculture

Statehood
April 30, 1812; 18th state

GEO WHIZ

The brown pelican, the state bird of Louisiana, was placed on the endangered species list in 1970. The species has made a remarkable recovery in the Atlantic coastal states, but it is still considered endangered in the Gulf Coast area.

The magnolia, Louisiana's state flower, is the oldest flowering plant in the world. Some species are believed to be 100 million years old.

Cajuns, people whose French-speaking ancestors were exiled by the British from Acadia, in what is now Canada, live primarily in the bayou region of Louisiana. Their distinctive music and spicy food have become popular throughout the country.

BROWN PELICAN
MAGNOLIA

LOUISIANA

Louisiana's Native American heritage is evident in place-names such as Natchitoches and Opelousas. Spanish sailors explored the area in 1528, but the French, traveling down the Mississippi River, established permanent settlements in the mid-17th century and named the region for King Louis XIV. The U.S. gained possession of the territory as part of the Louisiana Purchase in 1803, and Louisiana became the 18th state in 1812. New Orleans and the Port of South Louisiana, located near the delta of the Mississippi River, are Louisiana's main ports. Trade from the interior of the U.S. moves through these ports and out to world markets. Oil and gas are drilled in the Mississippi Delta area, and coastal waters are an important source of seafood. Louisiana is vulnerable to tropical storms. In late August 2005 Hurricane Katrina roared in off the Gulf of Mexico, flooding towns, breaking through levees, and changing forever the lives of everyone in southern Louisiana.

⇧ TASTY HARVEST. Louisiana produces more than half of all shrimp caught in the U.S. Most of this harvest comes from the Barataria-Terrebonne region, an estuary at the mouth of the Mississippi River that supports shrimp, oysters, crabs, and fish.

⇦ AVENUE TO THE PAST. Stately live oaks, believed to be 300 years old, frame Oak Alley Plantation on the banks of the Mississippi River west of New Orleans. Built in 1839, the house has been restored to its former grandeur and is open to the public for tours and private events.

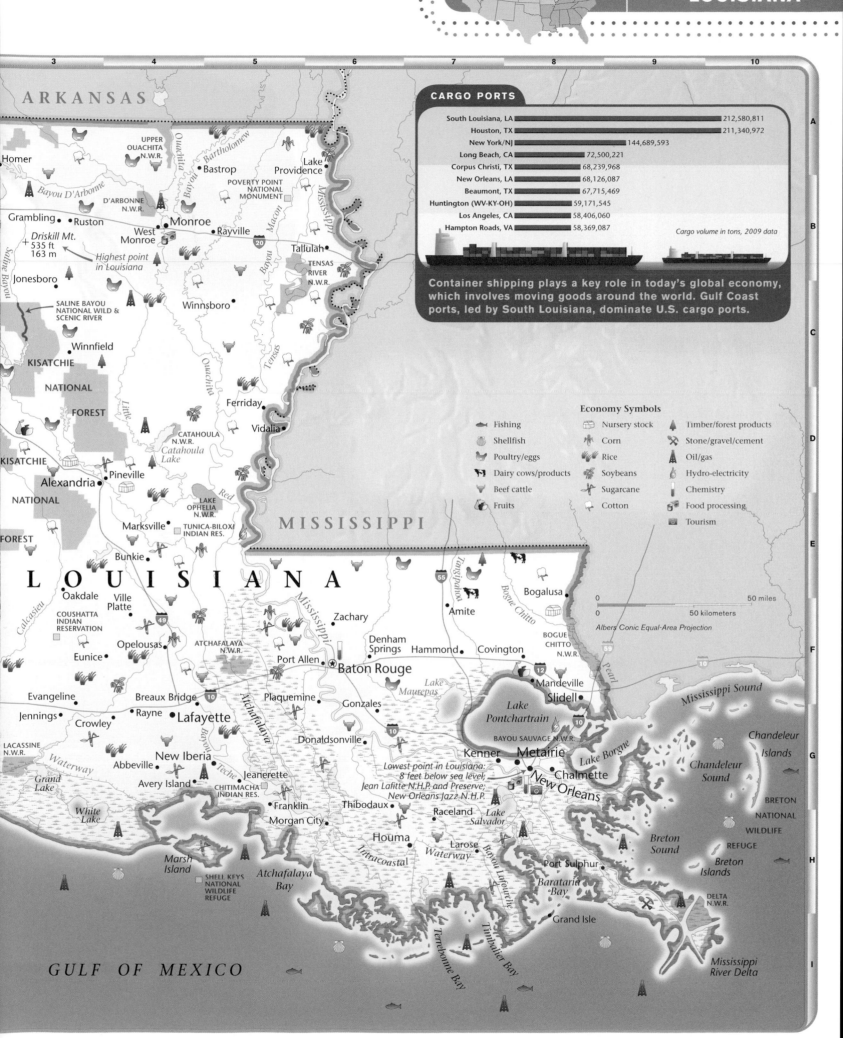

ARKANSAS

Homer

Bayou D'Arbonne
UPPER OUACHITA N.W.R.
Bastrop
Lake Providence
POVERTY POINT NATIONAL MONUMENT
D'ARBONNE N.W.R.
Grambling • Ruston
West Monroe • Monroe • Rayville
Driskill Mt. + 535 ft 163 m
Highest point in Louisiana
Tallulah
TENSAS RIVER N.W.R.
Jonesboro
Saline Bayou
SALINE BAYOU NATIONAL WILD & SCENIC RIVER
Winnsboro
Winnfield
KISATCHIE
NATIONAL
FOREST
Ferriday
Vidalia
CATAHOULA N.W.R.
Catahoula Lake
KISATCHIE
Alexandria • Pineville
NATIONAL
LAKE OPHELIA N.W.R.
Marksville
TUNICA-BILOXI INDIAN RES.
FOREST
Bunkie

MISSISSIPPI

CARGO PORTS

Port	Cargo volume (tons)
South Louisiana, LA	212,580,811
Houston, TX	211,340,972
New York/NJ	144,689,593
Long Beach, CA	72,500,221
Corpus Christi, TX	68,239,968
New Orleans, LA	68,126,087
Beaumont, TX	67,715,469
Huntington (WV-KY-OH)	59,171,545
Los Angeles, CA	58,406,060
Hampton Roads, VA	58,369,087

Cargo volume in tons, 2009 data

Container shipping plays a key role in today's global economy, which involves moving goods around the world. Gulf Coast ports, led by South Louisiana, dominate U.S. cargo ports.

Economy Symbols

- Fishing
- Shellfish
- Poultry/eggs
- Dairy cows/products
- Beef cattle
- Fruits
- Nursery stock
- Corn
- Rice
- Soybeans
- Sugarcane
- Cotton
- Timber/forest products
- Stone/gravel/cement
- Oil/gas
- Hydro-electricity
- Chemistry
- Food processing
- Tourism

LOUISIANA

Oakdale
Ville Platte
COUSHATTA INDIAN RESERVATION
Opelousas
Eunice
Zachary
Denham Springs • Hammond • Covington
Port Allen
Baton Rouge
ATCHAFALAYA N.W.R.
Amite
Bogalusa
BOGUE CHITTO N.W.R.
Bogue Chitto
Tangipahoa

0   50 miles
0   50 kilometers
Albers Conic Equal-Area Projection

Evangeline
Breaux Bridge
Plaquemine
Gonzales
Lake Maurepas
Mandeville
Slidell
Mississippi Sound
Jennings
Crowley • Rayne
Lafayette
Lake Pontchartrain
LACASSINE N.W.R.
Donaldsonville
BAYOU SAUVAGE N.W.R.
Kenner • Metairie
Lake Borgne
Chandeleur Islands
Abbeville
New Iberia
Lowest point in Louisiana: 8 feet below sea level; Jean Lafitte N.H.P. and Preserve; New Orleans Jazz N.H.P.
Chalmette
Chandeleur Sound
Grand Lake
Avery Island
Jeanerette
CHITIMACHA INDIAN RES.
New Orleans
White Lake
Franklin
Morgan City
Thibodaux
Raceland
Lake Salvador
Breton Sound
BRETON
Houma
Larose
NATIONAL WILDLIFE REFUGE
Marsh Island
SHELL KEYS NATIONAL WILDLIFE REFUGE
Atchafalaya Bay
Intracoastal Waterway
Bayou Lafourche
Port Sulphur
Barataria Bay
Breton Islands
DELTA N.W.R.
Grand Isle
Terrebonne Bay
Timbalier Bay
Mississippi River Delta

GULF OF MEXICO

Calcasieu
Waterway
Red
Little
Ouachita
Ouachita
Tensas
Bartholomew
Bayou Macon
Mississippi
Saline Bayou
Bayou D'Arbonne
Atchafalaya
Teche
Pearl

THE MAGNOLIA STATE:
MISSISSIPPI

THE BASICS

STATS

Area
48,430 sq mi (125,434 sq km)

Population
2,967,297

Capital
Jackson
Population 173,514

Largest city
Jackson
Population 173,514

Ethnic/racial groups
59.1% white; 37.0% African American; .9% Asian; .5% Native American. Hispanic (any race) 2.7%.

Industry
Petroleum products, health services, electronic equipment, transportation, banking, forest products, communications

Agriculture
Poultry and eggs, cotton, catfish, soybeans, cattle, rice, dairy products

Statehood
December 10, 1817; 20th state

GEO WHIZ

The Windsor Ruins, located near Port Gibson, are 23 monolithic columns that once made up the largest antebellum mansion in the state. The mansion survived the Civil War but was destroyed by a fire in 1890.

The Marine Life Oceanarium in Gulfport was almost completely destroyed by Hurricane Katrina in 2005. Eight of its 14 bottlenose dolphins were swept into the Gulf of Mexico by a 40-foot (12-m) wave. These animals and two sea lions named Splash and Elliot were eventually rescued. Others were not so lucky.

Greenville is the birthplace of Jim Henson, creator of Kermit the Frog, Miss Piggy, Big Bird, and other famous Muppets.

MOCKINGBIRD
MAGNOLIA

MISSISSIPPI

Mississippi is named for the river that forms its western boundary. The name comes from the Chippewa words *mici zibi,* meaning "great river." Indeed it is a great river, draining much of the interior U.S. and providing a trade artery to the world. Explored by the Spanish in 1540 and claimed by the French in 1699, the territory of Mississippi passed to the U.S. in 1783 and became the 20th state in 1817. For more than a hundred years following statehood, Mississippi was the center of U.S. cotton production and trade. The fertile soils and mild climate of the delta region in northwestern Mississippi provided a perfect environment for cotton, a crop that depended on slave labor. When the Civil War broke out, it took a heavy toll on the state. Today, poverty, especially in rural areas, is a major challenge for the state where agriculture—poultry, cotton, soybeans, and rice—is still the base of the economy.

⇧ SINGING THE BLUES. B. B. King sings the soulful sounds of the blues, a music form that traces its roots to Mississippi's cotton fields and the sorrows of West Africans traveling on slave ships to the Americas.

GONE FISHIN'

2011 data

Mississippi	147 million
Alabama	97 million
Arkansas	35 million

The Southeast, especially Mississippi, is the leading producer of pond-raised catfish. Mississippi also tops all other states in revenue for catfish sales.

DELTA QUEEN

⇨ BIG WHEEL TURNING. Now popular with tourists, paddlewheel boats made the Mississippi River a major artery for trade and travel in the 19th century.

Economy Symbols

- 🐟 Fishing
- 🐚 Shellfish
- 🐓 Poultry/eggs
- 🐖 Hogs
- 🐄 Dairy cows/products
- 🐂 Beef cattle
- 🍎 Fruits
- Nursery stock
- Wheat
- Corn
- Rice
- Soybeans
- Cotton
- Timber/forest products
- Furniture
- Stone/gravel/cement
- Oil/gas
- Machinery
- Shipbuilding
- Rubber/plastics
- Chemistry
- Food processing
- Computers/electronics
- Tourism

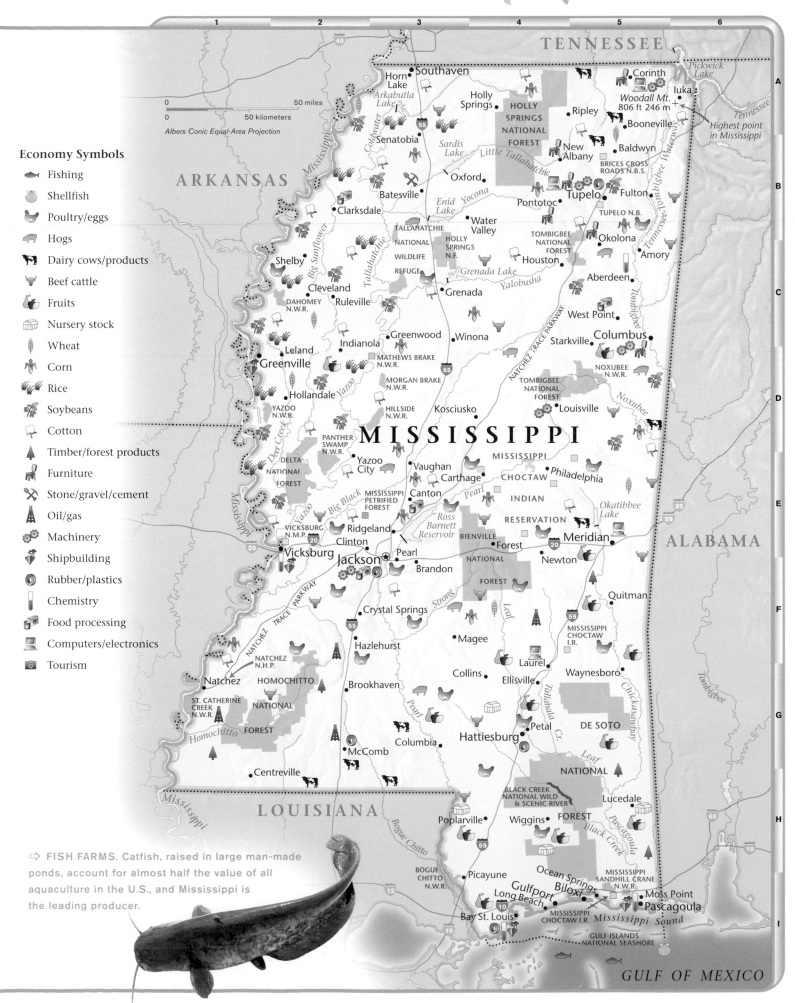

⇨ FISH FARMS. Catfish, raised in large man-made ponds, account for almost half the value of all aquaculture in the U.S., and Mississippi is the leading producer.

TENNESSEE

ARKANSAS

MISSISSIPPI

LOUISIANA

ALABAMA

GULF OF MEXICO

Woodall Mt. 806 ft 246 m
Highest point in Mississippi

THE TAR HEEL STATE:
NORTH CAROLINA

NORTH CAROLINA

THE BASICS

STATS

Area
53,819 sq mi (139,390 sq km)

Population
9,535,483

Capital
Raleigh
Population 403,892

Largest city
Charlotte
Population 731,424

Ethnic/racial groups
68.5% white; 21.5% African American;
2.2% Asian; 1.3% Native American.
Hispanic (any race) 8.4%.

Industry
Real estate, health services, chemicals,
tobacco products, finance, textiles

Agriculture
Poultry, hogs, tobacco, nursery stock,
cotton, soybeans

Statehood
November 21, 1789; 12th state

GEO WHIZ

The University of North Carolina at
Chapel Hill, which opened its doors
in 1795, is the oldest state university in
the United States.

The Biltmore estate in Asheville is the
largest private residence in the United
States. Built to resemble a French cha-
teau, the mansion is still
owned by descendants of Cornelius
Vanderbilt, who made the family's
original fortune in the late 1800s.

Standing 208 feet (63 m) high, Cape
Hatteras Light is the tallest lighthouse
in the U.S. Its beacon can be seen
some 20 miles (32 km) out to sea
and has warned sailors for more
than a century about the
shallow waters around a
group of treacherous sandbars
called Diamond Shoals.

CARDINAL

FLOWERING
DOGWOOD

Before European contact, the land that became North Carolina was inhabited by numerous Native American groups. Early attempts to settle the area met with strong resistance, and one early colony established in 1587 on Roanoke Island disappeared without a trace. More attempts at settlement came in 1650, and in 1663 King Charles granted a charter for the Carolina colony, which included present-day North Carolina, South Carolina, and part of Georgia. In 1789 North Carolina became the 12th state, but in 1861 it joined the Confederacy, supplying more men and equipment to the Southern cause than any other state. In 1903 the Wright brothers piloted the first successful airplane near Kitty Hawk, foreshadowing the change and growth coming to the Tar Heel State. Traditional industries included agriculture, textiles, and furniture making. Today, these, plus high-tech industries and education in the Raleigh-Durham Research Triangle area, as well as banking and finance in Charlotte, are important to the economy.

Map labels:
1   2   3

TENNESSEE

Highest point in North Carolina and east of the Mississippi

Boone

PISGAH

Grandfather Mountain 5,964 ft 1,818 m

NATIONAL SCENIC TRAIL

French Broad

NATIONAL

Mt. Mitchell 6,684 ft 2,037 m

FOREST

GREAT SMOKY MOUNTAINS

APPALACHIAN

Asheville

Morganton

NATIONAL PARK

Great Smoky Mts.

Black Mountain

BILTMORE HOUSE

CHEROKEE

CHEROKEE I.R.

Waynesville

PISGAH NATIONAL FOREST

Hendersonville

Forest City

INDIAN RESERVATION

Fontana

NANTAHALA NATIONAL

Franklin

Brevard

CARL SANDBURG HOME N.H.S.

Broad

Hiwassee L.

FOREST

CHATTOOGA NAT. WILD & SCENIC RIVER

HORSEPASTURE NATIONAL WILD & SCENIC RIVER

GEORGIA

Chattooga

SOUTH

⇨ FAVORITE PASTIME.
With four of the state's
major schools represented
in the powerful Atlantic
Coast Conference, it is not
surprising that basketball is
a popular sport among all
ages, whether on the court
or in the backyard.

⇦ TAKING FLIGHT.
The Wright Brothers
Memorial on Kill Devil
Hill, near Kitty Hawk on
North Carolina's Outer
Banks, marks the site
of the first successful
airplane flight in 1903.

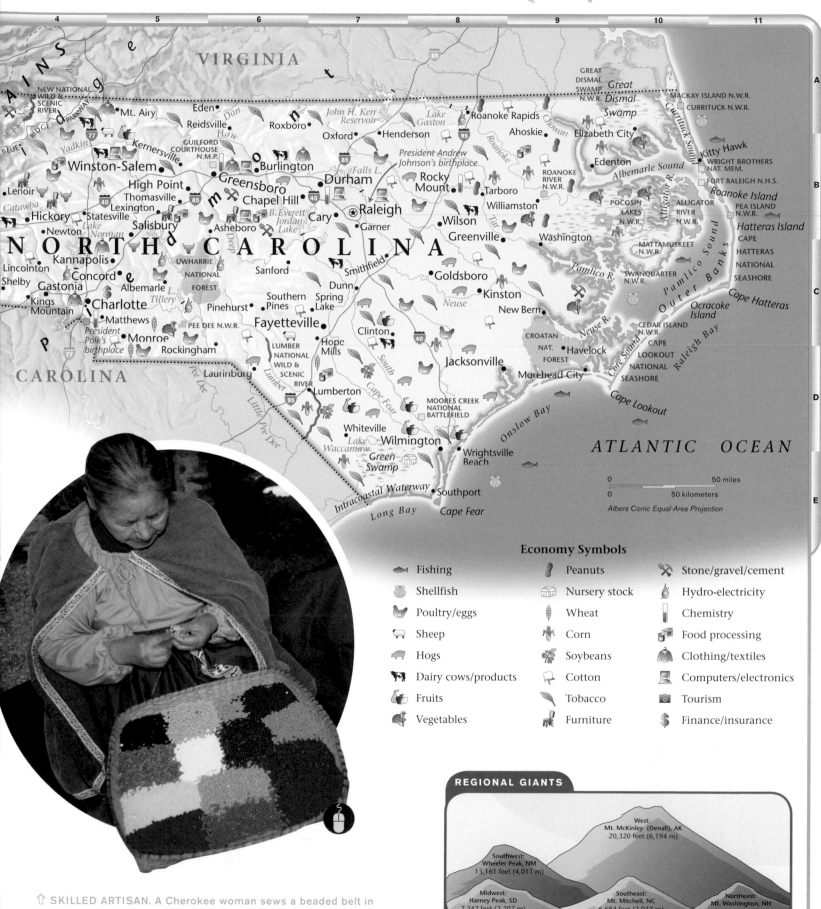

VIRGINIA

NEW NATIONAL WILD & SCENIC RIVER

Mt. Airy
Eden
Reidsville
Roxboro
Oxford
Henderson
John H. Kerr Reservoir
Lake Gaston
Roanoke Rapids
Ahoskie
Elizabeth City
GREAT DISMAL SWAMP N.W.R.
Great Dismal Swamp
MACKAY ISLAND N.W.R.
CURRITUCK N.W.R.

Kernersville
GUILFORD COURTHOUSE N.M.P.
Winston-Salem
Burlington
Durham
President Andrew Johnson's birthplace
Roanoke River
Edenton
Albemarle Sound
Kitty Hawk
WRIGHT BROTHERS NAT. MEM.
FORT RALEIGH N.H.S.

Lenoir
High Point
Greensboro
Chapel Hill
Falls L.
Rocky Mount
Tarboro
ROANOKE RIVER N.W.R.
POCOSIN LAKES N.W.R.
Roanoke Island

Thomasville
Lexington
Cary
Raleigh
Williamston
ALLIGATOR RIVER N.W.R.
PEA ISLAND N.W.R.
Hatteras Island

Hickory
Statesville
Salisbury
Asheboro
B. Everett Jordan Lake
Garner
Wilson
Greenville
Washington
MATTAMUSKEET N.W.R.
CAPE HATTERAS NATIONAL SEASHORE

NORTH CAROLINA

Newton
Kannapolis
UWHARRIE NATIONAL FOREST
Sanford
Smithfield
Goldsboro
Pamlico R.
SWANQUARTER N.W.R.
Pamlico Sound
Outer Banks

Lincolnton
Shelby
Concord
Albemarle
Dunn
Kinston
Neuse
Ocracoke Island
Cape Hatteras

Kings Mountain
Gastonia
Charlotte
Tillery
Pinehurst
Southern Pines
Spring Lake
New Bern
CEDAR ISLAND N.W.R.
CROATAN NAT. FOREST
Havelock
CAPE LOOKOUT NATIONAL SEASHORE
Raleigh Bay

Matthews
President Polk's birthplace
Monroe
Rockingham
PEE DEE N.W.R.
Fayetteville
Clinton
Jacksonville
Morehead City
Core Sound
Cape Lookout

CAROLINA
Laurinburg
LUMBER NATIONAL WILD & SCENIC RIVER
Hope Mills
Lumberton
MOORES CREEK NATIONAL BATTLEFIELD
Onslow Bay

Whiteville
Lake Waccamaw
Wilmington
Wrightsville Beach
ATLANTIC OCEAN

Green Swamp
Intracoastal Waterway
Southport
Long Bay
Cape Fear

0 — 50 miles
0 — 50 kilometers
Albers Conic Equal-Area Projection

Economy Symbols

Fishing	Peanuts	Stone/gravel/cement
Shellfish	Nursery stock	Hydro-electricity
Poultry/eggs	Wheat	Chemistry
Sheep	Corn	Food processing
Hogs	Soybeans	Clothing/textiles
Dairy cows/products	Cotton	Computers/electronics
Fruits	Tobacco	Tourism
Vegetables	Furniture	Finance/insurance

⇧ SKILLED ARTISAN. A Cherokee woman sews a beaded belt in Oconaluftee Indian Village in western North Carolina. Cherokees in this mountainous region are descendants of Indians who hid in the hills to avoid the forced migration known as the Trail of Tears. The village preserves traditional 18th-century crafts, customs, and lifestyles.

REGIONAL GIANTS

West:
Mt. McKinley (Denali), AK
20,320 feet (6,194 m)

Southwest:
Wheeler Peak, NM
13,161 feet (4,011 m)

Midwest:
Harney Peak, SD
7,242 feet (2,207 m)

Southeast:
Mt. Mitchell, NC
6,684 feet (2,037 m)

Northeast:
Mt. Washington, NH
6,288 feet (1,917 m)

Mt. Mitchell in the Southeast is the tallest peak east of the Mississippi, but young mountains in the West and Southwest tower above older eastern peaks.

SOUTH CAROLINA

THE BASICS

STATS

Area
32,020 sq mi (82,932 sq km)

Population
4,625,364

Capital
Columbia
Population 129,272

Largest city
Columbia
Population 129,272

Ethnic/racial groups
66.2% white; 27.9% African American; 1.3% Asian; .4% Native American. Hispanic (any race) 5.1%.

Industry
Service industries, tourism, chemicals, textiles, machinery, forest products

Agriculture
Chickens, tobacco, nursery stock, beef cattle, dairy products, cotton

Statehood
May 23, 1788; 8th state

GEO WHIZ

The loggerhead sea turtle, South Carolina's state reptile, is threatened throughout its range. These turtles weigh between 200–450 pounds (90–204 kg).

North America's largest remnant of old-growth bottomland hardwood forest towers above the Congaree River and is protected as a 22,000-acre (8,903-ha) refuge called Congaree National Park.

Sweetgrass basketmaking, a traditional art form of African origin, has been a part of the Mount Pleasant community for more than 300 years. The baskets were originally used by slaves in the planting and processing of rice in coastal lowland regions.

Bobcats are thriving on Kiawah Island, a resort community southeast of Charleston. The elusive, nocturnal cats, which are about twice the size of an average house cat, play an important role in controlling the island's deer population.

CAROLINA WREN

YELLOW JESSAMINE

Attempts in the 16th century by the Spanish and the French to colonize the area that would become South Carolina met fierce resistance from local Native American groups, but in 1670 the English were the first to establish a permanent European settlement at present-day Charleston. The colony prospered by relying on slave labor to produce first cotton, then rice and indigo. South Carolina became the 8th state in 1788 and the first to leave the Union just months before the first shots of the Civil War were fired on Fort Sumter in 1861. After the war, South Carolina struggled to rebuild its economy.

Early in the 20th century, textile mills introduced new jobs. Today, agriculture remains important, manufacturing and high-tech industries are expanding along interstate highway corridors, and tourists and retirees are drawn to the state's Atlantic coastline. But these coastal areas are not without risk. In 1989 Hurricane Hugo's 135-mile-per-hour (217-kmph) winds left a trail of destruction.

⬆ GLOW OF DAWN. The rising sun reflects off the water along the Atlantic coast. Beaches attract visitors year-round, contributing to tourism, the state's largest industry.

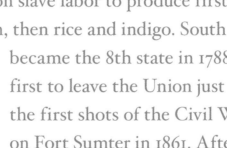

Highest point in South Carolina

Sassafras Mt. 3,560 ft 1,085 m

⬇ SOUTHERN CHARM. Twilight settles over antebellum homes in the historic district of Charleston. The city, established in 1670, is an important port located where the Ashley and Cooper Rivers merge before flowing to the Atlantic Ocean.

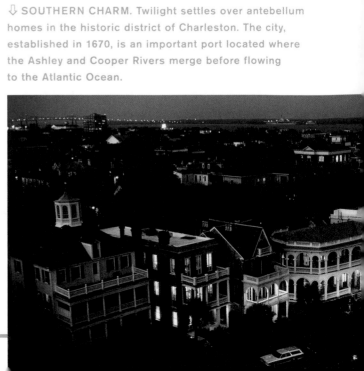

TRADE PARTNERS

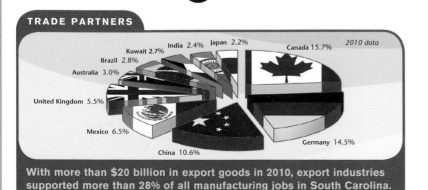

2010 data

Canada 15.7%
Japan 2.2%
India 2.4%
Kuwait 2.7%
Brazil 2.8%
Australia 3.0%
United Kingdom 5.5%
Mexico 6.5%
China 10.6%
Germany 14.5%

With more than $20 billion in export goods in 2010, export industries supported more than 28% of all manufacturing jobs in South Carolina. Transportation equipment is the leading manufactured export.

3   4   5   6   7   8   9   10

0 ____ 50 miles
0 ____ 50 kilometers
Albers Conic Equal-Area Projection

➡ **SHOWING OFF.** Feathers extended, a male wild turkey struts through Francis Beidler Forest, a wildlife sanctuary and the world's largest virgin cypress-tupelo swamp forest.

NORTH CAROLINA

COWPENS N.B.
Gaffney
Greer
Taylors
Spartanburg
Mauldin
Simpsonville
Union
Laurens
Clinton
SUMTER
NATIONAL
FOREST
Greenwood
Newberry
NINETY SIX
N.H.S.
SUMTER
NATIONAL
FOREST
Batesburg-
Leesville
Edgefield
North
Augusta
Clearwater
Aiken
Williston
Barnwell
Bamberg
GEORGIA
Allendale
Walterboro
Hampton
Burton
Beaufort
Port Royal
SAVANNAH
NATIONAL
WILDLIFE
REFUGE
PINCKNEY ISLAND
N.W.R.
Hilton Head
Island

KINGS
MOUNTAIN
N.M.P.
York
Rock Hill
Fort
Mill
CATAWBA
I.R.
Chester
Lancaster
Winnsboro
Camden
Lake
Murray
Irmo
Forest Acres
West Columbia
Columbia
Cayce
CONGAREE
NATIONAL
PARK
Orangeburg
SANTEE
N.W.R.
Lake
Marion
Santee
Dam
Lake
Moultrie
Moncks
Corner
Summerville
Ladson
Goose Creek
Hanahan
North
Charleston
Charleston
ACE BASIN
N.W.R.
Edisto
Island
St. Helena
Sound
St. Helena
Island
Parris Island
Port Royal Sound
Hilton Head Island
Daufuskie Island

Wylie Lake
Broad
Catawba
Cheraw
CAROLINA
SANDHILLS
N.W.R.
Bennettsville
Hartsville
Darlington
Florence
Sumter
Manning
Lake City
Kingstree
Santee
FRANCIS
MARION
NATIONAL
FOREST
Mt. Pleasant
FT. SUMTER NAT. MON.
CHARLES PINCKNEY N.H.S.
CAPE
ROMAIN
N.W.R.
Cape Island
North Island
Georgetown

Great Pee Dee
Dillon
Mullins
Marion
Loris
Conway
North
Myrtle Beach
Myrtle Beach
Socastee
Surfside Beach
Garden City
Waccamaw
Little Pee Dee
Lynches
Black
Great Pee Dee
Intracoastal Waterway
Long Bay

ATLANTIC
OCEAN

SEA ISLANDS

SOUTH
CAROLINA

Saluda
Congaree
Wateree
Edisto
N. Fork Edisto
S. Fork Edisto
Savannah
Coosawhatchie
Combahee
Cooper

Piedmont

Economy Symbols

- Fishing
- Shellfish
- Poultry/eggs
- Hogs
- Dairy cows/products
- Fruits
- Vegetables
- Peanuts
- Nursery stock
- Wheat
- Corn

- Soybeans
- Cotton
- Tobacco
- Timber/forest products
- Stone/gravel/cement
- Hydro-electricity
- Machinery
- Rubber/plastics
- Chemistry
- Clothing/textiles
- Tourism

THE BASICS

STATS

Area
42,143 sq mi (109,151 sq km)

Population
6,346,105

Capital
Nashville-Davidson
Population 601,222

Largest city
Memphis
Population 646,889

Ethnic/racial groups
77.6% white; 16.7% African American;
1.4% Asian; .3% Native American.
Hispanic (any race) 4.6%.

Industry
Service industries, chemicals,
transportation equipment, processed
foods, machinery

Agriculture
Cattle, cotton, dairy products, hogs,
poultry, nursery stock

Statehood
June 1, 1796; 16th state

GEO WHIZ

Twenty-seven species of salamanders
live in Great Smoky Mountains
National Park, earning it the
nickname Salamander Capital
of the World. Among the species
are the spotted; the Jordans, which
is found nowhere else; and the five-
foot-long hellbender (1.5 m).

The New Madrid Earthquakes of 1811–
1812, some of the largest earthquakes in
the history of the U.S., created Reelfoot
Lake in northwestern Tennessee. It is the
state's only large, natural lake; others
were created by damming waterways.

The Tennessee-Tombigbee Waterway
is a 234-mile (376-km)
artificial waterway
that connects the
Tennessee and
Tombigbee Rivers. This
water transportation route
provides inland ports with
an outlet to the Gulf of Mexico.

MOCKINGBIRD
IRIS

TENNESSEE

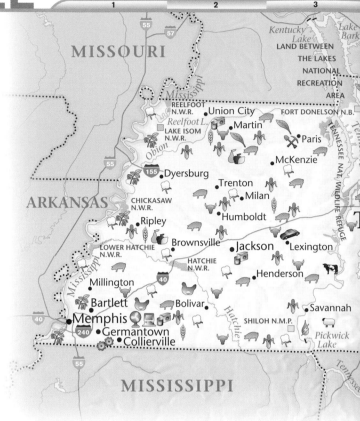

Following the last ice age, Native Americans moved onto the fertile lands of Tennessee. The earliest Europeans in Tennessee were Spanish explorers who passed through in 1541. In 1673 both the English and French made claims on the land, hoping to develop trade with the powerful Cherokees, whose town, called *Tanasi,* gave the state its name. Originally part of North Carolina, Tennessee was ceded to the federal government and became the 16th state in 1796. Tennessee was the last state to join the Confederacy and endured years of hardship after the war. Beginning in the 1930s, the federally funded Tennessee Valley Authority (TVA) set a high standard in water management in the state, and the hydropower it generated supported major industrial development. Tennessee played a key role in the civil rights movement of the 1960s. Today, visitors to Tennessee are drawn to national parks, Nashville's country music, and the mournful sound of the blues in Memphis.

⇦ OUT FOR A STROLL. Black bear cubs are usually born in January and remain with their mother for about 18 months. The Great Smoky Mountains National Park is one of the few remaining natural habitats for black bears in the eastern U.S.

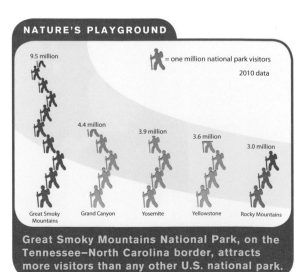

NATURE'S PLAYGROUND

9.5 million

= one million national park visitors
2010 data

4.4 million

3.9 million

3.6 million

3.0 million

Great Smoky Mountains

Grand Canyon

Yosemite

Yellowstone

Rocky Mountains

Great Smoky Mountains National Park, on the Tennessee–North Carolina border, attracts more visitors than any other U.S. national park.

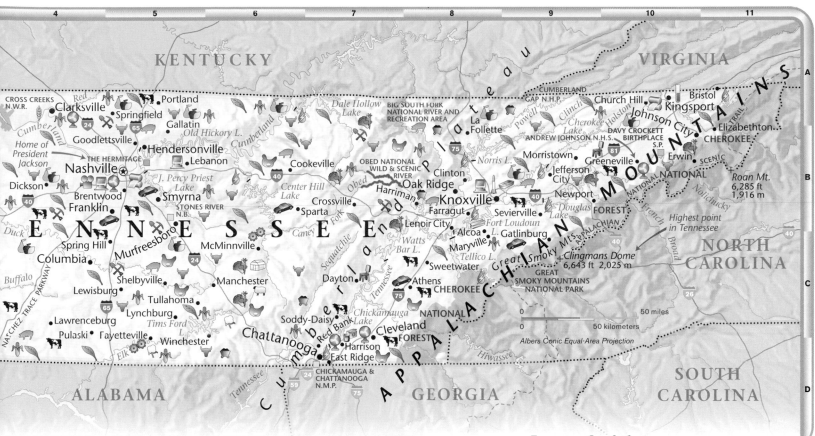

Economy Symbols

Symbol	Description	Symbol	Description
🐓	Poultry/eggs		Printing/publishing
	Sheep		Stone/gravel/cement
	Hogs		Mining
	Dairy cows/products		Coal
	Beef cattle		Hydro-electricity
	Fruits		Machinery
	Vegetables		Metal manufacturing
	Nursery stock		Motor vehicles/parts
	Wheat		Chemistry
	Corn		Food processing
	Soybeans		Electrical equipment
	Cotton		Computers/electronics
	Tobacco		Aerospace
	Furniture		Motion picture/music industry

⇧ WATTS BAR DAM is one of nine TVA dams built on the Tennessee River to aid navigation and flood control and to supply power. The large reservoir behind the dam provides a recreation area that attracts millions of vacationers each year. Without the dam, cities such as Chattanooga would face devastating floods.

⇨ SOUTHERN TRADITION. Nashville's Grand Ole Opry is the home of country music. Originally a 1925 radio show called "Barn Dance," the Opry now occupies a theater with a seating capacity of 4,400 and the largest broadcasting studio in the world. Country music, using mainly stringed instruments, evolved from traditional folk tunes of the Appalachians.

THE OLD DOMINION STATE:
VIRGINIA

THE BASICS

STATS

Area
42,774 sq mi (110,785 sq km)

Population
8,001,024

Capital
Richmond
Population 204,214

Largest city
Virginia Beach
Population 437,994

Ethnic/racial groups
68.6% white; 19.4% African American; 5.5% Asian; .4% Native American. Hispanic (any race) 7.9%.

Industry
Food processing, communication and electronic equipment, transportation equipment, printing, shipbuilding, textiles

Agriculture
Tobacco, poultry, dairy products, beef cattle, soybeans, hogs

Statehood
June 25, 1788; 10th state

GEO WHIZ

In the early 1700s the bustling port of Hampton was a major target for pirates, including the notorious Blackbeard. Today, each spring the city hosts the Blackbeard Festival, complete with pirate re-enactors, live music, games, and fireworks.

Virginia is the birthplace of eight U.S. presidents—more than any other state. They are: George Washington, Thomas Jefferson, James Madison, James Monroe, William Harrison, John Tyler, Zachary Taylor, and Woodrow Wilson. Learn about them and more in our book *Our Country's Presidents.*

During the Battle of Hampton Roads in 1862, the USS *Monitor* and the CSS *Virginia* (a rebuilt version of the USS *Merrimac*) met in one of the most famous naval engagements in U.S. history. It marked the dawn of a new era of naval warfare.

More than 200,000 telephone calls are made each day at the Pentagon, the headquarters for the U.S. Department of Defense, through phones connected by 100,000 miles (160,000 km) of telephone cable. It is one of the largest office buildings in the world.

CARDINAL
FLOWERING
DOGWOOD

VIRGINIA

Long before Europeans arrived in present-day Virginia, Native Americans populated the area. Early Spanish attempts to establish a colony failed, but in 1607 merchants established the first permanent English settlement in North America at Jamestown. Virginia became a prosperous colony, growing tobacco using slave labor. Virginia played a key role in the drive for independence, and the final battle of the Revolutionary War was at Yorktown, near Jamestown. In 1861 Virginia joined the Confederacy and became a major battleground of the Civil War, which left the state in financial ruin. Today, Virginia has a diversified economy. Farmers still grow tobacco, along with other crops. The Hampton Roads area, near the mouth of Chesapeake Bay, is a center for shipbuilding and home to major naval bases. Northern Virginia, across the Potomac River from Washington, D.C., boasts federal government offices and high-tech businesses. And the state's natural beauty and many historic sites attract tourists from around the world.

⇧ **EARLY ENTER-TAINMENT.** Dating back to ancient Greece and Rome, dice made of bone, ivory, or lead were popular during colonial times.

⇨ **NATURAL WONDER.**
Winding under the Appalachian Mountains, Luray Caverns formed as water dissolved limestone rocks and precipitated calcium deposits to form stalactites and stalagmites.

⇩ PAST AND PRESENT. Cyclists speed past a statue of Confederate General Robert E. Lee on Richmond's Monument Avenue. The street has drawn criticism for recognizing leaders of the Confederacy.

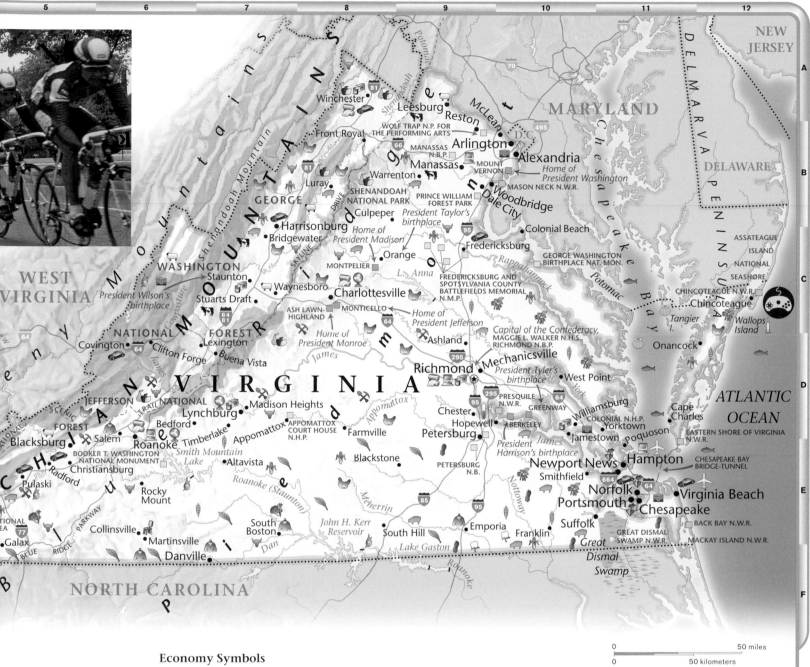

NEW JERSEY

MARYLAND

WEST VIRGINIA

DELAWARE

DELMARVA PENINSULA

ASSATEAGUE ISLAND

NATIONAL SEASHORE

Winchester
Leesburg
Reston
McLean
Front Royal
WOLF TRAP N.P. FOR THE PERFORMING ARTS
MANASSAS N.B.P.
Arlington
D.C.
Alexandria
Manassas
MOUNT VERNON
Home of President Washington
MASON NECK N.W.R.
Warrenton
Luray
SHENANDOAH NATIONAL PARK
Woodbridge
GEORGE
PRINCE WILLIAM FOREST PARK
Dale City
Harrisonburg
Culpeper
President Taylor's birthplace
Colonial Beach
Bridgewater
Home of President Madison
Fredericksburg
GEORGE WASHINGTON BIRTHPLACE NAT. MON.
Orange
MONTPELIER
CHINCOTEAGUE N.W.R.
WASHINGTON
Staunton
Chincoteague
President Wilson's birthplace
Waynesboro
Charlottesville
FREDERICKSBURG AND SPOTSYLVANIA COUNTY BATTLEFIELDS MEMORIAL N.M.P.
Tangier I.
Wallops Island
Stuarts Draft
ASH LAWN-HIGHLAND
MONTICELLO
Home of President Jefferson
Onancock
Covington
NATIONAL FOREST
Lexington
Home of President Monroe
Ashland
Capital of the Confederacy,
MAGGIE L. WALKER N.H.S.
RICHMOND N.B.P.
Clifton Forge
Buena Vista
Richmond
Mechanicsville
President Tyler's birthplace
West Point
JEFFERSON NATIONAL FOREST
Madison Heights
Lynchburg
295
PRESQUILE N.W.R.
GREENWAY
Williamsburg
Cape Charles
ATLANTIC OCEAN
Blacksburg
Bedford
Chester
BERKELEY
COLONIAL N.H.P.
Yorktown
EASTERN SHORE OF VIRGINIA N.W.R.
Salem
Roanoke
Timberlake
Appomattox
APPOMATTOX COURT HOUSE N.H.P.
Farmville
Hopewell
Petersburg
President Harrison's birthplace
Jamestown
Poquoson
BOOKER T. WASHINGTON NATIONAL MONUMENT
Smith Mountain Lake
Altavista
Blackstone
PETERSBURG N.B.
Newport News
Hampton
CHESAPEAKE BAY BRIDGE-TUNNEL
Christiansburg
Pulaski
Rocky Mount
Smithfield
Norfolk
Radford
Roanoke (Staunton)
Virginia Beach
Portsmouth
Chesapeake
Collinsville
South Boston
South Hill
Emporia
Franklin
Suffolk
BACK BAY N.W.R.
Galax
Martinsville
John H. Kerr Reservoir
Lake Gaston
GREAT DISMAL SWAMP N.W.R.
MACKAY ISLAND N.W.R.
Danville
Great Dismal Swamp

NORTH CAROLINA

VIRGINIA

Shenandoah
Potomac
Chesapeake Bay
Rappahannock
L. Anna
James
Appomattox
Meherrin
Nottoway
Dan
Roanoke

0   50 miles
0   50 kilometers
Albers Conic Equal-Area Projection

Economy Symbols

- Fishing
- Shellfish
- Poultry/eggs
- Sheep
- Hogs
- Dairy cows/products
- Beef cattle
- Fruits
- Vegetables
- Peanuts
- Wheat

- Corn
- Soybeans
- Cotton
- Tobacco
- Furniture
- Printing/publishing
- Stone/gravel/cement
- Coal
- Hydro-electricity
- Machinery
- Ship Building

- Motor vehicles/parts
- Chemistry
- Food processing
- Clothing/textiles
- Electrical equipment
- Computers/electronics
- Aircraft/parts
- Aerospace
- Tourism

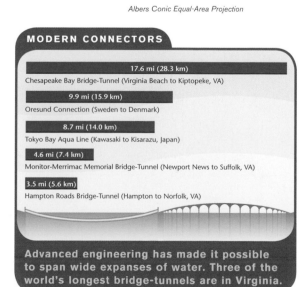

MODERN CONNECTORS

17.6 mi (28.3 km)	
Chesapeake Bay Bridge-Tunnel (Virginia Beach to Kiptopeke, VA)	
9.9 mi (15.9 km)	
Oresund Connection (Sweden to Denmark)	
8.7 mi (14.0 km)	
Tokyo Bay Aqua Line (Kawasaki to Kisarazu, Japan)	
4.6 mi (7.4 km)	
Monitor-Merrimac Memorial Bridge-Tunnel (Newport News to Suffolk, VA)	
3.5 mi (5.6 km)	
Hampton Roads Bridge-Tunnel (Hampton to Norfolk, VA)	

Advanced engineering has made it possible to span wide expanses of water. Three of the world's longest bridge-tunnels are in Virginia.

WEST VIRGINIA

Mountainous West Virginia was first settled by Native Americans who favored the wooded region for hunting. The first Europeans to settle in what originally was an extension of Virginia were Germans and Scotch-Irish, who came through mountain valleys of Pennsylvania in the early 1700s. Because farms in West Virginia did not depend upon slaves, residents opposed secession during the Civil War and broke away from Virginia, becoming the 35th state in 1863. In the early 1800s West Virginia harvested forest products and mined salt, but it was the exploitation of vast coal deposits that brought industrialization to the state. Coal fueled steel mills, steamboats, and trains, and jobs in the mines attracted immigrants from far and near. However, poor work conditions resulted in a legacy of poverty, illness, and environmental degradation— problems the state continues to face. Today, the state is working to build a tourist industry based on its natural beauty and mountain crafts and culture.

THE BASICS

STATS

Area
24,230 sq mi (62,755 sq km)

Population
1,852,994

Capital
Charleston
Population 51,400

Largest city
Charleston
Population 51,400

Ethnic/racial groups
93.9% white; 3.4% African American; .7% Asian; .2% Native American. Hispanic (any race) 1.2%.

Industry
Tourism, coal mining, chemicals, metal manufacturing, forest products, stone, clay, oil, glass products

Agriculture
Poultry and eggs, cattle, dairy products, apples

Statehood
June 20, 1863; 35th state

GEO WHIZ

The FBI crime data center in Clarksburg has the largest collection of fingerprints in the world. The center processes some 50,000 fingerprints each day.

The city of Weirton is nestled in the panhandle between Ohio and Pennsylvania. It is the only city in the U.S. that sits in one state and borders two others.

Bridge Day, held each October, is the only day of the year when it is legal to jump off the 876-foot- (267-m-) high New River Gorge Bridge using bungee cords, parachutes, or other equipment.

The first rural free mail delivery in the United States started in Charles Town on October 1, 1896.

CARDINAL
RHODODENDRON

⬆ HARD LABOR.
Coal miners work under difficult conditions. In 2010 West Virginia mined more than 178 million tons of coal, or 12.5 percent of U.S. production.

OHIO

Point Pleasant

Kanawha

Hurricane

Huntington 64 Nitro
Kenova   St. Alba

Ohio

Big Sandy

Madiso

Guyandotte

Logan

Tug Fork

Williamson

KENTUCKY

⬅ STRATEGIC LOCATION.
Founded in 1751 by Robert Harper, who built a ferry to cross the Shenandoah River, Harpers Ferry was a departure point for pioneers heading West as well as the site of many battles during the Civil War.

A

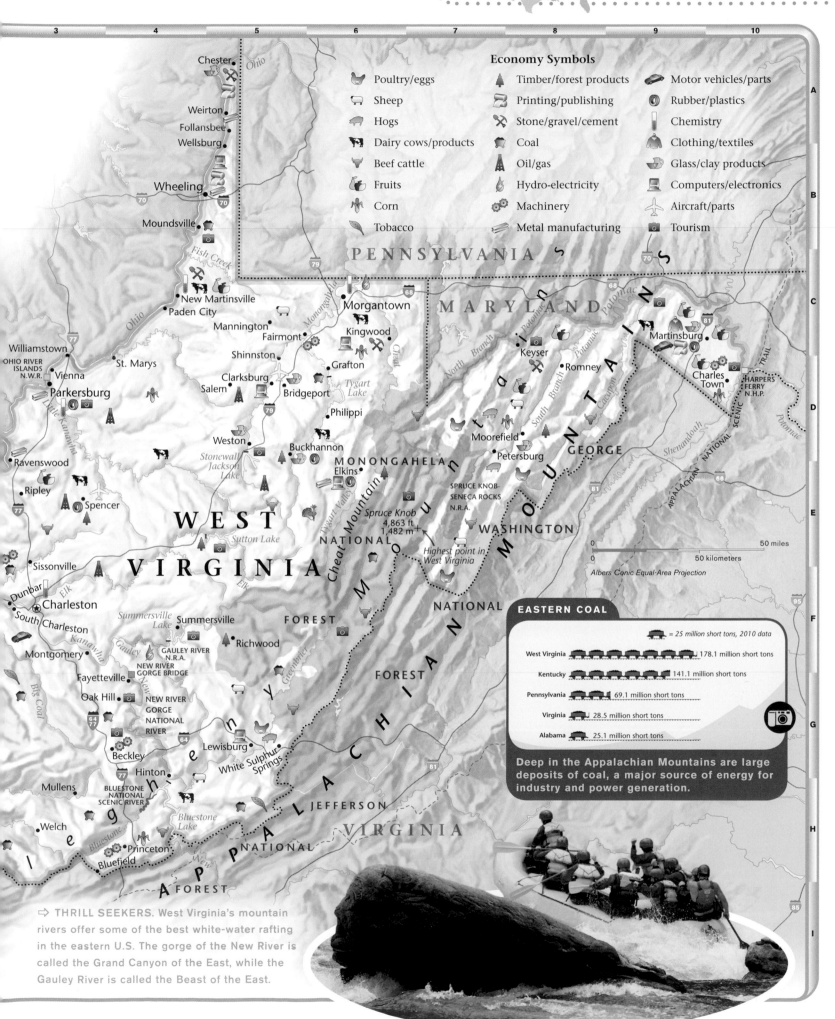

Economy Symbols

- Poultry/eggs
- Sheep
- Hogs
- Dairy cows/products
- Beef cattle
- Fruits
- Corn
- Tobacco
- Timber/forest products
- Printing/publishing
- Stone/gravel/cement
- Coal
- Oil/gas
- Hydro-electricity
- Machinery
- Metal manufacturing
- Motor vehicles/parts
- Rubber/plastics
- Chemistry
- Clothing/textiles
- Glass/clay products
- Computers/electronics
- Aircraft/parts
- Tourism

PENNSYLVANIA

MARYLAND

WEST VIRGINIA

Spruce Knob
4,863 ft
1,482 m
Highest point in
West Virginia

MONONGAHELA

NATIONAL

FOREST

APPALACHIAN MOUNTAINS

GEORGE WASHINGTON NATIONAL FOREST

JEFFERSON
NATIONAL
FOREST

VIRGINIA

Cities and places: Chester, Weirton, Follansbee, Wellsburg, Wheeling, Moundsville, New Martinsville, Paden City, Mannington, Fairmont, Kingwood, Shinnston, Morgantown, Grafton, Clarksburg, Salem, Bridgeport, Philippi, Weston, Buckhannon, Elkins, Williamstown, St. Marys, Vienna, Parkersburg, Ravenswood, Ripley, Spencer, Sissonville, Dunbar, Charleston, South Charleston, Montgomery, Fayetteville, Oak Hill, Beckley, Hinton, Mullens, Welch, Princeton, Bluefield, Summersville, Richwood, Lewisburg, White Sulphur Springs, Moorefield, Petersburg, Keyser, Romney, Martinsburg, Charles Town, Harpers Ferry N.H.P.

OHIO RIVER ISLANDS N.W.R.

Stonewall Jackson Lake
Sutton Lake
Summersville Lake
GAULEY RIVER N.R.A.
NEW RIVER GORGE BRIDGE
NEW RIVER GORGE NATIONAL RIVER
BLUESTONE NATIONAL SCENIC RIVER
Bluestone Lake
SPRUCE KNOB-SENECA ROCKS N.R.A.
APPALACHIAN NATIONAL SCENIC TRAIL
Shenandoah
Potomac
Ohio
Fish Creek
Monongahela
Cheat
Tygart Lake
Little Kanawha
Kanawha
Elk
Gauley
Greenbrier
New
Big Coal
Bluestone

Tygart Valley
Cheat Mountain
North Branch
South Branch
Cacapon

50 miles
50 kilometers
Albers Conic Equal-Area Projection

EASTERN COAL

= 25 million short tons, 2010 data

West Virginia	178.1 million short tons
Kentucky	141.1 million short tons
Pennsylvania	69.1 million short tons
Virginia	28.5 million short tons
Alabama	25.1 million short tons

Deep in the Appalachian Mountains are large deposits of coal, a major source of energy for industry and power generation.

⇨ THRILL SEEKERS. West Virginia's mountain rivers offer some of the best white-water rafting in the eastern U.S. The gorge of the New River is called the Grand Canyon of the East, while the Gauley River is called the Beast of the East.

THE REGION

PHYSICAL			POLITICAL	
Total area 821,739 sq mi (2,128,287 sq km)	**Lowest point** St. Francis River, MO 230 ft (70 m)	**Vegetation** Grassland; broadleaf, needleleaf, and mixed forest	**Total population** 66,927,001	**Smallest state** Indiana: 36,418 sq mi (94,322 sq km)
Highest point Harney Peak, SD 7,242 ft (2,207 m)	**Longest rivers** Mississippi, Missouri, Arkansas, Ohio	**Climate** Continental to mild, ranging from cold winters and cool	**States (12):** Illinois, Indiana, Iowa, Kansas, Michigan, Minnesota, Missouri, Nebraska, North Dakota, Ohio, South Dakota, Wisconsin	**Most populous state** Illinois: 12,830,632
	Largest lakes Superior, Michigan, Huron, Erie	summers in the north to mild winters and humid summers in the south	**Largest state** Michigan: 96,716 sq mi (250,495 sq km)	**Least populous state** North Dakota: 672,591
				Largest city proper Chicago, IL: 2,695,598

The Midwest

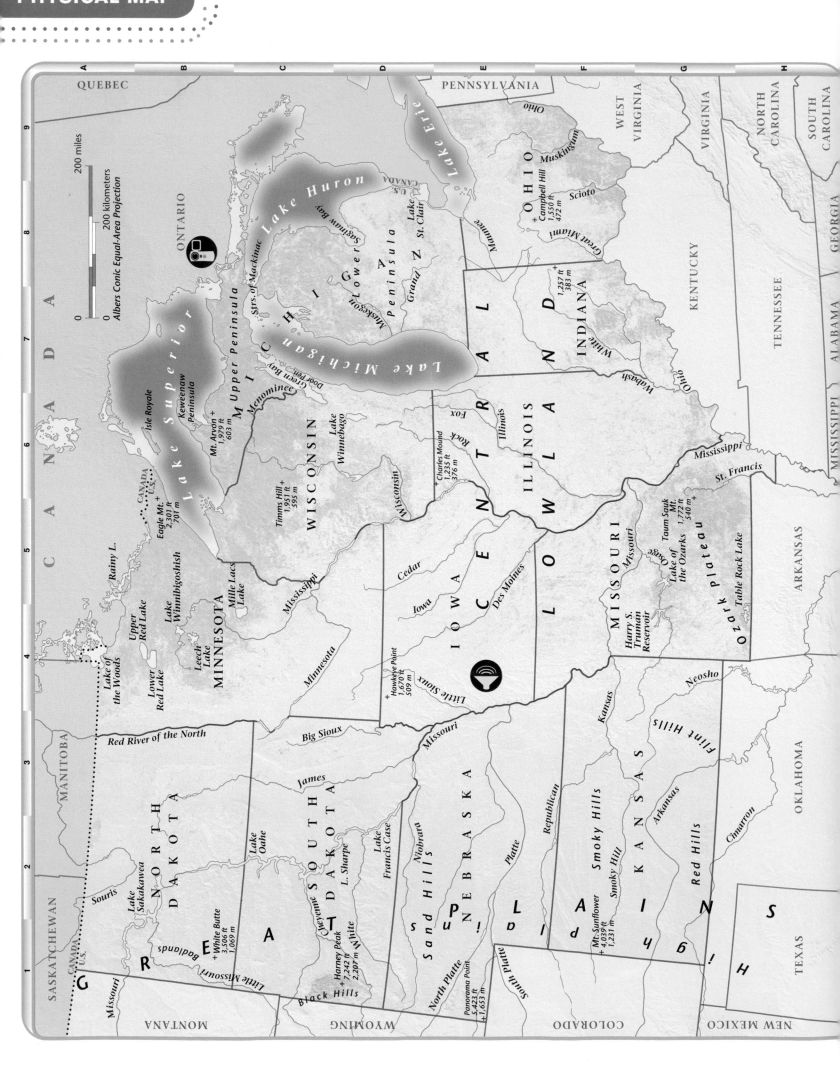

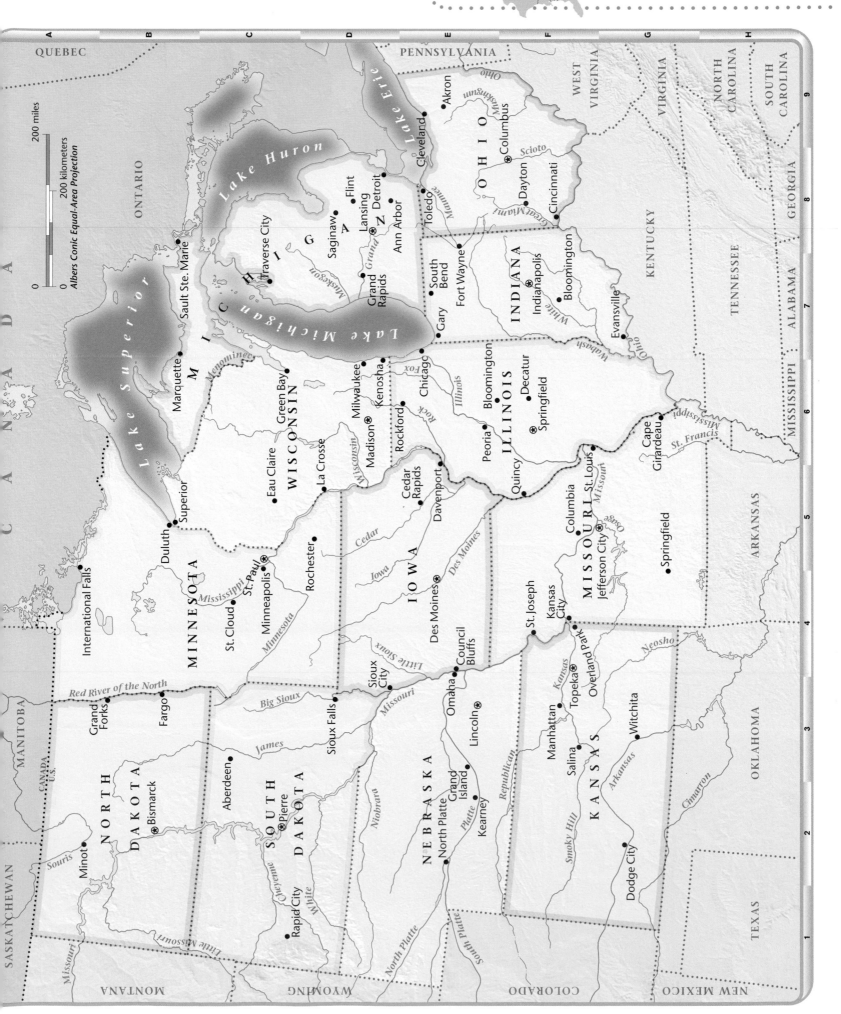

200 miles
200 kilometers
Albers Conic Equal-Area Projection

QUEBEC

PENNSYLVANIA

ONTARIO

WEST VIRGINIA

VIRGINIA

NORTH CAROLINA

SOUTH CAROLINA

Lake Huron

Lake Erie

Ohio

Muskingum

Akron

Cleveland

OHIO

Columbus

Scioto

GEORGIA

Dayton

Cincinnati

Great Miami

Maumee

Toledo

Flint

Lansing

Detroit

Saginaw

Ann Arbor

KENTUCKY

TENNESSEE

ALABAMA

Traverse City

MICHIGAN

Grand Rapids

Grand

South Bend

Fort Wayne

INDIANA

Indianapolis

Bloomington

Muskegon

Gary

White

Evansville

Ohio

MISSISSIPPI

Lake Superior

Lake Michigan

Marquette

Sault Ste. Marie

Menominee

Green Bay

Milwaukee

Kenosha

Chicago

Fox

Rock

Bloomington

Decatur

Springfield

Wabash

Illinois

ILLINOIS

CANADA

Eau Claire

WISCONSIN

La Crosse

Wisconsin

Madison

Rockford

Peoria

Cape Girardeau

St. Francis

Mississippi

Superior

Duluth

Cedar Rapids

Davenport

Quincy

St. Louis

Missouri

Columbia

MISSOURI

Springfield

ARKANSAS

International Falls

MINNESOTA

St. Cloud

St. Paul

Minneapolis

Rochester

Cedar

Iowa

IOWA

Des Moines

Des Moines

Jefferson City

Osage

Mississippi

Minnesota

Red River of the North

Grand Forks

Fargo

Big Sioux

Sioux Falls

Sioux City

Little Sioux

Council Bluffs

Omaha

Missouri

St. Joseph

Kansas City

Overland Park

Kansas

Topeka

Manhattan

Neosho

MANITOBA

CANADA
U.S.

James

Aberdeen

NORTH DAKOTA

Minot

Souris

Bismarck

SOUTH DAKOTA

Pierre

Rapid City

Cheyenne

White

Little Missouri

NEBRASKA

North Platte

Grand Island

Kearney

Lincoln

Niobrara

Platte

Republican

Salina

Witchita

KANSAS

Arkansas

Smoky Hill

Dodge City

Cimarron

OKLAHOMA

SASKATCHEWAN

MONTANA

WYOMING

COLORADO

NEW MEXICO

TEXAS

North Platte

South Platte

Missouri

⇨ FIERCE GIANT. Students in Chicago's Field Museum eye the skeleton of *Tyrannosaurus rex*, a dinosaur that roamed North America's plains 65 million years ago.

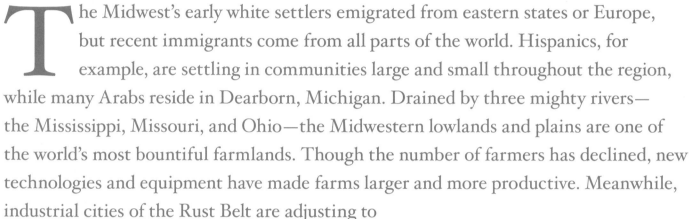

The Midwest
GREAT LAKES, GREAT RIVERS

The Midwest's early white settlers emigrated from eastern states or Europe, but recent immigrants come from all parts of the world. Hispanics, for example, are settling in communities large and small throughout the region, while many Arabs reside in Dearborn, Michigan. Drained by three mighty rivers—the Mississippi, Missouri, and Ohio—the Midwestern lowlands and plains are one of the world's most bountiful farmlands. Though the number of farmers has declined, new technologies and equipment have made farms larger and more productive. Meanwhile, industrial cities of the Rust Belt are adjusting to an economy focused more on information and services than on manufacturing.

⇩ CROP CIRCLES. Much of the western part of the region receives less than 20 inches (50 cm) of rain yearly—not enough to support agriculture. Large, circular center-pivot irrigation systems draw water from underground reserves called aquifers to provide life-giving water to crops.

⇩ DAIRY HEARTLAND. Dairy cows, such as these in Wisconsin, are sometimes treated with growth hormones to increase milk production. These animals play an important role in the economy of the Midwest, which supplies much of the country's milk, butter, and cheese.

⬇ MIDWEST URBAN HUB. Chicago, the third largest urban area in the U.S., with almost 10 million people, is the economic and cultural core of the Midwest and a major transportation hub.

⇨ PRESERVING THE PAST. A young Cherokee man, dressed in beaded costume and feathered headband, dances at a powwow in Milwaukee. Such gatherings provide Indians from across the country with a chance to share their traditions.

⬆ NATURE'S MOST VIOLENT STORMS. Parts of the midwestern U.S. have earned the nickname Tornado Alley because these destructive, swirling storms, which develop in association with thunderstorms along eastward-moving cold fronts, occur here more than any other place on Earth.

WHERE THE PICTURES ARE

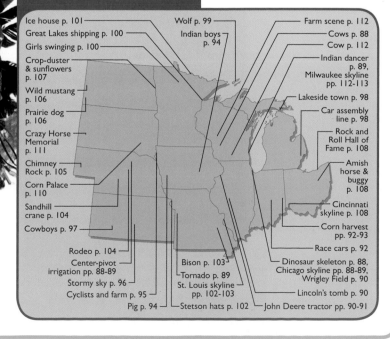

THE LAND OF LINCOLN STATE:
ILLINOIS

ILLINOIS

THE BASICS

STATS

Area
57,914 sq mi (149,998 sq km)

Population
12,830,632

Capital
Springfield
Population 116,250

Largest city
Chicago
Population 2,695,598

Ethnic/racial groups
71.5% white; 14.5% African American;
4.6% Asian; .3% Native American.
Hispanic (any race) 15.8%.

Industry
Industrial machinery, electronic
equipment, food processing, chemicals,
metals, printing and publishing, rubber
and plastics, motor vehicles

Agriculture
Corn, soybeans, hogs, cattle, dairy
products, nursery stock

Statehood
December 3, 1818; 21st state

GEO WHIZ

A giant fossilized rain forest has
been unearthed in an eastern
Illinois coal mine near the town
of Danville. Scientists believe an
earthquake buried the entire forest
300 million years ago.

The Great Chicago fire of 1871
destroyed the city's
waterworks, so fire-
men had to drag
water in buckets from
Lake Michigan and the
Chicago River. The fire
burned out of control for two
days until rain finally put it out.

CARDINAL
VIOLET

ILLINOIS

Two rivers that now form the borders of
Illinois aided the state's early white settlement.
Frenchmen first explored the area in 1673 by traveling down the Mississippi, and the Ohio brought
many 19th-century settlers to southern Illinois.
Most Indians were forced out by the 1830s, more
than a decade after Illinois became the 21st state.
Ethnically diverse Chicago, the most populous
city in the Midwest, is an economic giant and
one of the country's busiest rail, highway, and air
transit hubs. Barges from its port reach the Gulf
of Mexico via rivers and canals, while ships reach
the Atlantic Ocean via the Great Lakes and St.
Lawrence Seaway. Flat terrain and fertile prairie
soils in the northern and central regions help make the state a top producer
of corn and soybeans. The more rugged, forested south has deposits of
bituminous coal. Springfield, capital
of the Land of Lincoln,
welcomes tourists visiting
the home and tomb of the
country's 16th president.

⇧ REMEMBERING A PRESIDENT.
Dedicated in 1874, the National
Lincoln Monument in Springfield
honors Abraham Lincoln, who was
assassinated in 1865. A special
vault holds the remains of the
slain president, who led the
country during the Civil War.

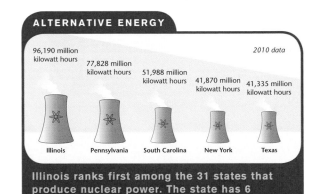

ALTERNATIVE ENERGY

2010 data

96,190 million kilowatt hours — Illinois
77,828 million kilowatt hours — Pennsylvania
51,988 million kilowatt hours — South Carolina
41,870 million kilowatt hours — New York
41,335 million kilowatt hours — Texas

Illinois ranks first among the 31 states that
produce nuclear power. The state has 6
nuclear power plants with 11 reactors.

⇧ PLAY BALL! Wrigley Field, home to the Chicago Cubs baseball
team, is affected by wind conditions more than any other major
league park due to its location near Lake Michigan.

⇧ FIELDS OF GRAIN. Illinois has long been a major grain
producer, but farming today is highly mechanized. Above,
a tractor moves bales of rolled hay.

Economy Symbols

- 🐔 Poultry/eggs
- 🐑 Sheep
- 🐷 Hogs
- 🐄 Dairy cows/products
- 🐂 Beef cattle
- 🥬 Vegetables
- 🏠 Nursery stock
- 🌾 Wheat
- 🌽 Corn
- 🌱 Soybeans
- 🖨 Printing/publishing
- ⚒ Stone/gravel/cement
- 🪨 Mining
- 🪵 Coal
- 🛢 Oil/gas
- ⚙ Machinery
- 🍳 Metal products
- 🚗 Motor vehicles/parts
- ⭕ Rubber/plastics
- ⚗ Chemistry
- 📷 Food processing
- 💻 Computers/electronics
- 🎥 Motion picture/music industry
- 📷 Tourism
- 💲 Finance/insurance

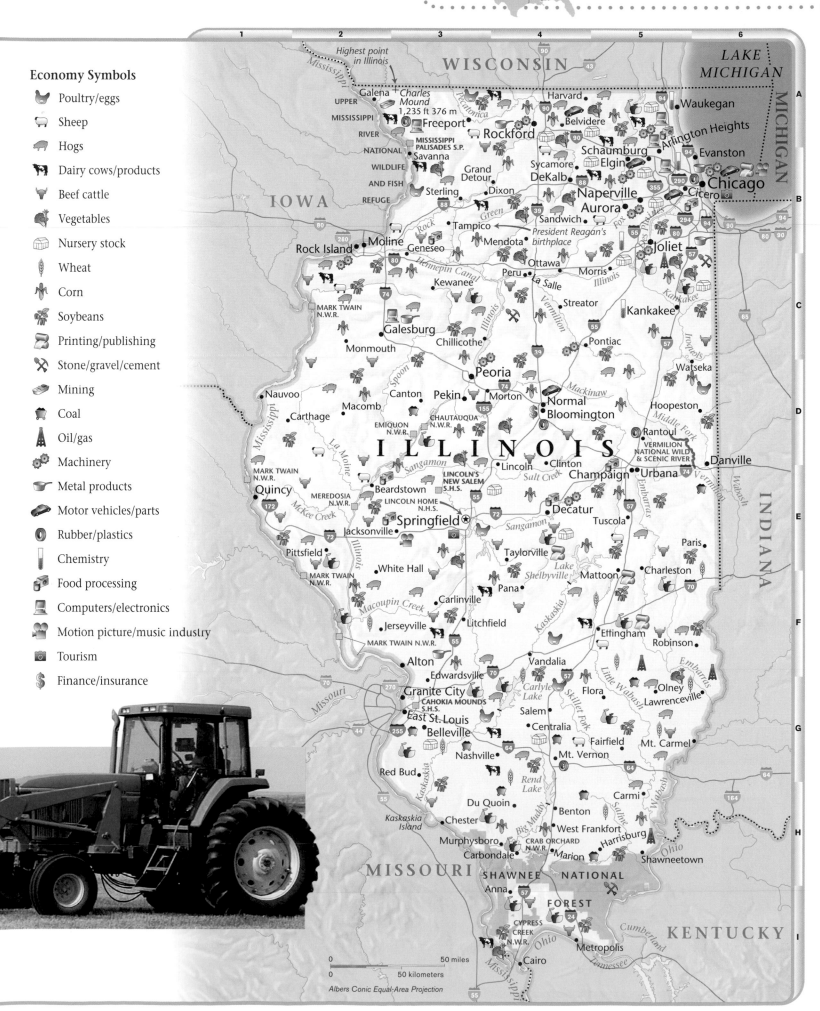

THE HOOSIER STATE: INDIANA

THE BASICS

STATS

Area
36,418 sq mi (94,322 sq km)

Population
6,483,802

Capital
Indianapolis
Population 820,445

Largest city
Indianapolis
Population 820,445

Ethnic/racial groups
84.3% white; 9.1% African American;
1.6% Asian; .3% Native American.
Hispanic (any race) 6.0%.

Industry
Transportation equipment, steel,
pharmaceutical and chemical products,
machinery, petroleum, coal

Agriculture
Corn, soybeans, hogs, poultry and eggs,
cattle, dairy products

Statehood
December 11, 1816; 19th state

GEO WHIZ

Every July during Circus Festival, in Peru, a couple hundred local kids and a couple thousand volunteers put on a three-ring circus complete with clowns, snow cones, and standing ovations from sellout crowds. The city is home to the International Circus Hall of Fame.

Every year Fort Wayne hosts the Johnny Appleseed Festival to honor John Chapman, the man who planted apple orchards from Pennsylvania to Illinois.

The Indianapolis Children's Museum, in partnership with National Geographic and the Environmental Research Systems Institute, has created an international traveling exhibit to teach children and parents that maps are tools of adventure.

CARDINAL

PEONY

INDIANA

Indiana's name, meaning "Land of the Indians," honors the tribes who lived in the region before the arrival of Europeans. The first permanent white settlement was Vincennes, established by the French in the early 1700s. Following statehood in 1816, most Indians were forced out to make way for white settlement. Lake Michigan, in the state's northwest corner, brings economic and recreational opportunities. The lakefront city of Gary anchors a major industrial region. Nearby, the natural beauty and shifting sands of the Indiana Dunes National Lakeshore attract many visitors. Corn, soybeans, and hogs are the most important products from Indiana's many farms. True to the state motto, "The Crossroads of America," highways from all directions converge at Indianapolis. Traveling at a much higher speed are cars on that city's famed Motor Speedway, home to the Indy 500 auto race since 1911. Cheering for a favorite high school or college team is a favorite pastime for many Hoosiers who catch basketball fever.

⇧ START YOUR ENGINES. The Indianapolis Motor Speedway seats 250,000 sports fans. Nicknamed the Brickyard, its track was once paved with 3.2 million bricks.

⇨ FUEL FARMING. Indiana farming is undergoing dramatic changes as corn is used in the production of ethanol, a non-fossil fuel energy source that is increasingly popular.

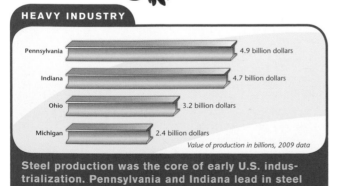

HEAVY INDUSTRY

Pennsylvania	4.9 billion dollars
Indiana	4.7 billion dollars
Ohio	3.2 billion dollars
Michigan	2.4 billion dollars

Value of production in billions, 2009 data

Steel production was the core of early U.S. industrialization. Pennsylvania and Indiana lead in steel production, but the U.S. also imports much of the steel it uses.

Economy Symbols

- Poultry/eggs
- Sheep
- Hogs
- Dairy cows/products
- Beef cattle
- Fruits
- Vegetables
- Nursery stock
- Wheat
- Corn
- Soybeans
- Tobacco
- Timber/forest products
- Stone/gravel/cement
- Coal
- Oil/gas
- Hydro-electricity
- Machinery
- Metal manufacturing
- Shipbuilding
- Motor vehicles/parts
- Chemistry
- Electrical equipment
- Aircraft/parts

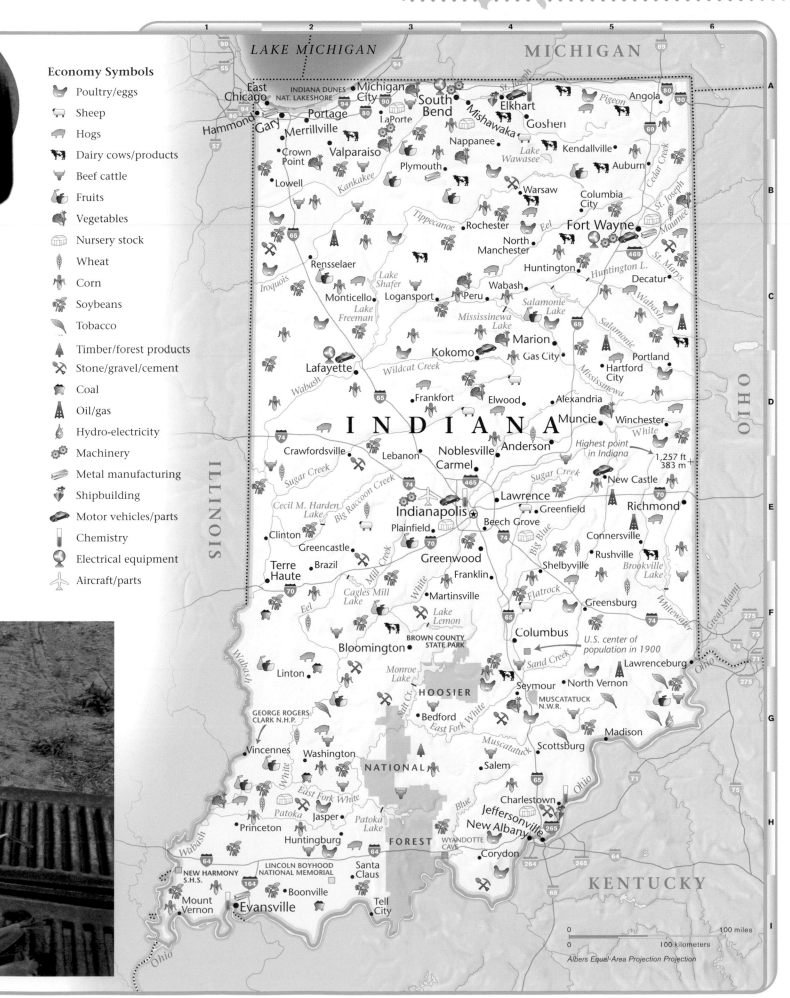

LAKE MICHIGAN

MICHIGAN

OHIO

ILLINOIS

KENTUCKY

INDIANA

East Chicago, Hammond, Gary, Portage, Merrillville, Crown Point, Lowell, Valparaiso, Michigan City, LaPorte, South Bend, Mishawaka, Elkhart, Goshen, Nappanee, Kendallville, Auburn, Angola, Plymouth, Warsaw, Columbia City, Rochester, Fort Wayne, North Manchester, Huntington, Decatur, Rensselaer, Wabash, Monticello, Logansport, Peru, Marion, Gas City, Portland, Hartford City, Kokomo, Lafayette, Frankfort, Elwood, Alexandria, Muncie, Winchester, Crawfordsville, Lebanon, Noblesville, Carmel, Anderson, New Castle, Indianapolis, Lawrence, Greenfield, Richmond, Plainfield, Beech Grove, Greenwood, Connersville, Rushville, Shelbyville, Clinton, Greencastle, Franklin, Terre Haute, Brazil, Martinsville, Greensburg, Columbus, Lawrenceburg, Bloomington, Linton, Seymour, North Vernon, Bedford, Scottsburg, Madison, Vincennes, Washington, Salem, Princeton, Jasper, Charlestown, Jeffersonville, New Albany, Huntingburg, Corydon, Santa Claus, Boonville, Mount Vernon, Evansville, Tell City

Highest point in Indiana → 1,257 ft 383 m

U.S. center of population in 1900

BROWN COUNTY STATE PARK

HOOSIER NATIONAL FOREST

GEORGE ROGERS CLARK N.H.P.

MUSCATATUCK N.W.R.

WYANDOTTE CAVE

LINCOLN BOYHOOD NATIONAL MEMORIAL

NEW HARMONY S.H.S.

INDIANA DUNES NAT. LAKESHORE

Lake Wawasee, Lake Shafer, Lake Freeman, Salamonie Lake, Mississinewa Lake, Cecil M. Harden Lake, Cagles Mill Lake, Lake Lemon, Monroe Lake, Patoka Lake, Brookville Lake

Kankakee, Tippecanoe, Eel, Iroquois, Wabash, Wildcat Creek, Sugar Creek, Big Raccoon Creek, Mill Creek, White, Eel, Salt Cr., East Fork White, Patoka, Blue, Ohio, Great Miami, Whitewater, Flatrock, Big Blue, Sand Creek, Muscatatuck, St. Joseph, Maumee, St. Marys, Cedar Creek, Pigeon, Huntington L.

0 100 miles
0 100 kilometers

Albers Equal-Area Projection Projection

THE HAWKEYE STATE:
IOWA

IOWA

THE BASICS

STATS

Area
56,272 sq mi (145,743 sq km)

Population
3,046,355

Capital
Des Moines
Population 203,433

Largest city
Des Moines
Population 203,433

Ethnic/racial groups
91.3% white; 2.9% African American; 1.7% Asian; .4% Native American. Hispanic (any race) 5.0%.

Industry
Real estate, health services, industrial machinery, food processing, construction

Agriculture
Hogs, corn, soybeans, oats, cattle, dairy products

Statehood
December 28, 1846; 29th state

GEO WHIZ

The most famous house in Iowa and one of the most famous houses in America is in Eldon. It was immortalized in Grant Wood's famous painting "American Gothic." The stern-faced, pitchfork-holding farmer and his wife shown in the art were not farmers at all. Wood's sister and his dentist posed for the painting.

Effigy Mounds National Monument, in the northeast corner of Iowa, is the only place in the country with such a large collection of mounds in the shapes of mammals, birds, and reptiles. Of the 191 mounds, 29 are shaped like animals. Eastern Woodland Indians built these mounds from about 500 B.C. to 1300 A.D.

Iowa ranks number 7 among leading U.S. wind energy producers, which are led by Texas and Kansas.

AMERICAN GOLDFINCH

WILD ROSE

IOWA

Iowa's prehistoric inhabitants built earthen mounds—some shaped like birds and bears—that are visible in the state's northeast. Nineteenth-century white settlers found rolling prairies covered by a sea of tall grasses that soon yielded to the plow. A decade after statehood in 1846, a group of religious German immigrants established the Amana Colonies, a communal society that still draws visitors. Blessed with ample precipitation and rich soils, Iowa is the heart of one of the world's most productive farming regions. The state is the country's top producer of corn, soybeans, hogs, and eggs. Food processing and manufacturing machinery are two of the biggest industries. Much of the grain crop feeds livestock destined to reach dinner plates in the U.S. and around the world. An increasing amount of corn is used to make ethanol, which is mixed with gasoline to fuel cars and trucks. Des Moines, the capital and largest city, is a center of insurance and publishing.

⬆ PIG BUSINESS. Hogs outnumber people more than six to one in Iowa. The state raises 30 percent of the nation's hogs, making it the leading producer.

GREEN ENERGY

2010 production capacity in millions of gallons (liters)

Iowa	Nebraska	Illinois	Minnesota	South Dakota
3,595 (13,609)	1,839 (6,961)	1,480 (5,602)	1,119 (4,234)	1,016 (3,846)

Iowa is the leading producer of ethanol fuel, a clean-burning, renewable, non-fossil fuel energy source made mainly from corn.

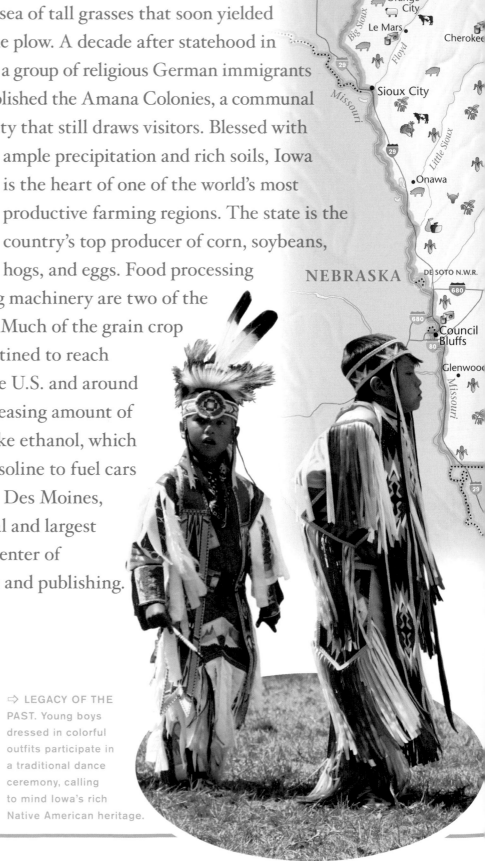

⮕ LEGACY OF THE PAST. Young boys dressed in colorful outfits participate in a traditional dance ceremony, calling to mind Iowa's rich Native American heritage.

Hawkeye Point 1,670 ft 509 m
Highest point in Iowa

SOUTH DAKOTA

Sioux Center
Sheldon
Orange City
Le Mars
Cherokee
Sioux City
Big Sioux
Floyd
Little Sioux
Missouri
Onawa

NEBRASKA

DE SOTO N.W.R.
Council Bluffs
Glenwood
Missouri

MINNESOTA

3   4   5   6   7   8   9   10

WISCONSIN

0   50 miles
0   50 kilometers
Albers Conic Equal-Area Projection

Spirit Lake
West Okoboji L.
East Okoboji Lake
Estherville
Spencer
UNION SLOUGH N.W.R.
Forest City
Emmetsburg
Algona
Clear Lake
Mason City
Osage
Cresco
Decorah
Waukon
EFFIGY MOUNDS N.M.
Charles City
New Hampton
Storm Lake
Humboldt
Hampton
Waverly
Oelwein
Manchester
Dyersville
Dubuque
Des Moines
Fort Dodge
Webster City
Iowa Falls
Cedar Falls
Waterloo
Independence
Monticello
Anamosa
Maquoketa
Story City
Carroll
Jefferson
Boone
Ames
Nevada
Marshalltown
Vinton
SAC AND FOX/ MESKWAKI INDIAN RESERVATION
Central City
Marion
Cedar Rapids
De Witt
Clinton
Perry
AMANA COLONIES
Ankeny
Urbandale
Windsor Heights
Newton
Grinnell
HERBERT HOOVER N.H.S.
Coralville
Iowa City
Bettendorf
Davenport
Harlan
West Des Moines
Des Moines
NEAL SMITH N.W.R.
Muscatine
Atlantic
Winterset
Indianola
Pella
Washington
MARK TWAIN N.W.R.
Red Oak
Creston
Osceola
Knoxville
Lake Red Rock
Oskaloosa
Chariton
Ottumwa
Fairfield
Mount Pleasant
Shenandoah
Clarinda
Blanchard
Bedford
Rathbun Lake
Centerville
Bloomfield
Burlington
Fort Madison
Keokuk

Boyer
Raccoon
Des Moines
Boone
Winnebago
Iowa
Cedar
Shell Rock
Wapsipinicon
Upper Iowa
Turkey
Maquoketa
Mississippi
UPPER MISSISSIPPI RIVER NATIONAL WILDLIFE AND FISH REFUGE
Cedar
Iowa
Thompson
E. Nodaway
Chariton
Des Moines
Mississippi

I O W A

MISSOURI

ILLINOIS

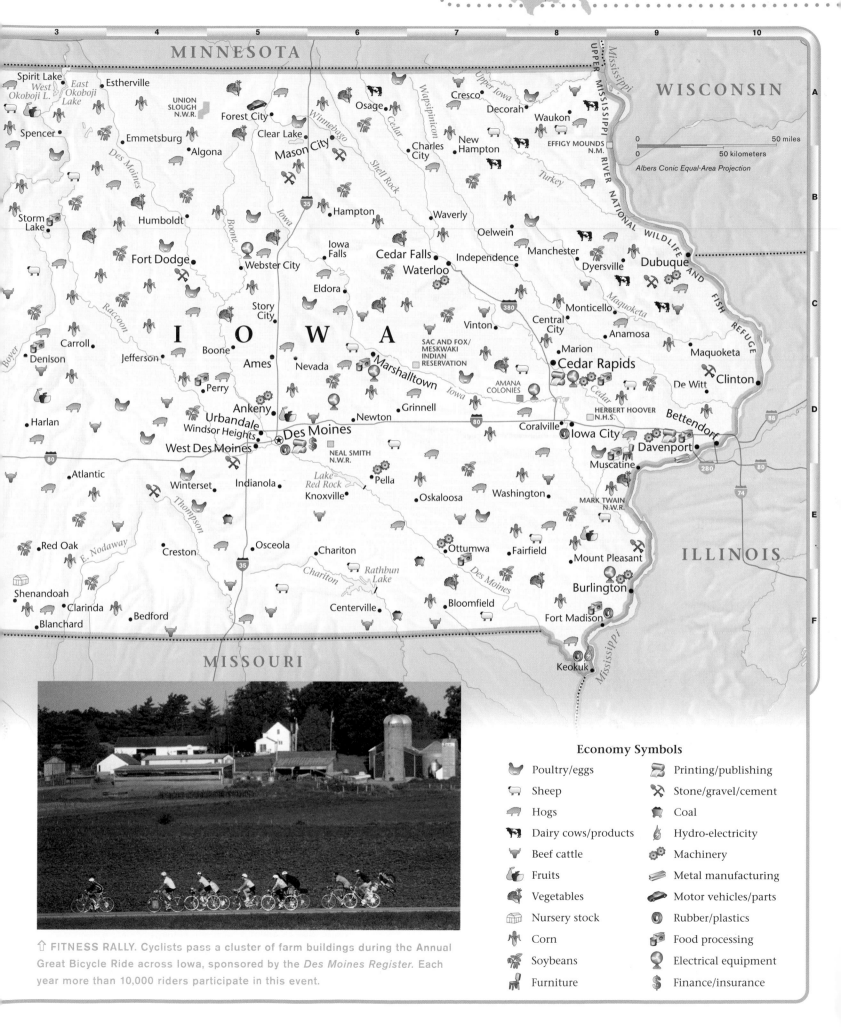

⇧ **FITNESS RALLY.** Cyclists pass a cluster of farm buildings during the Annual Great Bicycle Ride across Iowa, sponsored by the *Des Moines Register.* Each year more than 10,000 riders participate in this event.

Economy Symbols

Poultry/eggs	Printing/publishing
Sheep	Stone/gravel/cement
Hogs	Coal
Dairy cows/products	Hydro-electricity
Beef cattle	Machinery
Fruits	Metal manufacturing
Vegetables	Motor vehicles/parts
Nursery stock	Rubber/plastics
Corn	Food processing
Soybeans	Electrical equipment
Furniture	Finance/insurance

KANSAS

THE BASICS

STATS

Area
82,277 sq mi (213,097 sq km)

Population
2,853,118

Capital
Topeka
Population 127,473

Largest city
Wichita
Population 382,368

Ethnic/racial groups
83.8% white; 5.9% African American;
4.8% Asian; 1.0% Native American.
Hispanic (any race) 10.5%.

Industry
Aircraft manufacturing, transportation
equipment, construction, food processing, printing and publishing, health care

Agriculture
Cattle, wheat, sorghum, soybeans,
hogs, corn

Statehood
January 29, 1861; 34th state

GEO WHIZ

Plesiosaur skeletons and many other
marine reptile fossils have been
unearthed in Kansas. In 2007
National Geographic released the
IMAX film *Sea Monsters*, which
explores the kinds of animals that
lived in the prehistoric sea that
covered Kansas and much of North
America 82 million years ago.

The Tallgrass Prairie National
Preserve, the nation's last great
expanse of tallgrass prairie,
anchors a world renewed by fire.
It is in the Flint Hills of Kansas.

Lindsborg is proud of its Swedish
heritage and the fact that it
is home to the Anatoly
Karpov International School
of Chess. The school is
named for the Russian player
who succeeded American Bobby
Fischer as world champion in 1975.

WESTERN MEADOWLARK
SUNFLOWER

KANSAS

Considered by whites to be unsuitable for settlement, Kansas was made part of Indian Territory—a vast tract of land between Missouri and the Rockies—in the 1830s. By the 1850s whites were fighting Indians for more land and among themselves over the issue of slavery. In 1861 Kansas entered the Union as a free state. After the Civil War, cowboys drove Texas cattle to railheads in the Wild West towns of Abilene and Dodge City, where waiting trains hauled cattle to slaughterhouses in the East. Today, the state remains a major beef producer and the country's top wheat grower. Oil and natural gas wells dot the landscape, while factories in Wichita, the largest city, make aircraft equipment. A preserve in the Flint Hills boasts one of the few tallgrass prairies to escape farmers' plows. Heading west toward the Rockies, elevations climb slowly, and the climate gets drier. Threats of fierce thunderstorms accompanied by tornados have many Kansans keeping an eye on the sky.

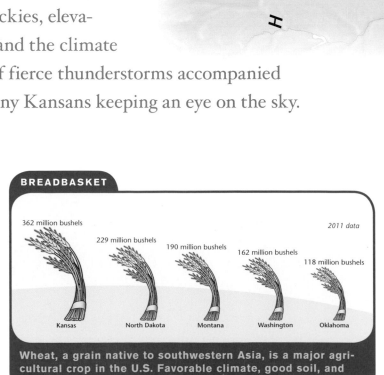

⇧ OMINOUS SKY. Lightning splits the sky as black clouds of a thunderstorm roll across a field of wheat. Such storms bring heavy rain and often spawn dangerous tornadoes.

BREADBASKET

362 million bushels
229 million bushels
190 million bushels
162 million bushels
118 million bushels

2011 data

Kansas
North Dakota
Montana
Washington
Oklahoma

Wheat, a grain native to southwestern Asia, is a major agricultural crop in the U.S. Favorable climate, good soil, and
technology advances have made Kansas the leading producer.

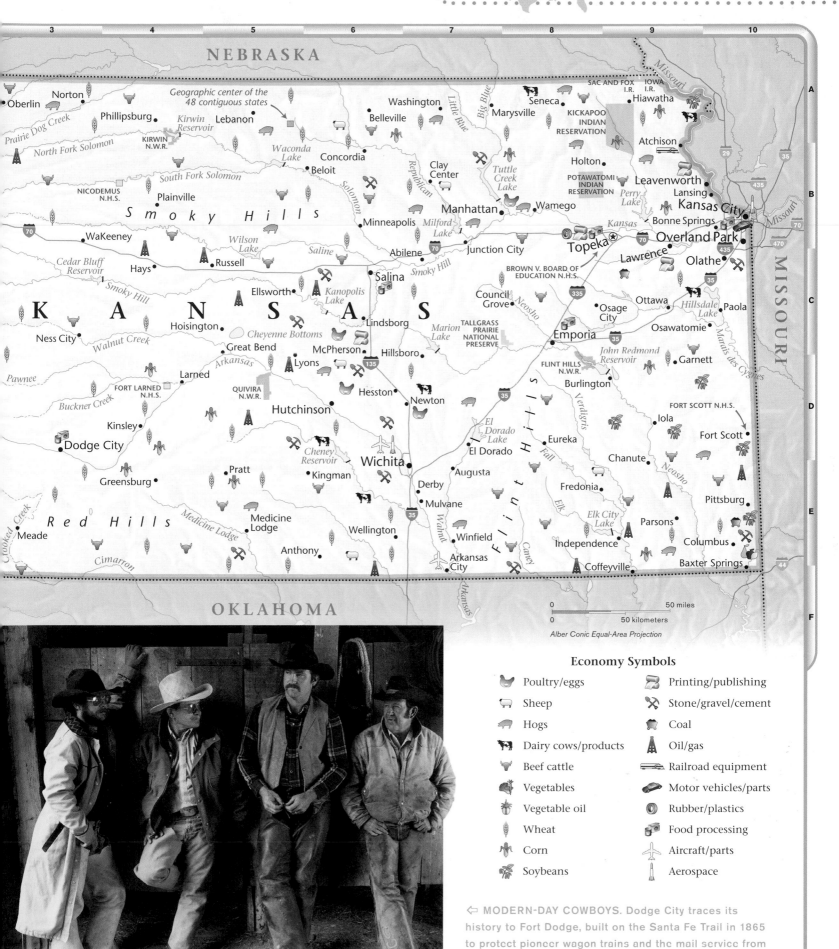

NEBRASKA

3   4   5   6   7   8   9   10

Oberlin
Norton
Phillipsburg
Prairie Dog Creek
Kirwin Reservoir
KIRWIN N.W.R.
Lebanon
Geographic center of the 48 contiguous states
Washington
Belleville
Little Blue
Marysville
Big Blue
Seneca
SAC AND FOX I.R.
IOWA I.R.
Hiawatha
KICKAPOO INDIAN RESERVATION
Atchison

North Fork Solomon
Waconda Lake
Concordia
Beloit
Republican
Clay Center
Tuttle Creek Lake
Holton
POTAWATOMI INDIAN RESERVATION
Perry Lake
Holton
Leavenworth
Lansing
Kansas City
29
35
435

NICODEMUS N.H.S.
Plainville
Smoky Hills
South Fork Solomon
Solomon
Minneapolis
Manhattan
Wamego
Bonne Springs
Missouri

70
WaKeeney
Wilson Lake
Saline
Abilene
Junction City
Topeka
Kansas
Overland Park
Lawrence
Olathe
70
470

Cedar Bluff Reservoir
Hays
Russell
Smoky Hill
Salina
Smoky Hill
BROWN V. BOARD OF EDUCATION N.H.S.
335
35
MISSOURI

KANSAS
Ness City
Walnut Creek
Ellsworth
Kanopolis Lake
Lindsborg
Neosho
Council Grove
TALLGRASS PRAIRIE NATIONAL PRESERVE
Osage City
Ottawa
Hillsdale Lake
Paola
Osawatomie
Marais des Cygnes

Pawnee
Hoisington
Great Bend
Cheyenne Bottoms
McPherson
Hillsboro
Marion Lake
Emporia
John Redmond Reservoir
Garnett
135

Buckner Creek
Larned
Arkansas
Lyons
FLINT HILLS N.W.R.
Burlington
FORT SCOTT N.H.S.
FORT LARNED N.H.S.
QUIVIRA N.W.R.
Hesston
Newton
35
Verdigris
Iola
Fort Scott

Kinsley
Hutchinson
El Dorado Lake
Eureka
Chanute
Neosho

Dodge City
Cheney Reservoir
Wichita
El Dorado
Fall
Fredonia

Greensburg
Pratt
Kingman
Augusta
Pittsburg

Red Hills
Medicine Lodge
Medicine Lodge
Derby
Mulvane
Walnut
Elk
Elk City Lake
Parsons
Columbus

Meade
Cimarron
Wellington
Anthony
Winfield
Flint Hills
Caney
Independence
35
44

Arkansas City
Coffeyville
Baxter Springs
Arkansas

0   50 miles
0   50 kilometers
Alber Conic Equal-Area Projection

OKLAHOMA

A
B
C
D
E
F

Economy Symbols

Poultry/eggs		Printing/publishing	
Sheep		Stone/gravel/cement	
Hogs		Coal	
Dairy cows/products		Oil/gas	
Beef cattle		Railroad equipment	
Vegetables		Motor vehicles/parts	
Vegetable oil		Rubber/plastics	
Wheat		Food processing	
Corn		Aircraft/parts	
Soybeans		Aerospace	

⇐ MODERN-DAY COWBOYS. Dodge City traces its history to Fort Dodge, built on the Santa Fe Trail in 1865 to protect pioneer wagon trains and the mail service from Indian attacks. Frequented by cattle herders and buffalo hunters, the town was known for its lawlessness.

THE BASICS

STATS

Area
96,716 sq mi (250,495 sq km)

Population
9,883,640

Capital
Lansing
Population 114,297

Largest city
Detroit
Population 713,777

Ethnic/racial groups
78.9% white; 14.2% African American;
2.4% Asian; .6% Native American.
Hispanic (any race) 4.4%.

Industry
Motor vehicles and parts, machinery,
metal products, office furniture,
tourism, chemicals

Agriculture
Dairy products, cattle, vegetables,
hogs, corn, nursery stock, soybeans,
hay, fruit

Statehood
January 26, 1837; 26th state

GEO WHIZ

Researchers at the Seney National
Wildlife Refuge near Seney, Michigan,
have discovered that male loons change
the sound of their call when they move
to a new territory. The reason is still a
mystery, but it does explain why people
say that loons sound different on different lakes.

The Keweenaw Peninsula is an adven-
turer's paradise. There's a 100-mile
(161-km) water trail for canoers, scores
of wrecks for divers, 14 miles (23 km)
of forested bike paths, and more than
150 miles (240 km) of hiking trails on
nearby Isle Royale National Park.

Climate change is causing Lake
Michigan and the other Great
Lakes to shrink, a fact that is
very costly to shipping. For every
inch (2.5 cm) of draft that a ship
loses, a freighter must lighten
its cargo by as much as 270 tons
to keep from running aground. The
collective annual cost can be in the
billions of dollars.

ROBIN
APPLE BLOSSOM

MICHIGAN

Indians had friendly relations with early French fur traders who came to what is now Michigan, but they waged battles with the British who later assumed control. Completion of New York's Erie Canal in 1825 made it easier for settlers to reach the area, and statehood came in 1837. Michigan consists of two large peninsulas that border four of the five Great Lakes— Erie, Huron, Michigan, and Superior.

⇧ ROLLING OFF THE ASSEMBLY LINE. Motor vehicle production is one of the largest manu-facturing sectors in the U.S., and Michigan is the center of the industry. At Chrysler's Sterling Heights assembly plant, almost 800 robots speed production by making it possible to build different car models on the same assembly line.

Most of the population is on the state's Lower Peninsula, while the Upper Peninsula, once a productive mining area, now is popular among vacation-ing nature lovers. The five-mile-long Mackinac Bridge (8 km) has linked the peninsulas since 1957. In the 20th century, Michigan became the center of the American auto industry, and the state's fortunes have risen and fallen with those of the Big Three car companies. Though it remains a big producer of cars and trucks, the state is working to diversify its economy. Michigan's farms grow crops ranging from grains to fruits and vegetables.

WINTER SPORT

Registered snowmobiles
2010, 2011 data

301,805	277,290	232,320	146,662	96,600
Michigan	Minnesota	Wisconsin	New York	Maine

Snowmobiling has become a popular winter sport. Michigan and other states of the upper Midwest lead in number of registered snowmobiles.

⇧ REFLECTION OF THE PAST. Victorian-style summer homes, built on Mackinac Island in the late 19th century by wealthy railroad families, now welcome vacationers to the island. To protect the environment, cars are not allowed.

⇦ SLY PREDATOR. Wolves on Isle Royale, in upper Lake Superior, live in packs that hunt moose in this isolated national park.

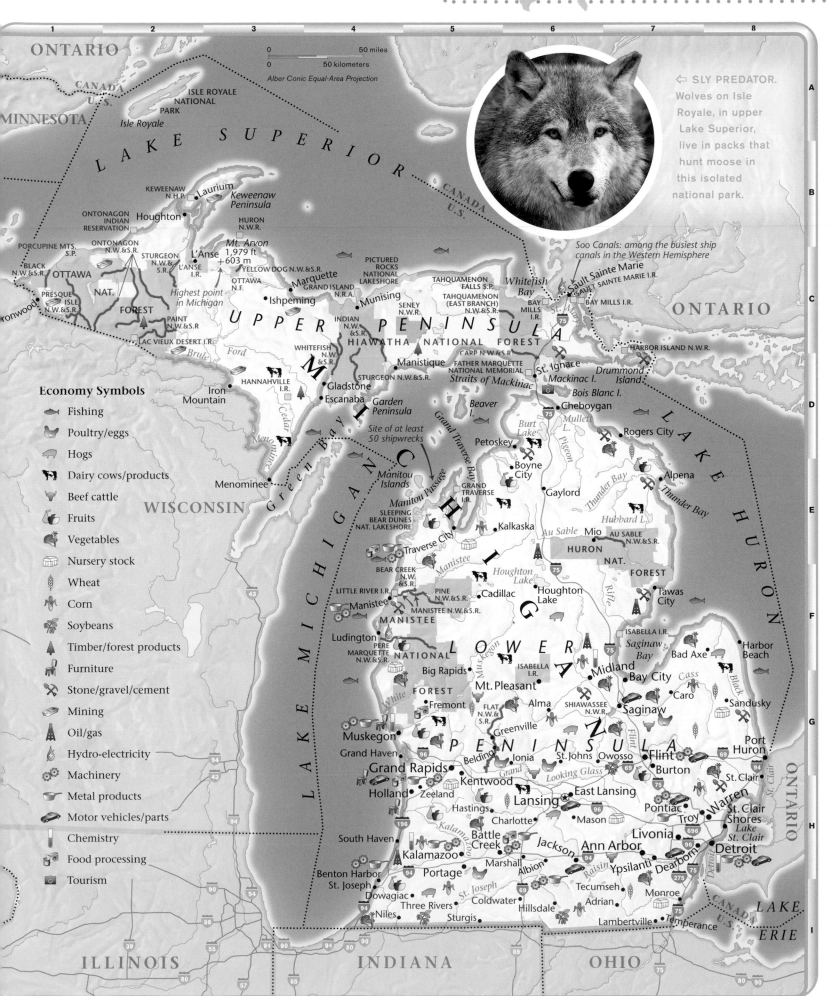

Soo Canals: among the busiest ship canals in the Western Hemisphere

Economy Symbols

- Fishing
- Poultry/eggs
- Hogs
- Dairy cows/products
- Beef cattle
- Fruits
- Vegetables
- Nursery stock
- Wheat
- Corn
- Soybeans
- Timber/forest products
- Furniture
- Stone/gravel/cement
- Mining
- Oil/gas
- Hydro-electricity
- Machinery
- Metal products
- Motor vehicles/parts
- Chemistry
- Food processing
- Tourism

0   50 miles
0   50 kilometers
Alber Conic Equal-Area Projection

ONTARIO
CANADA U.S.
MINNESOTA
ISLE ROYALE NATIONAL PARK
Isle Royale

LAKE SUPERIOR

KEWEENAW N.H.P.
Laurium
Keweenaw Peninsula
ONTONAGON INDIAN RESERVATION
Houghton
PORCUPINE MTS. S.P.
ONTONAGON N.W.&S.R.
BLACK N.W.&S.R.
Ironwood
PRESQUE ISLE N.W.&S.R.
OTTAWA
NAT. FOREST
STURGEON N.W.& S.R.
L'Anse
L'ANSE I.R.
HURON N.W.R.
Mt. Arvon 1,979 ft +603 m
Highest point in Michigan
YELLOW DOG N.W.&S.R.
Marquette
GRAND ISLAND N.R.A.
OTTAWA N.F.
PICTURED ROCKS NATIONAL LAKESHORE
PAINT N.W.&S.R.
LAC VIEUX DESERT I.R.
Brule
Ford
Ishpeming
Munising
SENEY N.W.R.
TAHQUAMENON FALLS S.P.
TAHQUAMENON (EAST BRANCH) N.W.&S.R.
Whitefish Bay
Sault Sainte Marie
SAULT SAINTE MARIE I.R.
BAY MILLS N.W.R.
BAY MILLS I.R.
St. Marys
ONTARIO

UPPER PENINSULA

WHITEFISH N.W.&S.R.
HIAWATHA NATIONAL FOREST
CARP N.W.&S.R.
Manistique
FATHER MARQUETTE NATIONAL MEMORIAL
St. Ignace
HARBOR ISLAND N.W.R.
HANNAHVILLE I.R.
Gladstone
STURGEON N.W.&S.R.
Straits of Mackinac
Mackinac I.
Drummond Island
Iron Mountain
Escanaba
Garden Peninsula
Beaver I.
Bois Blanc I.
Cheboygan
Menominee
Cedar
Green Bay
Site of at least 50 shipwrecks
Manitou Islands
Burt Lake
Mullett L.
Petoskey
Boyne City
Rogers City
Alpena
WISCONSIN
Menominee
Manitou Passage
GRAND TRAVERSE I.R.
Gaylord
Thunder Bay
Thunder Bay
SLEEPING BEAR DUNES NAT. LAKESHORE
Kalkaska
Au Sable
Mio
AU SABLE N.W.&S.R.
Hubbard L.
Traverse City
HURON NAT. FOREST
BEAR CREEK N.W. &S.R.
Manistee
Houghton Lake
Tawas City
LITTLE RIVER I.R.
PINE N.W.&S.R.
Cadillac
Houghton Lake
MANISTEE N.W.&S.R.
Rifle
Ludington
PERE MARQUETTE N.W.&S.R.
MANISTEE NATIONAL FOREST
Big Rapids
ISABELLA I.R.
Mt. Pleasant
Saginaw Bay
Bad Axe
Harbor Beach
White
Fremont
FLAT N.W.& S.R.
Alma
SHIAWASSEE N.W.R.
Midland
Bay City
Caro
Sandusky
LOWER PENINSULA
Muskegon
Greenville
Saginaw
Grand Haven
Belding
Ionia
St. Johns
Owosso
Flint
Port Huron
Grand Rapids
Kentwood
Grand
Looking Glass
Burton
St. Clair
Holland
Zeeland
Lansing
East Lansing
Pontiac
Warren
St. Clair Shores
Hastings
Mason
Troy
Livonia
South Haven
Charlotte
Battle Creek
Jackson
Ann Arbor
Detroit
Kalamazoo
Marshall
Albion
Ypsilanti
Dearborn
Benton Harbor
Portage
Kalamazoo
Raisin
Monroe
St. Joseph
Dowagiac
St. Joseph
Coldwater
Tecumseh
Adrian
Three Rivers
Hillsdale
Lambertville
Temperance
Niles
Sturgis
LAKE MICHIGAN
LAKE HURON
Lake St. Clair
LAKE ERIE
ILLINOIS
INDIANA
OHIO
ONTARIO
CANADA U.S.

THE BASICS

STATS

Area
86,939 sq mi (225,172 sq km)

Population
5,303,925

Capital
St. Paul
Population 285,068

Largest city
Minneapolis
Population 382,578

Ethnic/racial groups
85.3% white; 5.2% African American;
4.0% Asian; 1.1% Native American.
Hispanic (any race) 4.7%.

Industry
Health services, tourism, real estate,
banking and insurance, industrial
machinery, printing and publishing,
food processing, scientific equipment

Agriculture
Corn, soybeans, dairy products, hogs,
cattle, turkeys, wheat

Statehood
May 11, 1858; 32nd state

GEO WHIZ

Nett Lake on the Bois Forte Chippewa
reservation, in northern Minnesota,
is the largest contiguous wild
rice lake in the world. Native
people have been gathering
what the Indians call *manoomin*
for thousands of years.

The Mayo Clinic, a world-famous medical research center founded in 1889 by
Dr. William W. Mayo, is in Rochester.

The Boundary Waters Canoe Area
Wilderness, along the Minnesota-
Ontario border, was the
first wilderness
area in the U.S. to
be set aside for canoeing.

COMMON LOON

SHOWY LADY'S
SLIPPER

MINNESOTA

French fur traders began arriving in present-day Minnesota in the mid-17th century. Statehood was established in 1858, and most remaining Indians were forced from the state after a decisive battle in 1862. During the late 1800s large numbers of Germans, Scandinavians, and other immigrants settled a land rich in wildlife, timber, minerals, and fertile soils. Today, farming is concentrated in the south and west. In the northeast, the Mesabi Range's open-pit mines make the state the country's source of iron ore. Most of the ore is shipped from Duluth. It, along with Superior, in nearby Wisconsin (see p. 113), is the leading Great Lakes port. Ships from the port reach the Atlantic Ocean via the St. Lawrence Seaway. Scattered across the state's landscape are thousands of lakes—ancient footprints of retreating glaciers—that draw anglers and canoeists. One of those lakes, Lake Itasca, is the source of the mighty Mississippi River, which flows through the Twin Cities of Minneapolis and St. Paul.

⇧ SUMMER FUN. Young girls play on a rope swing near Leech Lake in northern Minnesota. The state's many lakes are remnants of the last ice age, when glaciers gouged depressions that filled with water as the ice sheets retreated.

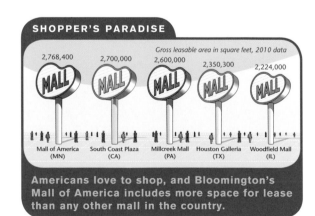

SHOPPER'S PARADISE

Gross leasable area in square feet, 2010 data

2,768,400	2,700,000	2,600,000	2,350,300	2,224,000
MALL	MALL	MALL	MALL	MALL
Mall of America (MN)	South Coast Plaza (CA)	Millcreek Mall (PA)	Houston Galleria (TX)	Woodfield Mall (IL)

Americans love to shop, and Bloomington's
Mall of America includes more space for lease
than any other mall in the country.

⇦ INLAND PORT. Duluth, on the northern shore of Lake Superior, is the westernmost deep-water port on the St. Lawrence Seaway. Barges and container ships move products such as iron ore and grain along the Great Lakes to the Atlantic Ocean and to markets around the world.

The "Northwest Angle" is the northernmost point in the 48 contiguous states

0 ___ 100 miles
0 ___ 100 kilometers
Albers Conic Equal-Area Projection

MANITOBA

RED LAKE
INDIAN RES.

Lake of the Woods

Rainy Lake

ONTARIO

CANADA
U.S.

• Hallock

Roseau •

Roseau

Baudette •

Rainy

International Falls •

Namakan Lake

VOYAGEURS NATIONAL PARK

AGASSIZ N.W.R.

Mud Lake

• Warren

Thief River Falls •

Red Lake

RED LAKE INDIAN RESERVATION

Upper Red Lake

Big Fork

BOIS FORTE I.R.

Vermilion Lake

BOUNDARY WATERS CANOE AREA WILDERNESS

Highest point in Minnesota
Eagle Mt. +
2,301 ft
701 m

Pigeon

GRAND PORTAGE I.R.

GRAND PORTAGE NAT. MON.

CANADA
U.S.

• East Grand Forks

• Crookston

Red Lake

Lower Red Lake

Red Lake •

BOIS FORTE (VERMILION LAKE) I.R.

Ely •

SUPERIOR

Grand Marais •

NORTH DAKOTA

Red River of the North

Source of the Mississippi River

Winnibigoshish Lake

CHIPPEWA

BOIS FORTE (DEER CREEK) I.R.

Mesabi Range

Virginia •

Chisholm •

NATIONAL

LAKE SUPERIOR

Bemidji •

Mississippi

WHITE EARTH INDIAN RESERVATION

NATIONAL

LEECH LAKE INDIAN RES.

Lake Itasca

FOREST

Leech Lake

Hibbing •

FOREST

• Grand Rapids

Two Harbors •

Wild Rice

Walker •

HAMDEN SLOUGH N.W.R.

TAMARAC N.W.R.

Park Rapids •

SANDY LAKE I.R.

FOND DU LAC I.R.

Duluth

Proctor •

MICHIGAN

• Moorhead

Detroit Lakes •

Menahga •

Mississippi

Cloquet •

Bois de Sioux

Pelican Rapids •

Perham •

Wadena •

Crow Wing

Aitkin •

RICE LAKE N.W.R.

Mille Lacs Lake

St. Croix

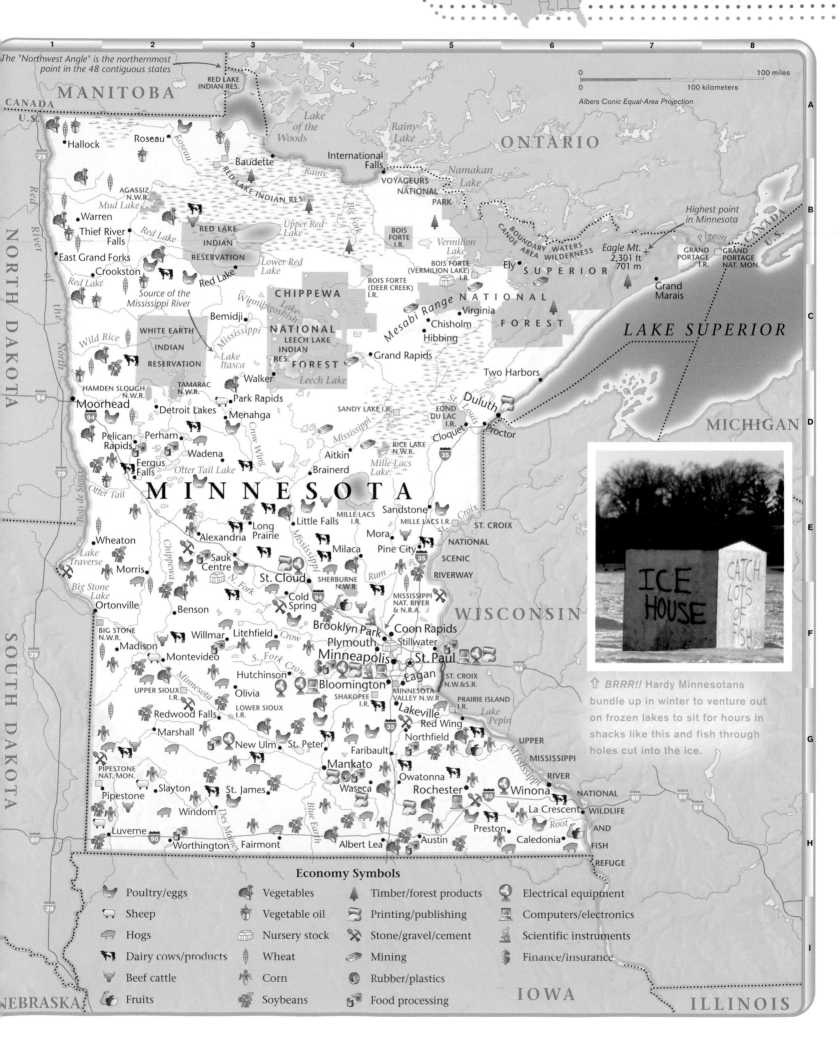

Fergus Falls •

Otter Tail Lake

Brainerd •

Otter Tail

M I N N E S O T A

• Wheaton

Lake Traverse

Alexandria •

Long Prairie •

Chippewa

Little Falls •

MILLE LACS I.R.

Sandstone •

Mille Lacs I.R.

ST. CROIX

• Morris

Big Stone Lake

Sauk Centre •

N. Fork

Mississippi

Milaca •

Mora •

Pine City •

NATIONAL

SCENIC

ICE HOUSE   CATCH LOTS OF FISH

• Ortonville

Benson •

St. Cloud •

SHERBURNE N.W.R.

Cold Spring •

Rum

RIVERWAY

BIG STONE N.W.R.

Willmar •

Litchfield •

Crow

Brooklyn Park •

Coon Rapids •

MISSISSIPPI NAT. RIVER & N.R.A.

WISCONSIN

• Madison

Montevideo •

S. Fork Crow

Plymouth •

Stillwater •

⬆ *BRRR!!* Hardy Minnesotans bundle up in winter to venture out on frozen lakes to sit for hours in shacks like this and fish through holes cut into the ice.

SOUTH DAKOTA

Hutchinson •

Minnesota

Minneapolis

St. Paul

Eagan •

ST. CROIX N.W.&S.R.

UPPER SIOUX I.R.

Olivia •

Bloomington •

SHAKOPEE I.R.

PRAIRIE ISLAND I.R.

LOWER SIOUX I.R.

Redwood Falls •

MINNESOTA VALLEY N.W.R.

Lakeville •

Lake Pepin

• Marshall

New Ulm •

St. Peter •

Red Wing •

UPPER

PIPESTONE NAT. MON.

Faribault •

Northfield •

MISSISSIPPI

• Pipestone

• Slayton

St. James •

Mankato •

Owatonna •

RIVER

Winona •

Windom •

Waseca •

Rochester •

La Crescent •

NATIONAL

• Luverne

Worthington •

Fairmont •

Blue Earth

Des Moines

Albert Lea •

Austin •

Preston •

Caledonia •

Root

WILDLIFE

AND

FISH

REFUGE

NEBRASKA

IOWA

ILLINOIS

Economy Symbols

Poultry/eggs	Vegetables	Timber/forest products	Electrical equipment	
Sheep	Vegetable oil	Printing/publishing	Computers/electronics	
Hogs	Nursery stock	Stone/gravel/cement	Scientific instruments	
Dairy cows/products	Wheat	Mining	Finance/insurance	
Beef cattle	Corn	Rubber/plastics		
Fruits	Soybeans	Food processing		

THE SHOW-ME STATE:
MISSOURI

THE BASICS

STATS

Area
69,704 sq mi (180,534 sq mi)

Population
5,988,927

Capital
Jefferson City
Population 43,079

Largest city
Kansas City
Population 459,787

Ethnic/racial groups
82.8% white; 11.6% African American; 1.6% Asian; .5% Native American. Hispanic (any race) 3.5%.

Industry
Transportation equipment, food processing, chemicals, electrical equipment, metal products

Agriculture
Cattle, soybeans, hogs, corn, poultry and eggs, dairy products

Statehood
August 10, 1821; 24th state

GEO WHIZ

Camp Wood, near St. Louis, was the starting point for Lewis and Clark's Corps of Discovery, commissioned by President Thomas Jefferson to seek a water route to the Pacific. Along the way their encounters included hundreds of new species of plants and animals, nearly 50 Indian tribes, and the Rocky Mountains.

In Ash Grove, near Springfield, Father Moses Berry has turned his family history into a museum for slavery education. His family was one of the few who didn't flee the area after three falsely accused black men were lynched in 1906. The museum is the only one of its kind in the Ozark region.

EASTERN BLUEBIRD
HAWTHORN

MISSOURI

The Osage people were among the largest tribes in present-day Missouri when the French began establishing permanent settlements in the 1700s. The U.S. obtained the territory in the 1803 Louisiana Purchase, and Lewis and Clark began exploring the vast wilderness by paddling up the Missouri River from the St. Louis area. Missouri entered the Union as a slave state in 1821. Though it remained in the Union during the Civil War, sympathies were split between the North and South. For much of the 1800s the state was the staging ground for pioneers traveling to western frontiers on the Santa Fe and Oregon Trails. Today, Missouri leads the country in lead mining. Farmers raise cattle, hogs, poultry, corn, and soybeans. Cotton and rice are grown in the southeastern Bootheel region. Cross-state river-port rivals St. Louis and Kansas City are centers of transportation, manufacturing, and finance. Lakes, caves, scenic views, and Branson's country music shows bring many tourists to the Ozarks.

⇧ TALL HATS. Since its founding in 1865 in St. Joseph, the Stetson Company has been associated with western hats worn by men and women around the world.

HISTORICAL MARKERS

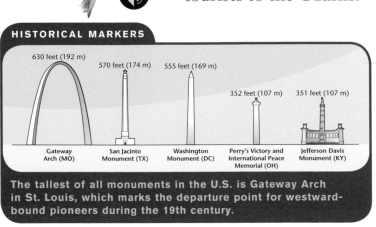

630 feet (192 m) — Gateway Arch (MO)
570 feet (174 m) — San Jacinto Monument (TX)
555 feet (169 m) — Washington Monument (DC)
352 feet (107 m) — Perry's Victory and International Peace Memorial (OH)
351 feet (107 m) — Jefferson Davis Monument (KY)

The tallest of all monuments in the U.S. is Gateway Arch in St. Louis, which marks the departure point for westward-bound pioneers during the 19th century.

⇨ HEADING WEST. The 630-foot (192-m) Gateway Arch honors the role St. Louis played in U.S. westward expansion. Trams carry one million tourists to the top of the arch each year.

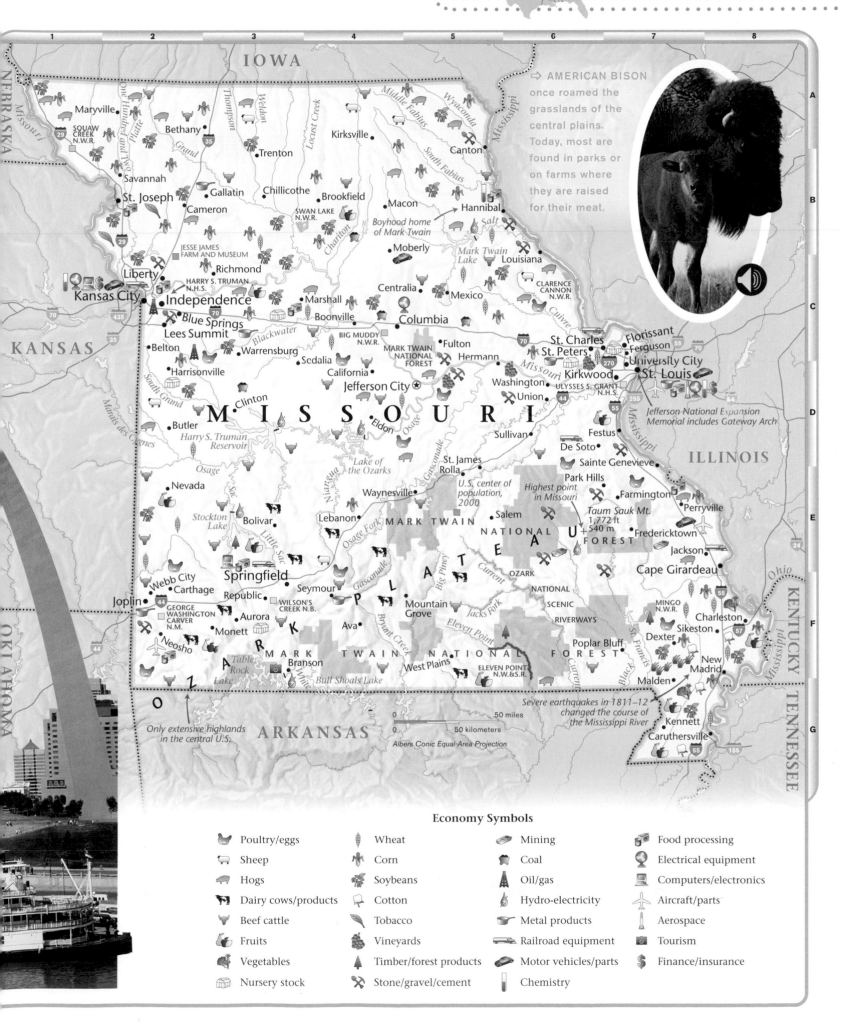

⇨ AMERICAN BISON once roamed the grasslands of the central plains. Today, most are found in parks or on farms where they are raised for their meat.

IOWA

NEBRASKA

KANSAS

MISSOURI

Boyhood home of Mark Twain

Maryville
Bethany
Savannah
St. Joseph
Cameron
Gallatin
Chillicothe
Brookfield
Macon
Kirksville
Trenton
Canton
Hannibal
SWAN LAKE N.W.R.
SQUAW CREEK N.W.R.
JESSE JAMES FARM AND MUSEUM
Richmond
Moberly
Louisiana
Liberty
HARRY S. TRUMAN N.H.S.
Independence
Marshall
Boonville
Centralia
Mexico
CLARENCE CANNON N.W.R.
Kansas City
Blue Springs
Lees Summit
Belton
Warrensburg
Sedalia
Columbia
BIG MUDDY N.W.R.
Fulton
Hermann
St. Charles
St. Peters
Florissant
Ferguson
University City
Kirkwood
St. Louis
Harrisonville
California
MARK TWAIN NATIONAL FOREST
Washington
Union
ULYSSES S. GRANT N.H.S.
Clinton
Jefferson City
Eldon
Sullivan
Festus
De Soto
Sainte Genevieve
Butler
Harry S. Truman Reservoir
Osage
Lake of the Ozarks
St. James
Rolla
U.S. center of population, 2000
Park Hills
Highest point in Missouri
Nevada
Waynesville
Taum Sauk Mt. 1,772 ft +540 m
Farmington
Perryville
Stockton Lake
Bolivar
Lebanon
MARK TWAIN
NATIONAL
FOREST
Salem
Fredericktown
Jackson
Webb City
Carthage
Springfield
Seymour
Mountain Grove
OZARK NATIONAL SCENIC RIVERWAYS
Cape Girardeau
Joplin
GEORGE WASHINGTON CARVER N.M.
Republic
WILSON'S CREEK N.B.
Ava
MINGO N.W.R.
Charleston
Aurora
Sikeston
Monett
Neosho
Table Rock Lake
Branson
West Plains
Poplar Bluff
Dexter
New Madrid
MARK TWAIN NATIONAL FOREST
ELEVEN POINT N.W.&S.R.
Malden
Bull Shoals Lake
Kennett
Caruthersville

Only extensive highlands in the central U.S.

Severe earthquakes in 1811–12 changed the course of the Mississippi River

Jefferson National Expansion Memorial includes Gateway Arch

ILLINOIS

KENTUCKY

TENNESSEE

ARKANSAS

OKLAHOMA

0   50 miles
0   50 kilometers
Albers Conic Equal-Area Projection

Economy Symbols

Poultry/eggs	Wheat	Mining	Food processing
Sheep	Corn	Coal	Electrical equipment
Hogs	Soybeans	Oil/gas	Computers/electronics
Dairy cows/products	Cotton	Hydro-electricity	Aircraft/parts
Beef cattle	Tobacco	Metal products	Aerospace
Fruits	Vineyards	Railroad equipment	Tourism
Vegetables	Timber/forest products	Motor vehicles/parts	Finance/insurance
Nursery stock	Stone/gravel/cement	Chemistry	

THE CORNHUSKER STATE: NEBRASKA

THE BASICS

STATS

Area
77,354 sq mi (200,346 sq km)

Population
1,826,341

Capital
Lincoln
Population 258,379

Largest city
Omaha
Population 408,958

Ethnic/racial groups
86.1% white; 4.5% African American; 1.8% Asian; 1.0% Native American. Hispanic (any race) 9.2%.

Industry
Food processing, machinery, electrical equipment, printing and publishing

Agriculture
Cattle, corn, hogs, soybeans, wheat, sorghum

Statehood
March 1, 1867; 37th state

GEO WHIZ

Many of Nebraska's early settlers were called sodbusters because they cut chunks of the grassy prairie (sod) to build their houses. These building blocks became known as "Nebraska marble."

Nebraska's state fossil is the mammoth. Fossils of these prehistoric elephants have been found in all 93 counties. The state estimates that as many as ten mammoths are buried beneath an average square mile of territory.

Boys Town, founded in 1917 as a home for troubled boys, has provided a haven for girls since 1979. They now make up about half the population of 500 kids in this village-style community near Omaha.

WESTERN MEADOWLARK
GOLDENROD

NEBRASKA

For thousands of westbound pioneers on the Oregon and California Trails, Scotts Bluff and Chimney Rock were unforgettable landmarks, towering above the North Platte River. Once reserved for Indians by the government, Nebraska was opened for white settlement in 1854. Following statehood in 1867, ranchers clashed with farmers in an unsuccessful bid to preserve open rangelands. Before white settlers arrived, Indians hunted bison and grew corn, pumpkins, beans, and squash. Today, farms and ranches cover nearly all of the state. Ranchers graze beef cattle on the grass-covered Sand Hills, while farmers grow corn, soybeans, and wheat elsewhere. The vast underground Ogallala Aquifer feeds center-pivot irrigation systems needed to water crops in areas that do not receive enough rain. Processing the state's farm products, especially meatpacking, is a big part of the economy. Omaha, which sits along the Missouri River, is a center of finance, insurance, and agribusiness. Lincoln, the state capital, has the only unicameral, or one-house, legislature in the United States.

⬆ TAKING FLIGHT. Migratory Sandhill cranes pass through Nebraska in late winter, stopping in the Platte River Valley to feed and rest.

Map labels:
WYOMING
OGLALA NATIONAL GRASSLAND
White
Chadron
Crawford
Pine Ridge
Rushville
NEBRASKA NATIONAL FOREST
AGATE FOSSIL BEDS NAT. MON.
Fossils of extinct mammals that lived here about 20 million years ago
NORTH PLATTE N.W.R.
Alliance
Scottsbluff
Gering
SCOTTS BLUFF N.M.
CHIMNEY ROCK N.H.S.
Bridgeport
Pumpkin Creek
North Platte
Highest point in Nebraska
Kimball
Lodgepole Cr.
Sidney
Panorama Point +5,423 ft, 1,653 m
COLORADO

⬇ RIDER DOWN. The Big Rodeo is an annual event in tiny Burwell (population 1,130) in Nebraska's Sand Hills. The town, sometimes called "the place where the Wild West meets the 21st century," has hosted the rodeo for more than 80 years.

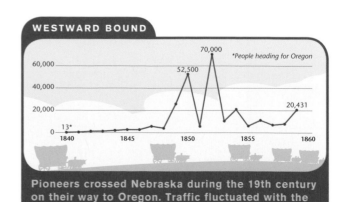

WESTWARD BOUND

People heading for Oregon
70,000
60,000
52,500
40,000
20,431
20,000
13*
1840   1845   1850   1855   1860

Pioneers crossed Nebraska during the 19th century on their way to Oregon. Traffic fluctuated with the occurrence of cholera epidemics and Indian wars.

SOUTH DAKOTA

IOWA

3   4   5   6   7   8   9   10

0   50 miles
0   50 kilometers
Albers Conic Equal-Area Projection

Gordon

Valentine

FORT NIOBRARA N.W.R.

NIOBRARA NATIONAL SCENIC RIVERWAY

Keya Paha

Niobrara

MISSOURI NATIONAL RECREATIONAL RIVER

SANTEE INDIAN RES.

Hartington

SAMUEL R. McKELVIE NATIONAL FOREST

Ainsworth

Atkinson

O'Neill

South Sioux City

Logan Creek

Verdigre Cr.

Gordon Cr.

VALENTINE N.W.R.

Holt Creek

Elkhorn

Neligh

Wayne

WINNEBAGO I.R.

Pender

OMAHA I.R.

29

20,000 square miles of grass-covered dunes, the largest such area in North America

S a n d   H i l l s

Mullen

North Loup

Calamus

Norfolk

Madison

West Point

Tekamah

RESCENT LAKE N.W.R.

Dismal

Middle Loup

NEBRASKA NAT. FOREST

Calamus Reservoir

Burwell

Cedar

Albion

Shell Cr.

Schuyler

Columbus

Blair

DE SOTO N.W.R.

BOYER CHUTE N.W.R.

680

80

Fremont

N E B R A S K A

Ord

Fullerton

Loup

David City

Wahoo

Omaha

80

President Ford's birthplace

Lake C.W. McConaughy

Wild West Show began in 1883

Broken Bow

South Loup

St. Paul

Central City

Papillion

Bellevue

Plattsmouth

South Platte

Ogallala

76

BUFFALO BILL S.H.P.

North Platte

Platte

80

Gothenburg

Ravenna

Grand Island

Aurora

York

Seward

Ashland

Waverly

Platte

Nine-Mile Prairie

Lincoln

Nebraska City

H I G H

Grant

Red Willow Creek

Cozad

Lexington

Gibbon

Kearney

Big Blue

Milford

Crete

Imperial

Largest mammoth fossil ever found, 1922

Minden

Hastings

Geneva

Wilber

Auburn

Hugh Butler Lake

Holdrege

Little Blue

Big Nemaha

Cambridge

Republican

Swanson Res.

McCook

Frenchman Cr.

Harlan County Lake

HOMESTEAD NAT. MON. OF AMERICA

Beatrice

Falls City

SAC AND FOX I.R.

Alma

Red Cloud

Superior

Hebron

Fairbury

IOWA I.R.

MISSOURI

KANSAS

Economy Symbols

Poultry/eggs	Printing/publishing
Sheep	Stone/gravel/cement
Hogs	Oil/gas
Dairy cows/products	Hydro-electricity
Beef cattle	Machinery
Vegetables	Railroad equipment
Vegetable oil	Food processing
Nursery stock	Computers/electronics
Wheat	Scientific instruments
Corn	Finance/insurance
Soybeans	

THE WAY WEST. Longhorn cattle and a bison stand knee-deep in grass below Chimney Rock, which rises more than 300 feet (91 m) above western Nebraska's rolling landscape. An important landmark on the Oregon Trail for 19th-century westbound pioneers and now a national historic site, the formation is being worn away by forces of erosion.

NORTH DAKOTA

THE BASICS

STATS

Area
70,700 sq mi (183,113 sq km)

Population
672,591

Capital
Bismarck
Population 61,272

Largest city
Fargo
Population 105,549

Ethnic/racial groups
90.0% white; 5.4% Native American; 1.2% African American; 1.0% Asian. Hispanic (any race) 2.0%.

Industry
Services, government, finance, construction, transportation, oil and gas

Agriculture
Wheat, cattle, sunflowers, barley, soybeans

Statehood
November 2, 1889; 39th state

GEO WHIZ

Teenage Indian guide Sacagawea (also known as Sakakawea) joined the Lewis and Clark expedition in the spring of 1805 after the explorers spent the winter in the Mandan-Hidatsa villages near present-day Washburn. Today, the state's largest reservoir is named in her honor.

Devils Lake has earned the title Perch Capital of the World for the large number of walleye—a kind of perch—that anglers catch there.

North Dakota's landscape boasts some of the world's largest outdoor animal sculptures, including Salem Sue, the world's largest Holstein cow; a 60-ton buffalo; a 40-by-60-foot (12-by-18-m) grasshopper; a giant snowmobiling turtle; and Wally the Giant Walleye.

WESTERN MEADOWLARK

WILD PRAIRIE ROSE

⬆ VIGILANT LOOKOUT. A black-tailed prairie dog watches for signs of danger. This member of the squirrel family lives in burrows in the Great Plains.

During the winter of 1804–05, Lewis and Clark camped at a Mandan village where they met Sacagawea, the Shoshone woman who helped guide them through the Rockies and onto the Pacific Ocean. White settlement of the vast grassy plains coincided with the growth of railroads, and statehood was gained in 1889. The geographic center of North America is southwest of Rugby. The state's interior location helps give it a huge annual temperature range. A record low temperature of -60°F (-51°C) and record high of 121°F (49°C) were recorded in 1936. Fargo, located on the northward flowing Red River of the North, is the state's largest city. Garrison Dam, on the Missouri River, generates electricity and provides water for irrigation. The state leads the country in the production of flaxseed, canola, sunflowers, and barley, but it is wheat, cattle, and soybeans that provide the greatest income. Oil and lignite coal are important in the western part of the state.

OIL FROM SEEDS

1.0 billion lbs
(454 million kg)
2010 data

616 million lbs
(279 million kg)

145 million lbs
(66 million kg)

124 million lbs
(56 million kg)

77 million lbs
(35 million kg)

North Dakota | South Dakota | Kansas | Colorado | Minnesota

Sunflowers are an important source of seeds and edible oil obtained by crushing the seeds of the flower.

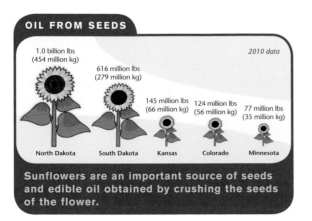

⇒ RUNNING FREE. A wild horse runs through a landscape dramatically eroded by the Little Missouri River in Theodore Roosevelt National Park in North Dakota's Badlands region.

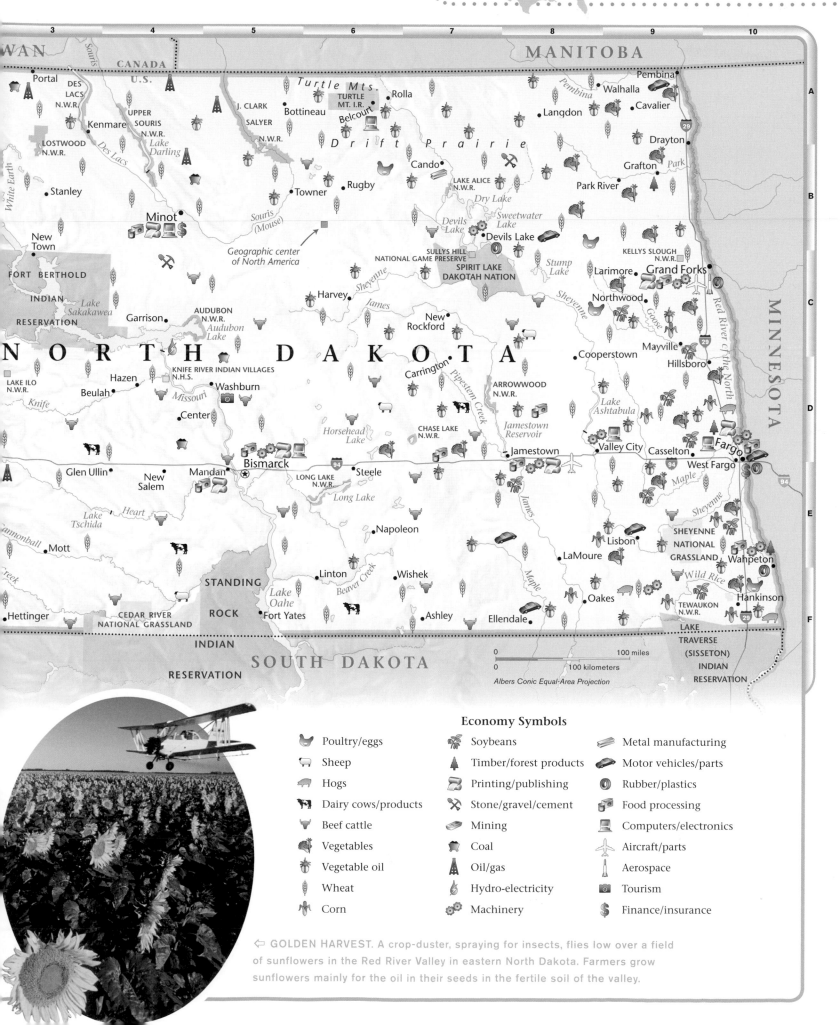

MANITOBA

CANADA
U.S.

Portal
DES LACS N.W.R.
UPPER SOURIS N.W.R.
Kenmare
LOSTWOOD N.W.R.
Lake Darling
J. CLARK SALYER N.W.R.
Bottineau
Turtle Mts.
TURTLE MT. I.R.
Belcourt
Rolla
Pembina
Walhalla
Cavalier
Langdon
Drayton
I-29

Drift Prairie

White Earth
Stanley
New Town
FORT BERTHOLD
INDIAN RESERVATION
Lake Sakakawea
Garrison
Minot
Souris (Mouse)
Towner
Rugby
Cando
LAKE ALICE N.W.R.
Dry Lake
Devils Lake
Sweetwater Lake
Devils Lake
SULLYS HILL NATIONAL GAME PRESERVE
SPIRIT LAKE DAKOTAH NATION
Stump Lake
KELLYS SLOUGH N.W.R.
Park River
Larimore
Grand Forks
Northwood
Grafton
Park River

Geographic center of North America
Sheyenne
Harvey
James
New Rockford
Cooperstown
Mayville
Hillsboro

NORTH DAKOTA

LAKE ILO N.W.R.
Hazen
Beulah
AUDUBON N.W.R.
Audubon Lake
KNIFE RIVER INDIAN VILLAGES N.H.S.
Washburn
Center
Missouri
Knife
Carrington
Pipestem Creek
ARROWWOOD N.W.R.
Lake Ashtabula
Valley City
Casselton
Fargo

Horsehead Lake
CHASE LAKE N.W.R.
Jamestown Reservoir
Jamestown
I-94
West Fargo
I-94

Glen Ullin
New Salem
Mandan
Bismarck
Steele
LONG LAKE N.W.R.
Long Lake
I-94
Maple

Lake Tschida
Heart
Napoleon
Lisbon
SHEYENNE NATIONAL GRASSLAND
Wahpeton

Mott
Cannonball
Linton
Beaver Creek
Wishek
LaMoure
James
Maple
Sheyenne
Wild Rice
Hankinson

Hettinger
CEDAR RIVER NATIONAL GRASSLAND
STANDING ROCK INDIAN RESERVATION
Lake Oahe
Fort Yates
Ashley
Ellendale
Oakes
TEWAUKON N.W.R.
Wild Rice

SOUTH DAKOTA

LAKE TRAVERSE (SISSETON) INDIAN RESERVATION

MINNESOTA

0 ———— 100 miles
0 ———— 100 kilometers
Albers Conic Equal-Area Projection

Economy Symbols

- Poultry/eggs
- Sheep
- Hogs
- Dairy cows/products
- Beef cattle
- Vegetables
- Vegetable oil
- Wheat
- Corn
- Soybeans
- Timber/forest products
- Printing/publishing
- Stone/gravel/cement
- Mining
- Coal
- Oil/gas
- Hydro-electricity
- Machinery
- Metal manufacturing
- Motor vehicles/parts
- Rubber/plastics
- Food processing
- Computers/electronics
- Aircraft/parts
- Aerospace
- Tourism
- Finance/insurance

⇐ GOLDEN HARVEST. A crop-duster, spraying for insects, flies low over a field of sunflowers in the Red River Valley in eastern North Dakota. Farmers grow sunflowers mainly for the oil in their seeds in the fertile soil of the valley.

THE BASICS

STATS

Area
44,825 sq mi (116,097 sq km)

Population
11,536,504

Capital
Columbus
Population 787,033

Largest city
Columbus
Population 787,033

Ethnic/racial groups
82.7% white; 12.2% African American; 1.7% Asian; .2% Native American. Hispanic (any race) 3.1%.

Industry
Transportation equipment, metal products, machinery, food processing, electrical equipment

Agriculture
Soybeans, dairy products, corn, hogs, cattle, poultry and eggs

Statehood
March 1, 1803; 17th state

GEO WHIZ

Cedar Point Amusement Park, in Sandusky, is known as the Roller Coaster Capital of the World. Top Thrill Dragster, the tallest and fastest roller coaster on Earth when it was built in 2003, is 420 feet (128 m) high with a top speed of 120 miles per hour (193 kmph)!

Ohio's state tree is the buckeye, so-called because the nut it produces resembles the eye of a buck. A buck is a male deer.

Ohio's state insect is the ladybird beetle, more commonly known as the ladybug. Use of these beetles to control plant-eating pests greatly reduces the need for chemical pesticides.

CARDINAL
SCARLET CARNATION

OHIO

Ohio and the rest of the Northwest Territory became part of the United States after the Revolutionary War. The movement of white settlers into the region led to conflicts with the native inhabitants until 1794 when Indian resistance was defeated at Fallen Timbers. Ohio entered the Union nine years later. Lake Erie in the north and the Ohio River in the south, along with canals and railroads, provided transportation links that spurred early immigration and commerce. The state became an industrial giant, producing steel, machinery, rubber, and glass. From 1869 to 1923, 7 of 12 U.S. presidents were Ohioans. With 18 electoral votes, seventh highest in the country, Ohio is still a big player in presidential elections. Education, government, and finance employ many people in Columbus, the capital and largest city. Manufacturing in Cleveland, Toledo, Cincinnati, and other cities remains a vital segment of the state's economy. Farmers on Ohio's western, glaciated plains grow soybeans and corn, the two largest cash crops.

⇑ INLAND URBAN CENTER. Cincinnati's skyline sparkles in the red glow of twilight. Founded in 1788, the modern city boasts education and medical centers as well as headquarters for companies such as Procter & Gamble.

⇓ TRADITIONAL TRAVEL. Horse and buggy are a familiar sight in central Ohio, location of the world's largest Amish population.

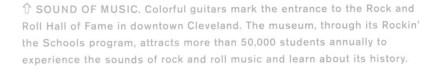

⇑ SOUND OF MUSIC. Colorful guitars mark the entrance to the Rock and Roll Hall of Fame in downtown Cleveland. The museum, through its Rockin' the Schools program, attracts more than 50,000 students annually to experience the sounds of rock and roll music and learn about its history.

LAKE ERIE

ONTARIO
CANADA
U.S.

MICHIGAN

PENNSYLVANIA

INDIANA

OHIO

KENTUCKY

WEST VIRGINIA

WAYNE NATIONAL FOREST

Cities and places:
Conneaut, Ashtabula, Geneva, Painesville, Mentor, Euclid, Cleveland, Shaker Heights, JAMES A. GARFIELD N.H.S., DAVID BERGER NAT. MEM., Pymatuning Reservoir, Mosquito Creek Lake, President McKinley's birthplace, Lorain, North Olmsted, Elyria, Parma, Strongsville, Brunswick, Medina, CUYAHOGA VALLEY N.P., Cuyahoga Falls, Akron, Kent, Austintown, Warren, Niles, Youngstown, Salem, Berlin Lake, Lake Milton, Barberton, Alliance, Orrville, North Canton, Canton, Massillon, Wooster, FIRST LADIES N.H.S., LITTLE BEAVER CREEK NAT. SCENIC RIVER, East Liverpool, Toronto, Steubenville, Uhrichsville, Dover, New Philadelphia, Atwood Lake, Leesville Lake, Piedmont L., Coshocton, Salt Fork Lake, Martins Ferry, Bellaire, Senecaville Lake, Cambridge, Zanesville, Newark, Marietta, Belpre, Nelsonville, Athens, Gallipolis, Ironton, South Point, Wheelersburg

Sylvania, Toledo, Maumee, Oregon, Perrysburg, OTTAWA N.W.R., Port Clinton, S. Bass I., Kelleys I., PERRY'S VICTORY AND INT'L. PEACE MEMORIAL, Wauseon, Bryan, Napoleon, Defiance, Bowling Green, Fremont, Sandusky, Bellevue, Norwalk, Willard, Fostoria, Tiffin, Findlay, Van Wert, Delphos, Upper Sandusky, Bucyrus, Shelby, Ashland, Loudonville, Mansfield, Galion, Blooming Grove, President Harding's birthplace, Lima, Kenton, Marion, Wapakoneta, Celina, St. Marys, Grand Lake (St. Marys), Indian Lake, Delaware Lake, Mt. Vernon, President Hayes' birthplace, Bellefontaine, Campbell Hill +1,550 ft 472 m, Highest point in Ohio, Sidney, Delaware, Piqua, Urbana, Troy, Marysville, Dublin, Westerville, Gahanna, Greenville, Columbus, Upper Arlington, Reynoldsburg, Newark, Springfield, Huber Heights, Englewood, Trotwood, Fairborn, Dayton, DAYTON AVIATION HERITAGE N.H.P., Kettering, Centerville, Xenia, Circleville, Lancaster, New Lexington, Logan, Middletown, Oxford, Hamilton, Lebanon, Mason, Fairfield, President Benjamin Harrison's birthplace, North Bend, Cincinnati, Norwood, WILLIAM HOWARD TAFT N.H.S., Washington Court House, Wilmington, Greenfield, HOPEWELL CULTURE N.H.P., Chillicothe, Hillsboro, Waverly, Wellston, Jackson, SERPENT MOUND STATE MEMORIAL, President Grant's birthplace, Point Pleasant, Georgetown, Manchester, Portsmouth, Gallipolis

BIG DARBY CREEK NATIONAL SCENIC RIVER, LITTLE MIAMI NATIONAL SCENIC RIVER, Buckeye Lake, Caesar Creek Lake, Deer Creek Lake, East Fork Lake

Rivers/features: St. Joseph, Maumee, Maumee Bay, Sandusky Bay, Portage, Blanchard, Auglaize, Sandusky, St. Marys, Stillwater, Great Miami, Little Miami, Scioto, Olentangy, Big Darby Cr., Little Darby Cr., Deer Cr., Paint Creek, E. Fk. Little Miami, Licking, Wills Creek, Tuscarawas, Muskingum, Mohican, Hocking, Raccoon Cr., Ohio, Mahoning, Grand

BIG BUSINESS

Sales of rubber and plastic products, 2007 data

$17.4 billion	$15.8 billion	$13.8 billion	$13.1 billion	$10.7 billion	$10.7 billion
Ohio	California	Illinois	Texas	Michigan	Pennsylvania

With more than 1,200 rubber and plastic manufacturers, Ohio leads the country in income generated by these important industries.

Economy Symbols

- Poultry/eggs
- Sheep
- Hogs
- Dairy cows/products
- Beef cattle
- Fruits
- Vegetables
- Vegetable oil
- Nursery stock
- Wheat
- Corn
- Soybeans
- Tobacco
- Stone/gravel/cement
- Mining
- Coal
- Oil/gas
- Hydro-electricity
- Machinery
- Metal manufacturing
- Metal products
- Motor vehicles/parts
- Rubber/plastics
- Food processing
- Glass/clay products
- Electrical equipment
- Aerospace
- Tourism
- Finance/insurance

Albers Conic Equal-Area Projection

0 50 miles
0 50 kilometers

THE BASICS

STATS

Area
77,117 sq mi (199,732 sq km)

Population
814,180

Capital
Pierre
Population 13,646

Largest city
Sioux Falls
Population 153,888

Ethnic/racial groups
85.9% white; 8.8% Native American; 1.3% African American; .9% Asian. Hispanic (any race) 2.7%.

Industry
Finance, services, manufacturing, government, retail trade, transportation and utilities, wholesale trade, construction, mining

Agriculture
Cattle, corn, soybeans, wheat, hogs, hay, dairy products

Statehood
November 2, 1889; 40th state

GEO WHIZ

Thirty years ago, black-footed ferrets were on the brink of extinction. Now, thanks to captive breeding programs, the world's largest wild black-footed ferret population is thriving in a black-tailed prairie dog colony in south-central South Dakota.

Called Shrine of Democracy by its creator Gutzon Borglum, Mount Rushmore National Monument features the faces of George Washington, Thomas Jefferson, Abraham Lincoln, and Theodore Roosevelt. Each is 60 feet (18 m) tall.

The Black Hills Institute of Geological Research in Hill City has been involved in digging up eight *Tyrannosaurus rex* skeletons, including Sue, Stan, Bucky, and WREX. In addition to research work, the institute prepares museum-quality reproductions.

RING-NECKED PHEASANT

PASQUEFLOWER

SOUTH DAKOTA

After the discovery of Black Hills gold in 1874, prospectors poured in and established lawless mining towns such as Deadwood. Indians fought this invasion but were defeated, and statehood came in 1889. Today, South Dakota has several reservations, and nearly 9 percent of the state's people are Native Americans. The Missouri River flows through the center of the state, creating two distinct regions. To the east, farmers grow corn and soybeans on the fertile, rolling prairie. To the west, where it is too dry for most crops, farmers grow wheat and graze cattle and sheep on the vast plains. In the southwest, the Black Hills, named for the dark coniferous trees blanketing their slopes, are still a rich source of gold. Millions of tourists visit the area to see Mount Rushmore and a giant sculpture of Crazy Horse that has been in the works since 1948. Nearby, the fossil-rich Badlands, a region of eroded buttes and pinnacles, dominate the landscape.

⇨ HONORING AGRICULTURE. The face of the Corn Palace in Mitchell is renewed each year using thousands of bushels of grain to create pictures depicting the role of agriculture in the state's history.

ALTERNATIVE BEEF

Bison sold 2007 data

South Dakota	Nebraska	North Dakota	Colorado	Montana	Wyoming
10,862	7,266	6,042	5,456	5,270	4,668

Bison meat is popular among health-conscious consumers because it is lower in calories, fat, and cholesterol than other meats.

MITCHELL CORN PALACE

LIFE ON THE FARM 2005

Map of South Dakota

3 4 5 6 7 8 9 10

NORTH DAKOTA

STANDING ROCK

Lemmon
McIntosh
INDIAN
POCASSE N.W.R.
Eureka
SAND LAKE N.W.R.
Britton
TRAVERSE (SISSETON)
Lake Traverse

GRAND RIVER
NATIONAL
GRASSLAND
Bison
RESERVATION
Mobridge
Leola
Sisseton
INDIAN RES.

Thunder Butte Creek
Moreau
Timber Lake
Selby
Ipswich
Aberdeen
Groton
Waubay L.
WAUBAY N.W.R.
Webster
Big Stone Lake
Milbank

Dupree
CHEYENNE RIVER
SIOUX
Lake Oahe
Gettysburg
Faulkton
Redfield
Clark
Watertown
Clear Lake

Sulphur Creek
Cherry Creek
Cheyenne
INDIAN RESERVATION
Okobojo Creek
Onida
Highmore
Miller
De Smet
Lake Poinsett
Foster Creek
Big Sioux
Brookings
Volga

S O U T H   D A K O T A

Fort Pierre
★ Pierre
Huron
FLANDREAU I.R.
Flandreau

Missouri
Bad
FORT PIERRE NATIONAL GRASSLAND
Lake Sharpe
CROW CREEK INDIAN RESERVATION
LOWER BRULE INDIAN RESERVATION
Fort Thompson
Wessington Springs
Woonsocket
Madison
Howard

MINUTEMAN MISSILE N.H.S.
Wall
Philip
Murdo
Kennebec
Chamberlain
Crow Creek
Salem

point Dakota
BUFFALO GAP
NATIONAL
Kadoka
White
Plankinton
Mitchell
Sand Creek
229

GRASSLAND
Huge rock barrier sculptured into pinnacles and gullies by running water
Alexandria
Sioux Falls

NE RIDGE
RESERVATION
White River
Last major conflict of the Indian Wars, December 1890
Winner
Lake Francis Case
Platte
Parkston
James
Parker
Lennox
Canton

WOUNDED KNEE MASSACRE SITE
Martin
LACREEK N.W.R.
Rosebud
ROSEBUD INDIAN RESERVATION
Gregory
Burke
YANKTON
Lake Andes
LAKE ANDES N.W.R.
Armour
Freeman
Beresford

Pine Ridge
Little White
Keya Paha
INDIAN RES.
Wagner
Tyndall
Big Sioux
29

NEBRASKA

Lewis and Clark Lake
Yankton
Vermillion
Elk Point
N. Sioux City

MISSOURI NATIONAL RECREATIONAL RIVER
Missouri

MINNESOTA

IOWA

⬇ **BRAVE WARRIOR.** Begun in 1948, the Crazy Horse Memorial in South Dakota's Black Hills honors the culture, tradition, and living heritage of North American Indians. In the background sculptors are recreating the statue of the Lakota chief and his horse in the mountainside.

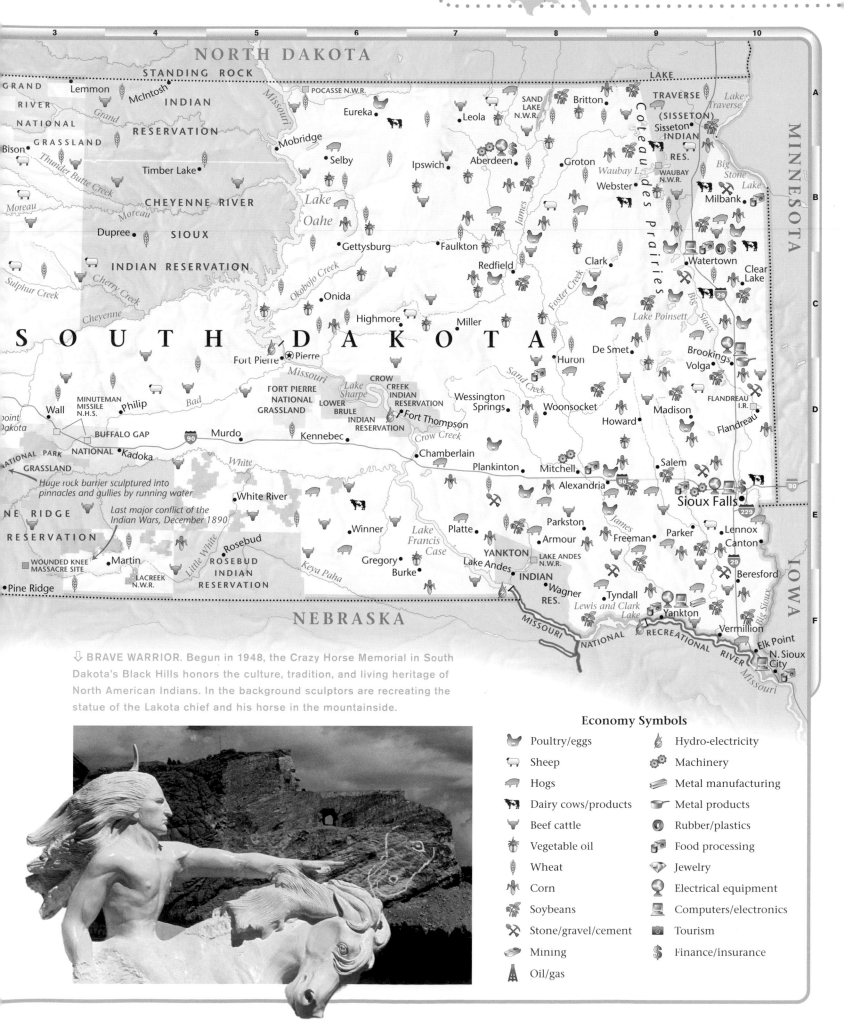

Economy Symbols

Poultry/eggs	Hydro-electricity
Sheep	Machinery
Hogs	Metal manufacturing
Dairy cows/products	Metal products
Beef cattle	Rubber/plastics
Vegetable oil	Food processing
Wheat	Jewelry
Corn	Electrical equipment
Soybeans	Computers/electronics
Stone/gravel/cement	Tourism
Mining	Finance/insurance
Oil/gas	

WISCONSIN

1848

THE BASICS

STATS

Area
65,498 sq mi (169,639 sq km)

Population
5,686,986

Capital
Madison
Population 233,209

Largest city
Milwaukee
Population 594,833

Ethnic/racial groups
86.2% white; 6.3% African American; 2.3% Asian; 1.0% Native American. Hispanic (any race) 5.9%.

Industry
Industrial machinery, paper products, food processing, metal products, electronic equipment, transportation

Agriculture
Dairy products, cattle, corn, poultry and eggs, soybeans

Statehood
May 29, 1848; 30th state

GEO WHIZ

The Indian Community School in Milwaukee offers courses in native languages, history, and rituals. In all of its programs—from math to tribal creation stories—seven core values are stressed: bravery, love, truth, wisdom, humility, loyalty, and respect.

Bogs left by retreating ice-age glaciers provide excellent conditions for raising cranberries. Wisconsin leads the nation in cranberry farming, producing more than half of the estimated 575 million pounds (261 million kg) consumed by Americans annually.

Wisconsin is nicknamed the Badger State, not for the animal but for the men who mined lead in the state during the 1820s. They dug living spaces by burrowing like badgers into the hillside.

ROBIN
WOOD VIOLET

WISCONSIN

Frenchman Jean Nicolet was the first European to reach present-day Wisconsin when he stepped ashore from Green Bay in 1634. After decades of getting along, relations with the region's Indians soured as the number of settlers increased. The Black Hawk War in 1832 ended the last major Indian resistance, and statehood came in 1848. Many Milwaukee residents are descendants of German immigrants who labored in the city's breweries and meatpacking plants. Even as the economic importance of health care and other services has increased, food processing and the manufacture of machinery and metal products remains significant for the state. More than one million dairy cows graze in America's Dairyland, as the state is often called. It leads the country in cheese production, and is the second-largest producer of milk and butter. Other farmers grow crops ranging from corn and soybeans to potatoes and cranberries. Northern Wisconsin is sparsely populated but heavily forested, and is the source of paper and paper products produced by the state.

⇧ CITY BY THE LAKE. Milwaukee, on the shore of Lake Michigan, derives its name from the Algonquian word for "beautiful land." The city, known for brewing and manufacturing, also has a growing service sector.

⇧ TASTY GRAZING. The largest concentration of Brown Swiss cows in the U.S. is in Wisconsin, where the milk of this breed is prized by cheese manufacturers.

⇦ RURAL ECONOMY. The dairy industry is an important part of Wisconsin's rural economy, and dairy farmers control most of the state's farmland.

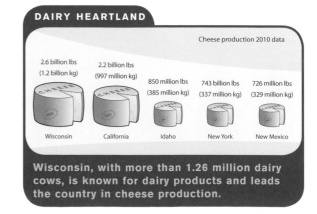

DAIRY HEARTLAND

Cheese production 2010 data

2.6 billion lbs (1.2 billion kg)	2.2 billion lbs (997 million kg)	850 million lbs (385 million kg)	743 billion lbs (337 million kg)	726 million lbs (329 million kg)
Wisconsin	California	Idaho	New York	New Mexico

Wisconsin, with more than 1.26 million dairy cows, is known for dairy products and leads the country in cheese production.

LAKE SUPERIOR

MICHIGAN

MINNESOTA

APOSTLE ISLANDS NATIONAL LAKESHORE
Apostle Islands

RED CLIFF I.R.
Madeline Island
BAD RIVER INDIAN RES.

Washburn
Superior
CHEQUAMEGON-
Ashland
Hurley

NICOLET

Bois Brule
St. Croix

Hayward
Land O'Lakes

Turtle-Flambeau Flowage

LAC DU FLAMBEAU INDIAN RES.
Park Falls
Eagle River
CHEQUAMEGON-

ST. CROIX
NATIONAL
Namekagon
LAC COURTE OREILLES I.R.
Spooner
Lake Chippewa

NATIONAL
Brule
Popple
Niagara
Menominee
NICOLET

SCENIC
RIVERWAY
ST. CROIX INDIAN RES.
Rhinelander
SOKAOGON CHIPPEWA I.R.
Peshtigo

Rice Lake
Ladysmith
Flambeau
Jump
Highest point in Wisconsin
+ Timms Hill 1,951ft 595 m
Tomahawk
FOREST COUNTY POTAWATOMI I.R.
Washington Island

St. Croix Falls
FOREST
Chippewa
Yellow
Medford
Merrill
Antigo
NATIONAL
Wolf
FOREST
Marinette

New Richmond
Chippewa Falls
Lake Wissota
Wausau
MENOMINEE INDIAN RES.
WOLF N.W.&S.R.
STOCKBRIDGE I.R.
Oconto
Oconto
Sturgeon Bay

Hudson
River Falls
Eau Claire
Altoona
Big Eau Pleine Reservoir
Marshfield
Lake Du Bay
Shawano
Ashwaubenon
Algoma

ST. CROIX N.W.&S.R.
Menomonie
Chippewa
W I S C O N S I N
ONEIDA INDIAN RES.
Green Bay
De Pere

Mississippi
Lake Pepin
Pepin
Black
WISCONSIN WINNEBAGO I.R.
Stevens Point
Plover
New London
Waupaca
Appleton
Kaukauna
Two Rivers
Manitowoc

Black River Falls
Wisconsin
Wisconsin Rapids
Menasha
Neenah
Oshkosh
Lake Winnebago

TREMPEALEAU N.W.R.
NECEDAH N.W.R.
Petenwell Lake
Lake Poygan
LAKE

Sparta
Onalaska
Tomah
Castle Rock Lake
Ripon
Fond du Lac
Sheboygan

La Crosse
MICHIGAN

Economy Symbols

Viroqua
Kickapoo
Reedsburg
Wisconsin Dells
Waupun
HORICON N.W.R.
West Bend
Port Washington

Fishing
Baraboo
Portage
Beaver Dam
Mequon

Poultry/eggs
Richland Center
Lake Wisconsin
Menomonee Falls
Wauwatosa

Sheep
Prairie du Chien
TALIESIN
Sun Prairie
Watertown
Brookfield
Milwaukee

Hogs
Wisconsin
Middleton
Monona
Fort Atkinson
Waukesha
West Allis

Dairy cows/products
Madison
Stoughton
Whitewater
S. Milwaukee

Beef cattle
Dodgeville
Pecatonica
Janesville
Burlington
Racine

Fruits
Lancaster
Sugar
Monroe
Lake Geneva
Pleasant Prairie
Kenosha

Vegetables
Platteville
Mississippi
Rock
Beloit

Nursery stock
IOWA

Corn

Soybeans

Tobacco   Machinery   Food processing

Timber/forest products   Metal products   Electrical equipment

Printing/publishing   Shipbuilding   Computers/electronics

Stone/gravel/cement   Railroad equipment Scientific instruments

Mining   Motor vehicles/parts   Aircraft/parts

Hydro-electricity   Chemistry   Tourism

ILLINOIS
INDIANA

Green Bay
Door Peninsula

NATIONAL WILDLIFE AND FISH REFUGE
UPPER MISSISSIPPI RIVER

THE REGION

PHYSICAL			POLITICAL	
Total area 574,067 sq mi (1,486,833 sq km)	**Lowest point** Sea level, shores of the Gulf of Mexico	**Vegetation** Mixed, broadleaf, and needleleaf forest; grassland; desert	**Total population** 37,348,108	**Smallest state** Oklahoma: 69,898 sq mi (181,036 sq km)
			States (4): Arizona, New Mexico, Oklahoma, Texas	**Most populous state** Texas: 25,145,561
Highest point Wheeler Peak, NM 13,161 ft (4,011 m)	**Longest rivers** Rio Grande, Arkansas, Colorado	**Climate** Humid subtropical, semiarid and arid, with warm to hot summers and cool winters		**Least populous state** New Mexico: 2,059,179
	Largest lakes Toledo Bend, Sam Rayburn, Eufaula (all reservoirs)		**Largest state** Texas: 268,581 sq mi (695,624 sq km)	**Largest city proper** Houston, TX: 2,099,451

The Southwest

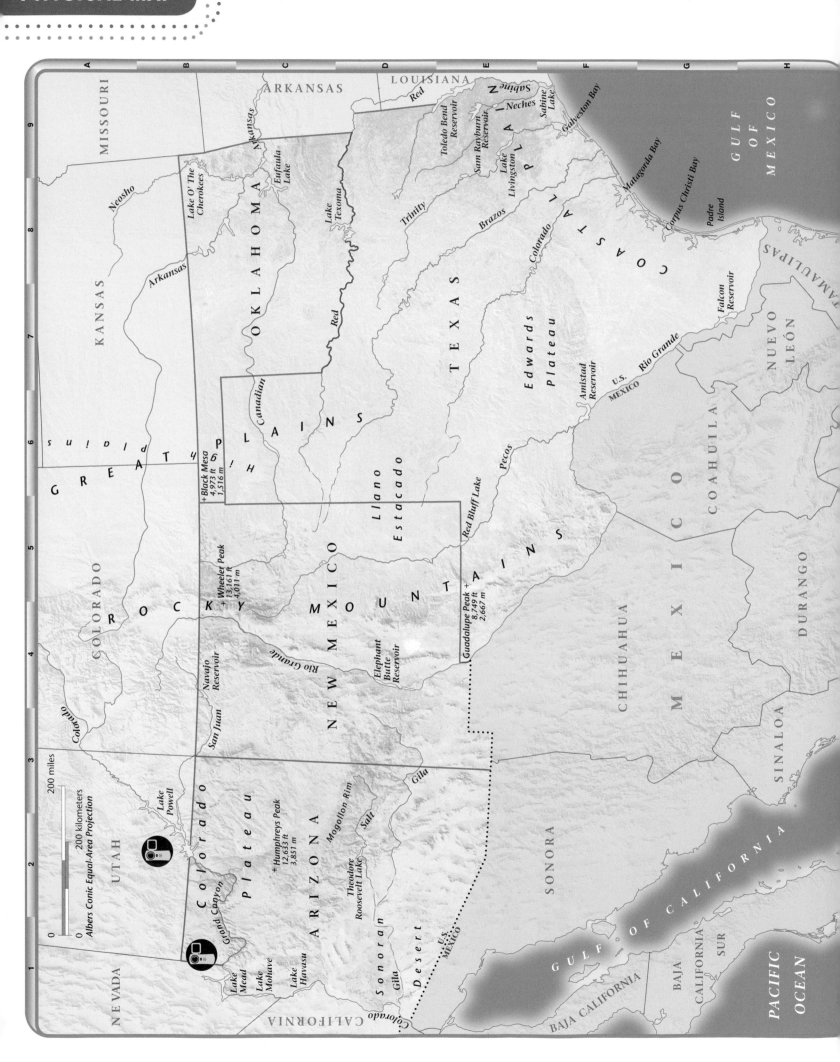

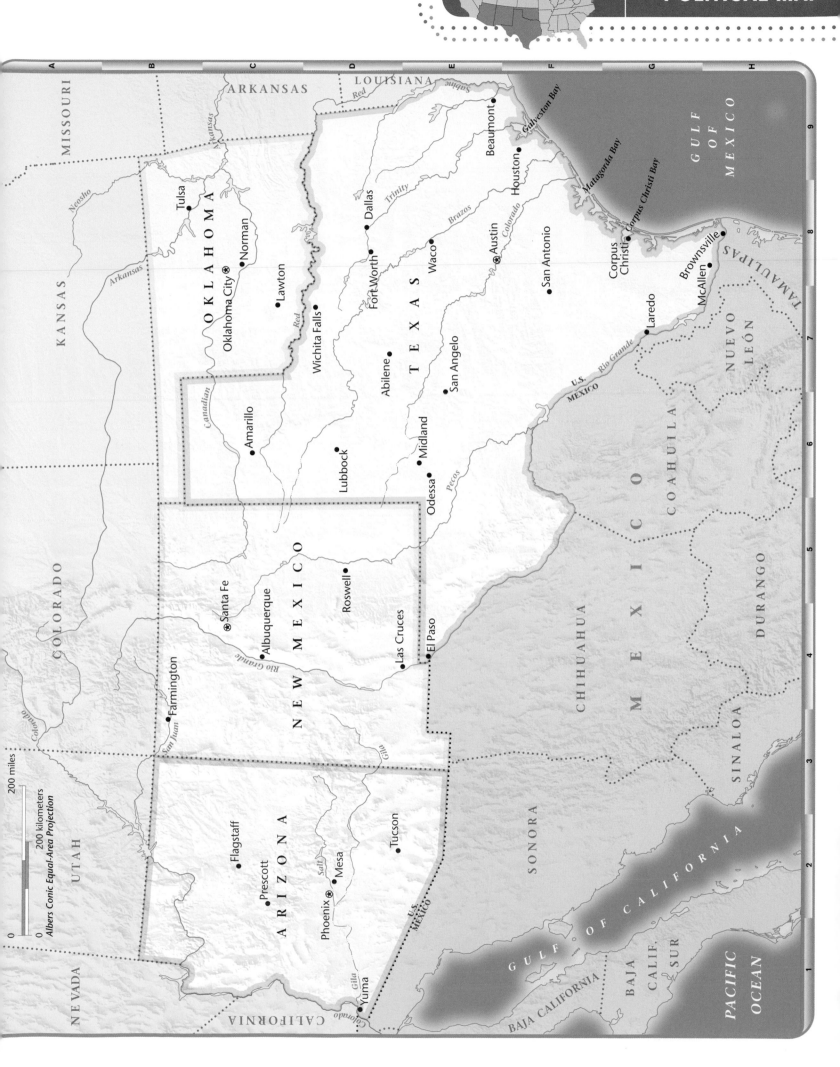

⇨ SKY STONE. According to Indian legend, turquoise stole its color from the sky. This Zuni woman is wearing turquoise jewelry for a festival in Phoenix. Zuni Indians, whose reservation is in western New Mexico, have made jewelry for more than one thousand years.

The Southwest
FROM CANYONS TO GRASSLANDS

L egendary cities of gold lured Spanish conquistadors to the Southwest in the 1500s. Today, the promise of economic opportunities brings people from other states as well as immigrants, both legal and illegal, from countries south of the border. This part of the Sunbelt region boasts future-oriented cities while preserving Wild West tales and Native American traditions. Stretching from the humid Gulf Coast to Arizona's deserts, the landscape is as diverse as its climate, ranging from sprawling plains in the east to plateaus cut by dramatic canyons in the west. Water is a major concern in the Southwest, one of the country's fastest-growing regions.

⇩ HIGH SOCIETY. Dressed in an elegant ball gown, a young woman participates in the Society of Martha Washington Pageant in Laredo, Texas. This event presents daughters of wealthy and long-established Hispanic families to the local community.

⇧ MODERN METROPOLIS. Lights sparkle in the skyline of Dallas, Texas. Although incorporated as a town in 1856, it was not until 1930 that it experienced explosive growth and prosperity due to the discovery of oil. Today, Dallas is a center of the U.S. oil industry and a leader in technology-based industries.

⇧ DEADLY VIPER. Shaking the rattles on the tip of its tail, this diamondback rattlesnake—coiled for attack—warns intruders to stay away. Common throughout the arid Southwest, the snake eats mainly small rodents.

⇦ STANDING TALL. The saguaro cactus, which often rises more than 30 feet (9 m) above the shrubs of the Sonoran Desert, frequently has several branches and produces creamy-white flowers that bloom at night. The Sonoran, hottest desert in North America, is located in the borderlands of southern Arizona and California and extends into northern Mexico.

WHERE THE PICTURES ARE

Copper worker p. 120

Grand Canyon p. 120

Rattlesnake p. 119

Bison grazing p. 124

Historic plane p. 125

Saguaro cactus pp. 118-119

Turquoise jewelry p. 118

Gila monster p. 122

Hot-air balloons p. 122

Los Alamos scientists p. 122

Dallas skyline pp. 118-119

Oil drillers p. 126

Rio Grande ferry pp. 126-127

Texas debutante p. 118

THE GRAND CANYON STATE:
ARIZONA

THE BASICS

STATS

Area
113,998 sq mi (295,256 sq km)

Population
6,392,017

Capital
Phoenix
Population 1,445,632

Largest city
Phoenix
Population 1,445,632

Ethnic/racial groups
73.0% white; 4.6% Native American;
4.1% African American; 2.8% Asian.
Hispanic (any race) 29.6%.

Industry
Real estate, manufactured goods,
retail, state and local government,
transportation and public utilities,
wholesale trade, health services,
tourism, electronics

Agriculture
Vegetables, cattle, dairy products,
cotton, fruit, nursery stock, nuts

Statehood
February 14, 1912; 48th state

GEO WHIZ

The California condor, once common
throughout the Southwest, nearly
became extinct in 1987. Through
captive breeding and other conservation measures, the species has
been reintroduced to the wild in areas
such as the Grand Canyon.

People have been carving pictures called
petroglyphs into rock cliffs in Verde
Valley near Flagstaff for thousands
of years. The meanings of most are
a mystery, but others reveal the
plants and animals of bygone eras.

Introduced as wild game for sports-
men, bullfrogs have made Arizona
their new home on the range. With
no natural predators and plenty to
eat, bullfrogs are taking over.

**CACTUS WREN
SAGUARO**

ARIZONA

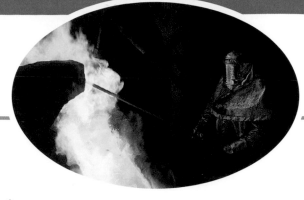

⬆ HOT WORK. A man in protective clothing works near a furnace that melts and refines copper ore at Magma Copper Company near Tucson. Arizona is one of the largest copper-producing regions in the world.

The Europeans to first visit what is now Arizona were the Spanish in the 1500s. The territory passed from Spain to Mexico and then to the United States over the next three centuries. In the 1800s settlers clashed with the Apache warriors Cochise and Geronimo—and with one another in lawless towns like Tombstone. Youngest of the 48 contiguous states, statehood arrived in 1912. Arizona's economy was long based on the Five C's—copper, cattle, cotton, citrus, and climate—but manufacturing and service industries have gained prominence. A fast-growing population, sprawling cities, and agricultural irrigation strain limited water supplies in this dry state, which depends on water from the Colorado River and underground aquifers. Tourists flock to the Colorado Plateau in the north to see stunning vistas of the Grand Canyon, Painted Desert, and Monument Valley. To the south, the Sonoran Desert's unique ecosystem includes the giant saguaro cactus. Indian reservations scattered around the state offer outsiders the chance to learn about tribal history and culture.

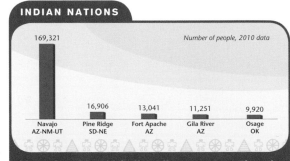

INDIAN NATIONS

Number of people, 2010 data

Navajo AZ-NM-UT	Pine Ridge SD-NE	Fort Apache AZ	Gila River AZ	Osage OK
169,321	16,906	13,041	11,251	9,920

More than 200,000 Indians live on reservations in the Southwest. The most populous is the Navajo Reservation in Arizona and adjoining states.

⬇ NATURAL WONDER. Carved by the rushing waters of the Colorado River, the Grand Canyon's geologic features and fossil record reveal almost two billion years of Earth's history. Archaeological evidence indicates human habitation dating back 12,000 years.

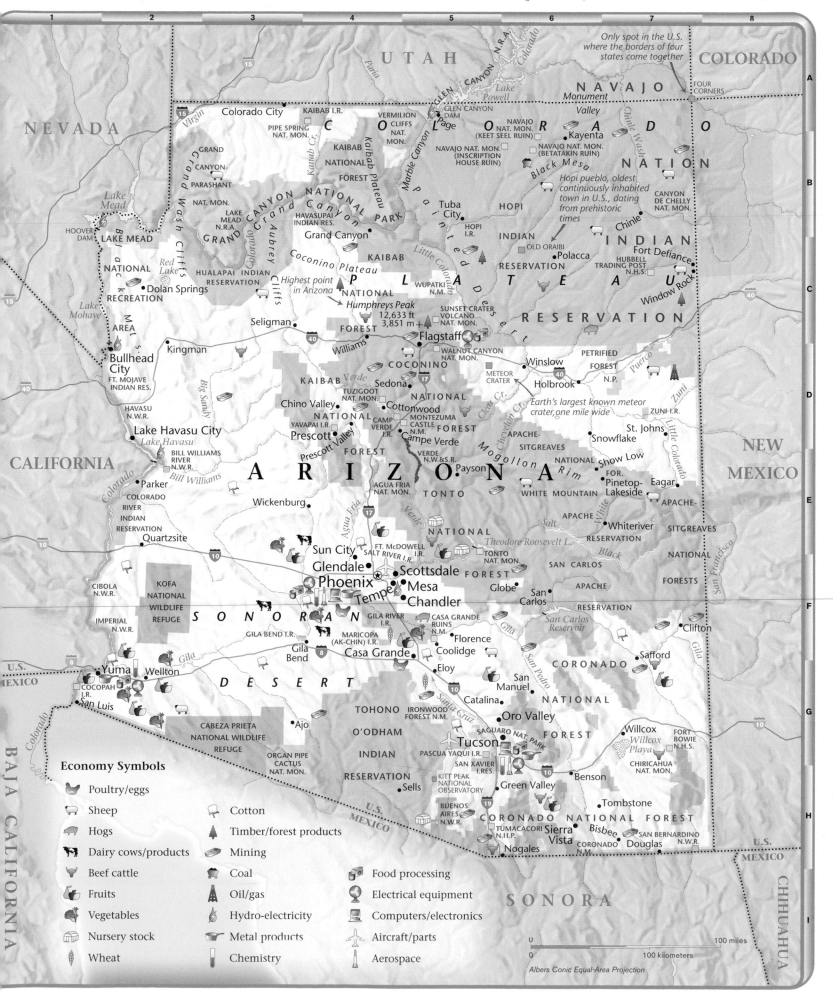

Only spot in the U.S. where the borders of four states come together

NEVADA
UTAH
COLORADO
CALIFORNIA
NEW MEXICO
BAJA CALIFORNIA
SONORA
CHIHUAHUA

A R I Z O N A

FOUR CORNERS

NAVAJO Monument Valley

COLORADO NATION

Colorado City
KAIBAB I.R.
VERMILION CLIFFS NAT. MON.
PIPE SPRING NAT. MON.
Page
GLEN CANYON DAM
Lake Powell
NAVAJO NAT. MON. (KEET SEEL RUIN)
Kayenta
Chinle Wash

KAIBAB NATIONAL FOREST
Kaibab Plateau
Marble Canyon
NAVAJO NAT. MON. (INSCRIPTION HOUSE RUIN)
NAVAJO NAT. MON. (BETATAKIN RUIN)
Black Mesa
CANYON DE CHELLY NAT. MON.

GRAND CANYON-PARASHANT NAT. MON.
GRAND CANYON NATIONAL PARK
HAVASUPAI INDIAN RES.
Grand Canyon
Tuba City
HOPI
Hopi pueblo, oldest continuously inhabited town in U.S., dating from prehistoric times
Chinle

Lake Mead
LAKE MEAD N.R.A.
Coconino Plateau
KAIBAB
HOPI I.R.
INDIAN RESERVATION
OLD ORAIBI
Polacca
Fort Defiance
HUBBELL TRADING POST N.H.S.

HOOVER DAM
LAKE MEAD
NATIONAL RECREATION AREA
HUALAPAI INDIAN RESERVATION
Highest point in Arizona
Humphreys Peak 12,633 ft 3,851 m
Painted Desert
Little Colorado
INDIAN
WUPATKI N.M.
PLATEAU
RESERVATION
Window Rock

Red Lake
Dolan Springs
Lake Mohave
Seligman
FOREST
SUNSET CRATER VOLCANO NAT. MON.
Flagstaff
WALNUT CANYON NAT. MON.
PETRIFIED FOREST
Puerco

Kingman
Williams
COCONINO
Winslow
Holbrook
PETRIFIED FOREST N.P.
Zuni

Bullhead City
FT. MOJAVE INDIAN RES.
KAIBAB
Verde
Sedona
17
METEOR CRATER
Earth's largest known meteor crater, one mile wide
ZUNI I.R.

HAVASU N.W.R.
Big Sandy
Chino Valley
TUZIGOOT NAT. MON.
Cottonwood
MONTEZUMA CASTLE N.M.
NATIONAL
APACHE-SITGREAVES
St. Johns
Little Colorado

Lake Havasu City
Lake Havasu
NATIONAL
YAVAPAI I.R.
Prescott
CAMP VERDE
Campe Verde
Snowflake

BILL WILLIAMS RIVER N.W.R.
Bill Williams
Prescott Valley
FOREST
VERDE N.W.&S.R.
Mogollon Rim
NATIONAL
Show Low

Parker
COLORADO RIVER INDIAN RESERVATION
Wickenburg
AGUA FRIA NAT. MON.
TONTO
Payson
WHITE MOUNTAIN
FOR.
Pinetop-Lakeside
Eagar
APACHE-SITGREAVES

Quartzsite
Sun City
FT. McDOWELL I.R.
SALT RIVER I.R.
NATIONAL
Theodore Roosevelt L.
APACHE
Whiteriver
NATIONAL FORESTS
San Francisco

CIBOLA N.W.R.
KOFA NATIONAL WILDLIFE REFUGE
Glendale
Phoenix
Scottsdale
Mesa
Tempe
Chandler
TONTO NAT. MON.
Globe
San Carlos
APACHE

IMPERIAL N.W.R.
SONORAN
GILA RIVER I.R.
CASA GRANDE RUINS N.M.
San Carlos Reservoir
CORONADO
Clifton

GILA BEND T.R.
MARICOPA (AK-CHIN) I.R.
Gila Bend
Casa Grande
Florence
Coolidge
Gila
Safford

Yuma
Wellton
DESERT
Eloy
San Manuel
San Pedro
NATIONAL

COCOPAH I.R.
San Luis
CABEZA PRIETA NATIONAL WILDLIFE REFUGE
Ajo
TOHONO
IRONWOOD FOREST N.M.
Catalina
Oro Valley
FOREST
Willcox
Willcox Playa
FORT BOWIE N.H.S.

ORGAN PIPE CACTUS NAT. MON.
O'ODHAM
SAGUARO NAT. PARK
Tucson
PASCUA YAQUI I.R.
CHIRICAHUA NAT. MON.

INDIAN RESERVATION
Sells
SAN XAVIER I.RES.
Benson
CORONADO NATIONAL FOREST

KITT PEAK NATIONAL OBSERVATORY
Green Valley
Tombstone

BUENOS AIRES N.W.R.
Sierra Vista
Bisbee
SAN BERNARDINO N.W.R.

TUMACACORI N.I.IP.
Nogales
CORONADO N.M.
Douglas

Virgin
Paria
GLEN CANYON N.R.A.
Colorado
Navajo

Economy Symbols

- 🐔 Poultry/eggs
- 🐑 Sheep
- 🐖 Hogs
- 🐄 Dairy cows/products
- Beef cattle
- 🍎 Fruits
- Vegetables
- Nursery stock
- 🌾 Wheat

- Cotton
- 🌲 Timber/forest products
- Mining
- Coal
- Oil/gas
- Hydro-electricity
- Metal products
- 🧪 Chemistry

- 📦 Food processing
- 🌐 Electrical equipment
- 💻 Computers/electronics
- ✈ Aircraft/parts
- Aerospace

100 miles
100 kilometers

Albers Conic Equal-Area Projection

THE LAND OF ENCHANTMENT STATE:
NEW MEXICO

THE BASICS

STATS

Area
121,590 sq mi (314,917 sq km)

Population
2,059,179

Capital
Santa Fe
Population 67,947

Largest city
Albuquerque
Population 545,852

Ethnic/racial groups
68.4% white; 9.4% Native American;
2.1% African American; 1.4% Asian.
Hispanic (any race) 46.3%.

Industry
Electronic equipment, state and
local government, real estate,
business services, federal
government, oil and gas
extraction, health services

Agriculture
Cattle, dairy products, hay,
chili peppers, onions

Statehood
January 6, 1912; 47th state

GEO WHIZ

Carlsbad Caverns National Park
has more than a hundred caves,
including the deepest limestone
cavern in the U.S. From May
through October, visitors can watch
hundreds of thousands of Mexican
free-tailed bats emerge from the
cavern on their nightly search for food.

Taos Pueblo, in north-central New
Mexico, has been continuously inhabited by Pueblo people for more than
1,000 years. When Spanish explorers
reached it in 1540, they thought they
had found one of the fabled golden
cities of Cibola.

In 2007 voters in a county
in south-central New
Mexico approved a tax
to help fund construction
of a spaceport where rockets
will launch tourists into space.

ROADRUNNER
YUCCA

NEW MEXICO

New Mexico is among the youngest states—statehood was established in 1912—but its capital city is the country's oldest. The Spanish founded Santa Fe in 1610, a decade before the *Mayflower* reached America. Beginning in the 1820s, the Santa Fe Trail brought trade and settlers, and the United States acquired all the territory from Mexico by 1853. Most large cities are in the center of the state, along the Rio Grande. The Rocky Mountains divide the plains in the east from eroded mesas and canyons in the west. Cattle and sheep ranching on the plains is the chief agricultural activity, but hay, onions, and chili peppers are also important. Copper, potash, and natural gas produce mineral wealth. Cultural richness created by the historic interaction of Indian, Hispanic, and Anglo peoples abounds. Visitors experience this unique culture in the state's spicy cuisine, the famous art galleries of Taos, and the crafts made by Indians on the state's many reservations.

⇧ PAINFUL BITE. The strikingly patterned gila monster, the most poisonous lizard native to the United States, lives in desert areas of the Southwest.

⇧ FLYING HIGH. Brightly colored balloons rise into a brilliant blue October sky during Albuquerque's annual International Balloon Fiesta, the largest such event in the world. During the 9-day festival more than 700 hot-air balloons drift on variable air currents created by surrounding mountains.

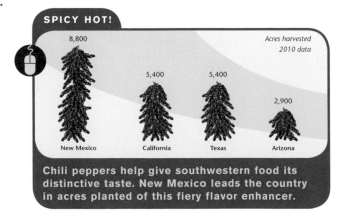

SPICY HOT!

8,800 — New Mexico
5,400 — California
5,400 — Texas
2,900 — Arizona

Acres harvested
2010 data

Chili peppers help give southwestern food its distinctive taste. New Mexico leads the country in acres planted of this fiery flavor enhancer.

⇦ NUCLEAR MYSTERIES. Scientists at Los Alamos National Laboratory, a leading scientific and engineering research institution responsible for national security, use 3-D simulations to study nuclear explosions.

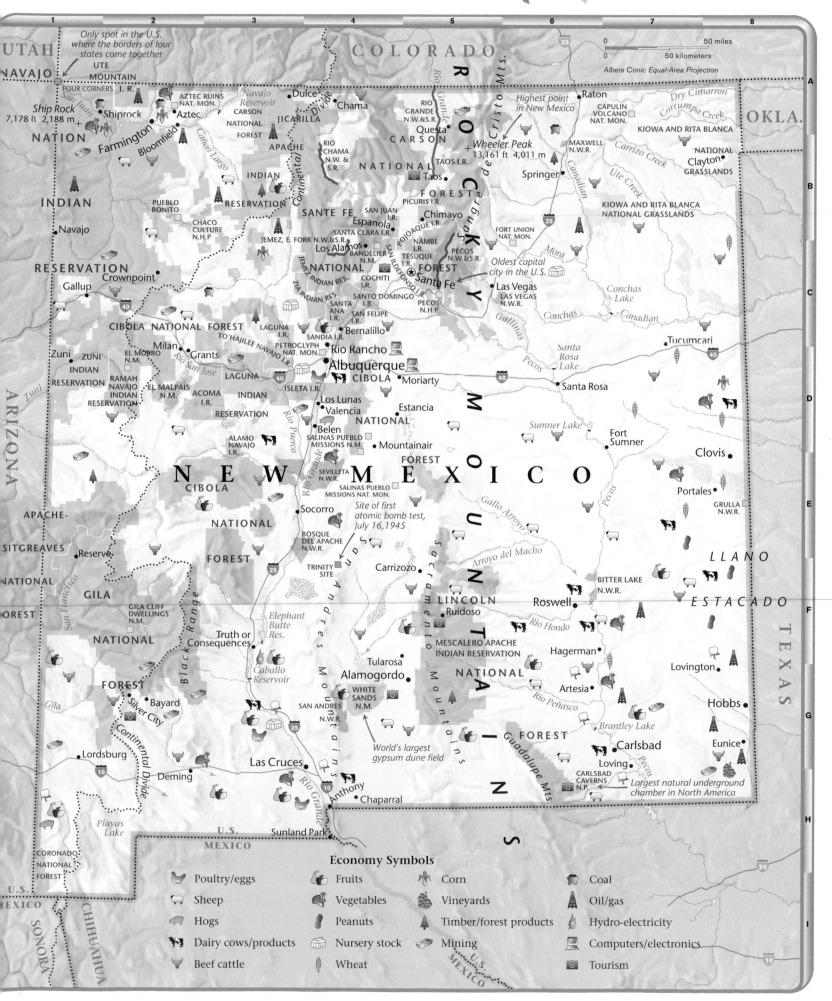

Only spot in the U.S. where the borders of four states come together

COLORADO

UTAH

Ship Rock 7,178 ft 2,188 m

Highest point in New Mexico

Wheeler Peak 13,161 ft 4,011 m

OKLA.

Oldest capital city in the U.S.

ARIZONA

NEW MEXICO

Site of first atomic bomb test, July 16, 1945

LLANO ESTACADO

TEXAS

World's largest gypsum dune field

Largest natural underground chamber in North America

U.S. MEXICO

CHIHUAHUA

SONORA

Economy Symbols

Poultry/eggs	Fruits	Corn	Coal
Sheep	Vegetables	Vineyards	Oil/gas
Hogs	Peanuts	Timber/forest products	Hydro-electricity
Dairy cows/products	Nursery stock	Mining	Computers/electronics
Beef cattle	Wheat		Tourism

THE SOONER STATE:
OKLAHOMA

OKLAHOMA

THE BASICS

STATS

Area
69,898 sq mi (181,036 sq km)

Population
3,751,351

Capital
Oklahoma City
Population 579,999

Largest city
Oklahoma City
Population 579,999

Ethnic/racial groups
72.2% white; 8.6% Native American; 7.4% African American; 1.7% Asian. Hispanic (any race) 8.9%.

Industry
Manufacturing, services, government, finance, insurance, real estate

Agriculture
Cattle, wheat, hogs, poultry, nursery stock

Statehood
November 16, 1907; 46th state

GEO WHIZ

An area of Oklahoma City has earned the nickname Little Saigon. In the 1960s the city opened its doors to tens of thousands of refugees from Vietnam. Today, the area is a thriving business district that includes people of other Asian nationalities.

"Hillbilly Speed Bump" is one of several nicknames for the armadillo. Native to South America, large populations of this armor-plated mammal are found as far north as Oklahoma.

Before it became a state in 1907, Oklahoma was known as Indian Territory. Today 39 tribes, including Cherokees, Osages, Creeks, and Choctaws, have their headquarters in the state.

SCISSOR-TAILED FLYCATCHER
MISTLETOE

OKLAHOMA

The U.S. government declared most of present-day Oklahoma Indian Territory in 1834. To reach this new homeland, southeastern Indians were forced to travel the Trail of Tears, named for its brutal conditions. By 1889 areas were opened for white homesteaders who staked claims in frenzied land runs. White and Indian lands were combined to form the state of Oklahoma in 1907. During the 1930s, many Okies fled drought and dust storms that smothered everything in sight. Some traveled as far as California in search of work. Better farming methods and the return of rain helped agriculture recover, and today cattle and wheat are the chief products. Oil and natural gas wells are found throughout the state. The Red River, colored by the region's iron-rich soils, marks the state's southern boundary. Along the eastern border, the Ozark Plateau and Ouachita Mountains form rugged bluffs and valleys. To the west, rolling plains rise toward the High Plains in the state's panhandle.

⇧ NATURAL LANDSCAPE. A bison herd grazes in the Tallgrass Prairie Preserve, near Pawhuska. In years when rain is abundant, the grasses can grow as tall as 8 feet (2.5 m). Tallgrass prairie once covered 140 million acres (57 million ha), extending from Minnesota to Texas, but today less than 10 percent remains because of urban sprawl and cropland expansion.

WEATHER ALERT

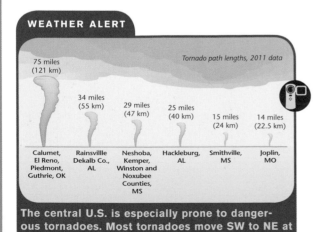

Tornado path lengths, 2011 data

75 miles (121 km) — Calumet, El Reno, Piedmont, Guthrie, OK

34 miles (55 km) — Rainsville, Dekalb Co., AL

29 miles (47 km) — Neshoba, Kemper, Winston and Noxubee Counties, MS

25 miles (40 km) — Hackleburg, AL

15 miles (24 km) — Smithville, MS

14 miles (22.5 km) — Joplin, MO

The central U.S. is especially prone to dangerous tornadoes. Most tornadoes move SW to NE at an average forward speed of 30 mph (48 km).

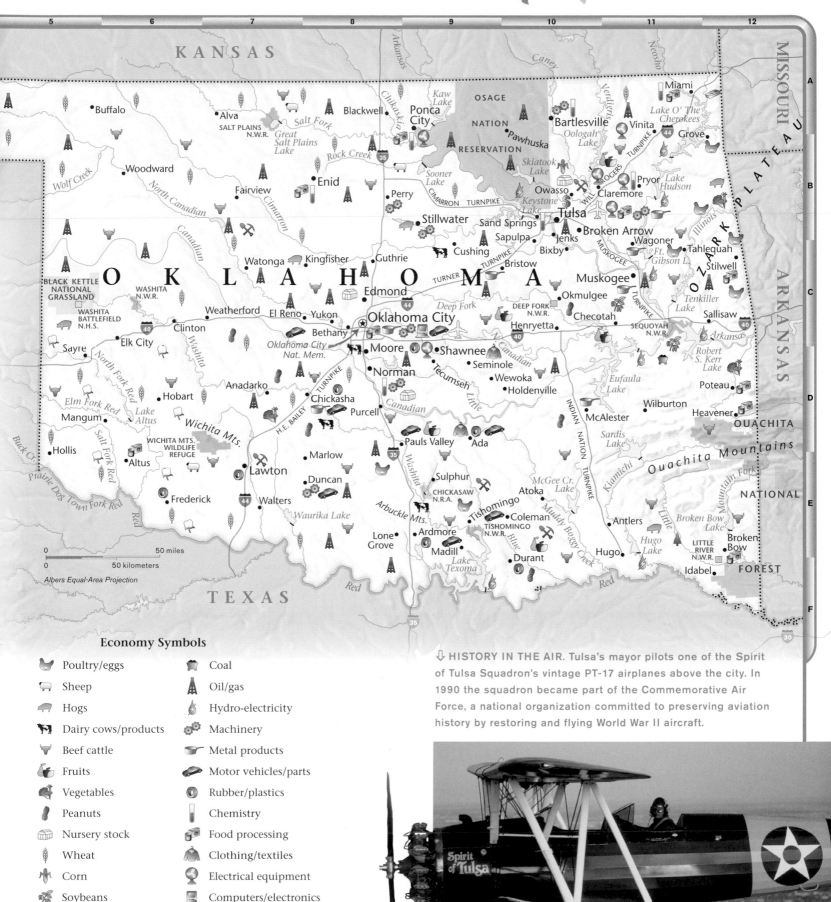

KANSAS

Buffalo · Alva · Blackwell · Ponca City · OSAGE NATION RESERVATION · Miami

SALT PLAINS N.W.R. · Great Salt Plains Lake · Salt Fork · Chikaska · Kaw Lake · Bartlesville · Vinita · Lake O' The Cherokees · Grove

Woodward · Rock Creek · Oologah Lake · Pawhuska · Skiatook Lake · Owasso · TURNPIKE

North Canadian · Fairview · Enid · Perry · Sooner Lake · CIMARRON TURNPIKE · Keystone Lake · Will Rogers · Claremore · Pryor · Lake Hudson

Wolf Creek · Cimarron · Stillwater · Sand Springs · Tulsa · Broken Arrow · Wagoner · Ft. Gibson L.

Watonga · Kingfisher · Guthrie · Cushing · Sapulpa · Jenks · Bixby · Tahlequah · Stilwell · Muskogee

O K L A H O M A · TURNER TURNPIKE · Bristow · Muskogee · OZARK

BLACK KETTLE NATIONAL GRASSLAND · WASHITA N.W.R. · Edmond · Deep Fork · DEEP FORK N.W.R. · Okmulgee · Checotah · Tenkiller Lake · Sallisaw

WASHITA BATTLEFIELD N.H.S. · Weatherford · El Reno · Yukon · Oklahoma City · Henryetta · SEQUOYAH N.W.R. · Arkansas · Robert S. Kerr Lake

Clinton · Bethany · Oklahoma City Nat. Mem. · Moore · Shawnee · Seminole · Wewoka · Eufaula Lake · Poteau

Sayre · Elk City · Norman · Tecumseh · Canadian · Holdenville · Wilburton · Heavener · OUACHITA

Mangum · North Fork Red · Lake Altus · Anadarko · Chickasha · Purcell · Canadian · McAlester · Sardis Lake · Ouachita Mountains · NATIONAL

Hollis · Salt Fork Red · WICHITA MTS. WILDLIFE REFUGE · Wichita Mts. · Marlow · Pauls Valley · Ada · Kiamichi · Broken Bow Lake

Altus · Lawton · Duncan · Sulphur · CHICKASAW N.R.A. · Atoka · McGee Cr. Lake · Little · Hugo Lake · LITTLE RIVER N.W.R. · Broken Bow

Frederick · Walters · Waurika Lake · Arbuckle Mts. · Tishomingo · Coleman · Muddy Boggy Creek · Antlers · Hugo · Idabel · FOREST

Prairie Dog Town Fork Red · Red · Lone Grove · Ardmore · Madill · TISHOMINGO N.W.R. · Durant · Blue · Mountain Fork

Lake Texoma · Red

TEXAS · **MISSOURI** · **ARKANSAS**

Scale:
0 — 50 miles
0 — 50 kilometers
Albers Equal-Area Projection

Economy Symbols

- Poultry/eggs
- Sheep
- Hogs
- Dairy cows/products
- Beef cattle
- Fruits
- Vegetables
- Peanuts
- Nursery stock
- Wheat
- Corn
- Soybeans
- Cotton
- Stone/gravel/cement
- Mining

- Coal
- Oil/gas
- Hydro-electricity
- Machinery
- Metal products
- Motor vehicles/parts
- Rubber/plastics
- Chemistry
- Food processing
- Clothing/textiles
- Electrical equipment
- Computers/electronics
- Aircraft/parts
- Finance/insurance

⇩ **HISTORY IN THE AIR.** Tulsa's mayor pilots one of the Spirit of Tulsa Squadron's vintage PT-17 airplanes above the city. In 1990 the squadron became part of the Commemorative Air Force, a national organization committed to preserving aviation history by restoring and flying World War II aircraft.

THE LONE STAR STATE:
TEXAS

TEXAS

Huge size, geographic diversity, and rich natural resources make Texas seem like its own country. In fact, it was an independent republic after throwing off Mexican rule in 1836. A famous battle in the fight for independence produced the Texan battle cry "Remember the Alamo!" In 1845 Texas was annexed by the United States. Texas is the second largest state (behind Alaska) and the second most populous (behind California). It is a top producer of many agricultural products, including cattle, sheep, cotton, citrus fruits, vegetables, rice, and pecans. It also has huge oil and natural gas fields and is a manufacturing powerhouse. Pine forests cover East Texas, the wettest region. The Gulf Coast has swamps and extensive barrier islands. Grassy plains stretch across the northern panhandle, while the rolling Hill Country is famous for beautiful wildflowers. Mountains, valleys, and sandy plains sprawl across dry West Texas. The Rio Grande, sometimes barely a trickle, separates Texas and Mexico.

THE BASICS

STATS

Area
268,581 sq mi (695,624 sq km)

Population
25,145,561

Capital
Austin
Population 790,390

Largest city
Houston
Population 2,099,451

Ethnic/racial groups
70.4% white; 11.8% African American; 3.8% Asian; .7% Native American. Hispanic (any race) 37.6%.

Industry
Chemicals, machinery, electronics and computers, food products, petroleum and natural gas, transportation equipment

Agriculture
Cattle, sheep, poultry, cotton, sorghum, wheat, rice, hay, peanuts, pecans

Statehood
December 29, 1845; 28th state

GEO WHIZ

The Fossil Rim Wildlife Research Center in the Texas Hill Country is breeding black rhinos and other endangered African animals. The goal is to reintroduce offspring into the wild in their native environment. Meanwhile, visitors get a chance to see a bit of Africa in Texas.

Six national flags have flown over Texas during the course of its history—the Spanish, French, Mexican, Texan, Confederate, and American.

Texas has a long history of Bigfoot sightings. The ape-man creature was part of local Indian lore, and white settlers told stories about a wild woman along the Navidad River. The Texas Bigfoot Research Center has collected hundreds of eyewitness reports, footprint casts, and hair samples of what locals call Wooly Booger.

MOCKINGBIRD
BLUEBONNET

⇑ BLACK GOLD. Workers plug an oil well. Discovery of oil early in the 20th century transformed life in Texas. Today, the state leads the U.S. in oil and natural gas production.

Chamizal National Memorial

NEW MEXICO

U.S.
MEXICO
El Paso
GUADALUPE MTS. N.P.
YSLETA DEL SUR I.R.
Fabens
CHIHUAHUA
Rio Grande
ROCKY MTS.
+ Guadalupe Peak
8,749 ft
2,667 m
Highest point in Texas
Pecos
Davis Mts.
FORT DAVIS N.H.S.
Alpine
Marfa
Presidio
BIG
NATIO
PA

ROUNDUP

2011 data

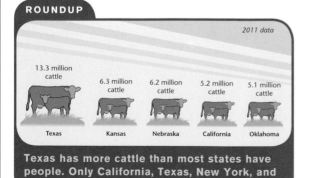

13.3 million cattle — Texas
6.3 million cattle — Kansas
6.2 million cattle — Nebraska
5.2 million cattle — California
5.1 million cattle — Oklahoma

Texas has more cattle than most states have people. Only California, Texas, New York, and Florida have larger human populations.

⇨ BORDERLAND RELIC. Los Ebanos Ferry, which takes its name from a grove of ebony trees growing nearby, is the last remaining government-licensed, hand-pulled ferry on any U.S. border. The privately owned ferry, near Mission, Texas, can carry three cars at a time across the Rio Grande.

THE REGION

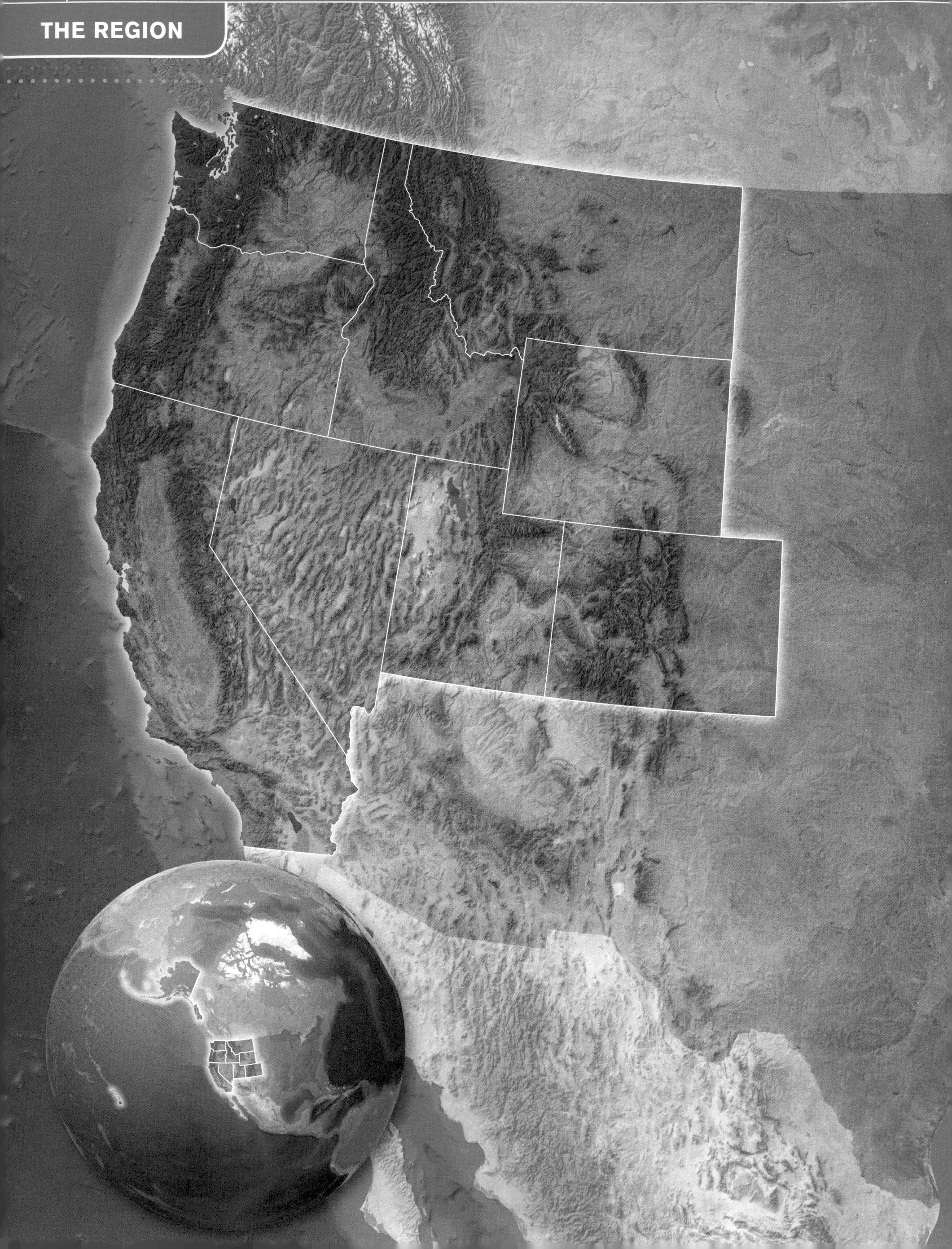

The West

PHYSICAL

Total area
1,635,555 sq mi
(4,236,083 sq km)

Highest point
Mount McKinley (Denali),
AK: 20,320 ft (6,194 m)

Lowest point
Death Valley, CA:
-282 ft (-86 m)

Longest rivers
Missouri, Yukon,
Rio Grande, Colorado

Largest lakes
Great Salt, Iliamna,
Becharof

Vegetation
Needleleaf, broadleaf, and mixed
forest; grassland; desert; tundra
(Alaska); tropical (Hawai'i)

Climate
Mild along the coast, with warm
summers and mild winters; semiarid
to arid inland; polar in parts of
Alaska; tropical in Hawai'i

POLITICAL

Total population
63,494,357

States (11):
Alaska, California, Colorado, Hawai'i,
Idaho, Montana, Nevada, Oregon,
Utah, Washington, Wyoming

Largest state
Alaska: 663,267 sq mi
(1,717,862 sq km)

Smallest state
Hawai'i: 10,931 sq mi (28,311 sq km)

Most populous state
California: 37,253,956

Least populous state
Wyoming: 563,626

Largest city proper
Los Angeles, CA: 3,792,621

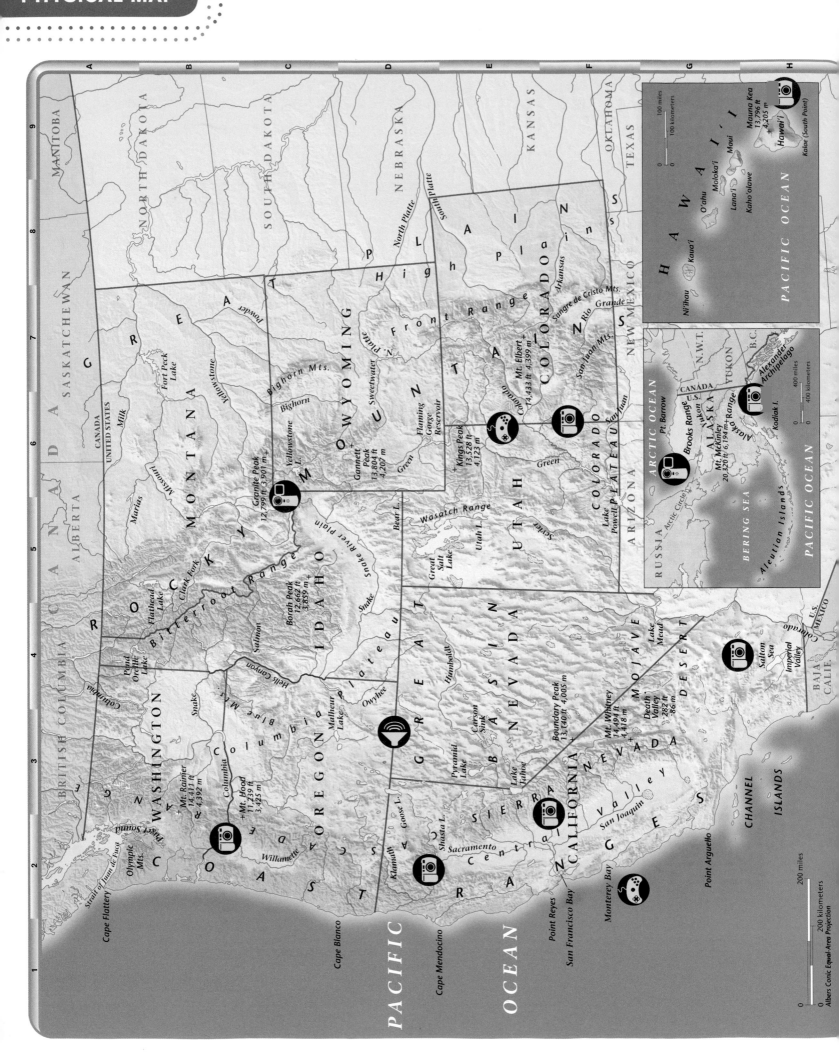

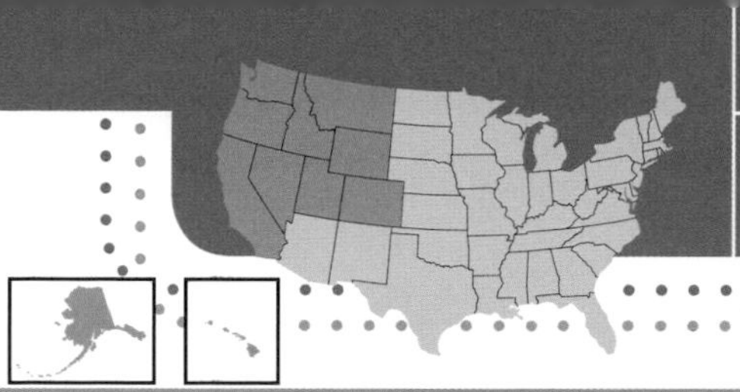

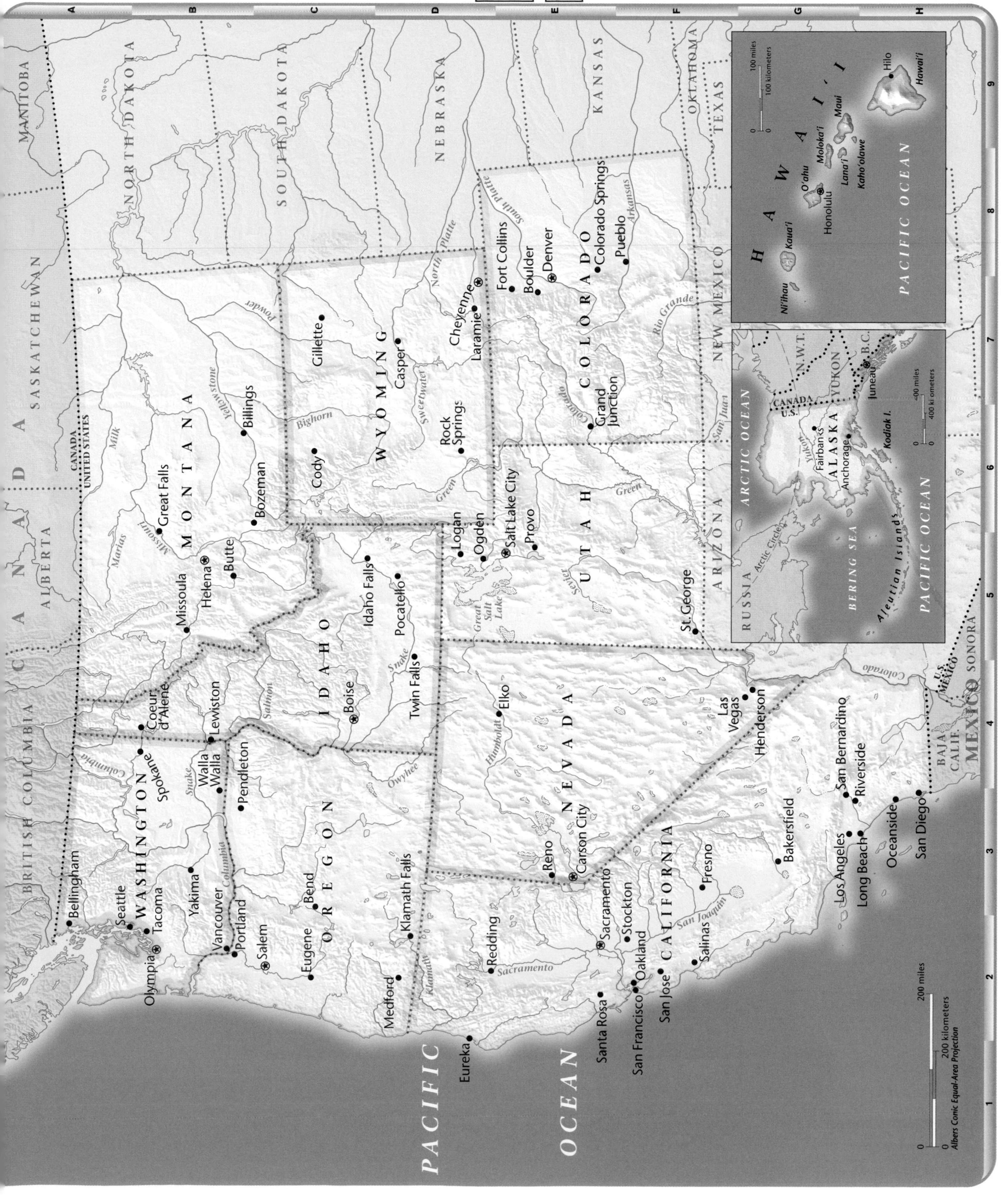

PACIFIC OCEAN

H A W A I ' I

100 miles
100 kilometers

Hilo
Hawai'i
Kaua'i
Ni'ihau
O'ahu
Moloka'i
Maui
Lana'i
Kaho'olawe
Honolulu

ARCTIC OCEAN

RUSSIA
CANADA
U.S.
N.W.T.
YUKON
B.C.
Juneau
Fairbanks
ALASKA
Anchorage
Yukon
Arctic Circle
Kodiak I.
BERING SEA
Aleutian Islands
PACIFIC OCEAN

400 miles
400 kilometers

MANITOBA
SASKATCHEWAN
ALBERTA
BRITISH COLUMBIA

C A N A D A
CANADA
UNITED STATES

NORTH DAKOTA
SOUTH DAKOTA
NEBRASKA
KANSAS
OKLAHOMA
TEXAS
NEW MEXICO

MONTANA
WYOMING
COLORADO
IDAHO
UTAH
ARIZONA
NEVADA
OREGON
CALIFORNIA
WASHINGTON

MEXICO
SONORA
BAJA CALIF.
U.S.
MEXICO

PACIFIC OCEAN

Milk
Missouri
Marias
Yellowstone
Powder
Bighorn
North Platte
South Platte
Arkansas
Rio Grande
San Juan
Colorado
Green
Sweetwater
Green
Snake
Salmon
Owyhee
Humboldt
Klamath
San Joaquin
Sacramento
Columbia
Snake
Great Salt Lake

Seattle
Tacoma
Olympia
Bellingham
Spokane
Yakima
Vancouver
Portland
Salem
Eugene
Bend
Medford
Klamath Falls
Redding
Eureka
Santa Rosa
San Francisco
Oakland
San Jose
Salinas
Fresno
Bakersfield
Los Angeles
Long Beach
Oceanside
San Diego
Riverside
San Bernardino
Henderson
Las Vegas
Carson City
Reno
Sacramento
Stockton
Elko
St. George
Boise
Idaho Falls
Pocatello
Twin Falls
Lewiston
Coeur d'Alene
Walla Walla
Pendleton
Missoula
Helena
Butte
Great Falls
Bozeman
Billings
Cody
Gillette
Casper
Cheyenne
Laramie
Rock Springs
Fort Collins
Boulder
Denver
Colorado Springs
Pueblo
Grand Junction
Salt Lake City
Ogden
Logan
Provo

200 miles
200 kilometers
Albers Conic Equal-Area Projection

⇨ OLD AND NEW. A cable car carries passengers on a steep hill in San Francisco. In the background modern buildings, including the Transamerica Pyramid, rise above older neighborhoods in this earthquake-prone city.

The West

THE HIGH FRONTIER

The western states, which make up almost half of the country's land area, have diverse landscapes and climates, ranging from the frozen heights of Denali, in Alaska, to the desolation of Death Valley, in California, and the lush, tropical islands of Hawai'i. More than half the region's population lives in California, and the Los Angeles metropolitan area is second only to New York City. Yet many parts of the region are sparsely populated, and much of the land is set aside as parkland and military bases. The region also faces many natural hazards—earthquakes, landslides, wild-fires, and even volcanic eruptions.

⇨ NORTHERN GIANT. Mount McKinley, called Denali—the "High One"—by native Athabascans, is North America's highest peak, rising more than 20,000 feet (6,100 m) in the Alaska Range. The same tectonic forces that trigger earthquakes in Alaska are slowly pushing this huge block of granite ever higher.

WHERE THE PICTURES ARE

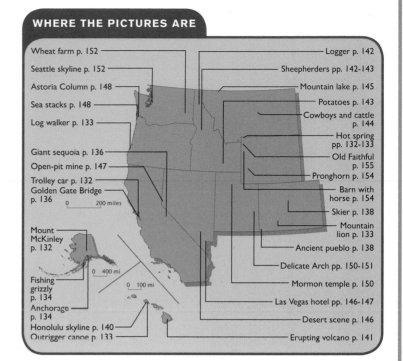

Wheat farm p. 152
Seattle skyline p. 152
Astoria Column p. 148
Sea stacks p. 148
Log walker p. 133
Giant sequoia p. 136
Open-pit mine p. 147
Trolley car p. 132
Golden Gate Bridge p. 136
Mount McKinley p. 132
Fishing grizzly p. 134
Anchorage p. 134
Honolulu skyline p. 140
Outrigger canoe p. 133

Logger p. 142
Sheepherders pp. 142-143
Mountain lake p. 145
Potatoes p. 143
Cowboys and cattle p. 144
Hot spring pp. 132-133
Old Faithful p. 155
Pronghorn p. 154
Barn with horse p. 154
Skier p. 138
Mountain lion p. 133
Ancient pueblo p. 138
Delicate Arch pp. 150-151
Mormon temple p. 150
Las Vegas hotel pp. 146-147
Desert scene p. 146
Erupting volcano p. 141

0   200 miles

0   400 mi

0   100 mi

⇧ ELUSIVE PREDATOR. Known by many names, including cougar and mountain lion, these big cats are found mainly in remote mountainous areas of the West, where they hunt deer and smaller animals.

⇦ STEAMY BATH. Colorful, mineral-rich hot springs are just one geothermal feature of Yellowstone National Park. Runoff from rain and snowmelt seeps into cracks in the ground, sinking to a depth of 10,000 feet (3,050 m), where it is heated by molten rock before rising back to the surface.

⇩ BALANCING ACT. For many years, rivers have been used to move logs from forest to market, taking advantage of the buoyancy of logs and the power of moving water. A logger stands on a floating log raft in Coos Bay, Oregon.

⇧ TRADITIONAL SAILING CRAFT. A Hawaiian outrigger canoe on Waikiki Beach promises fun in the surf for visitors to the 50th state. An important part of Polynesian culture, the canoes were once used to travel from island to island.

ALASKA

Alaska—from *Alyeska*, an Aleut word meaning "great land"—was purchased by the U.S. from Russia in 1867 for just two cents an acre. Many people thought it was a bad investment, but it soon paid off when gold was discovered, and again when major petroleum deposits were discovered in 1968. Today, an 800-mile-long pipeline (1,287 km) links North Slope oil fields to the ice-free port at Valdez, but opponents worry about long-term environmental impact.

Everything is big in Alaska. It is the largest state, with one-sixth of the country's land area; it has the highest peak in the U.S., Mt. McKinley (Denali); and the largest earthquake ever recorded in the U.S.—a 9.2 magnitude—occurred there in 1964. It is first in forestland, a leading source of seafood, and a major oil producer. Alaska's population includes a higher percentage of native people than that of any other state.

THE BASICS

STATS

Area
663,267 sq mi (1,717,862 sq km)

Population
710,231

Capital
Juneau
Population 31,275

Largest city
Anchorage
Population 291,826

Ethnic/racial groups
66.7% white; 14.8% Native American; 5.4% Asian; 3.3% African American. Hispanic (any race) 5.5%.

Industry
Petroleum products, government, services, trade

Agriculture
Shellfish, seafood, nursery stock, vegetables, dairy products, feed crops

Statehood
January 3, 1959; 49th state

GEO WHIZ

During the summer humpback whales migrate to Alaskan waters, where they work together to catch fish. While swimming in circles, the whales blow bubbles that form a net around schools of herring. Each whale can eat hundreds of fish in one gulp.

Global warming and population growth are changing the route of the Iditarod, the world's most famous sled-dog race. Since 2002 lack of snow in Wasilla has forced the starting point for the competition to move 30 miles (48 km) farther north to Willow.

The Tongass National Forest, where conservationists are battling to stop the harvesting of 1,000-year-old trees, is the largest national forest in the United States.

WILLOW PTARMIGAN
FORGET-ME-NOT

⇧ TIME FOR LUNCH. A grizzly bear wades into the rushing waters of Brooks Falls, in Katmai National Park, to catch a leaping salmon.

CHUKCHI SEA

RUSSIA

RUSSIA / U.S.

Bering Strait

Little Diomede I.

Cape Prince of Wales

only 2.5 miles from Russia

Nome

St. Lawrence I.

Yukon Delta

Emmonak

Mountain Village

St. Matthew I.
ALASKA MARITIME N.W.R.

Hooper Bay • YUKON

Nelson I.

NAT

WILD

Nunivak I.

B E R I N G

S E A

St. Paul
Pribilof Islands
ALASKA MARITIME N.W.R.

A L E U T I A N   I S L A N D S
IZEMBEK N.W.R.
Unimak I.
AL AS

Unalaska I.
Dutch Harbor
ALEUTIAN WORLD WAR II N.H.A.
Unalaska

Sanak I.

Umnak I.

Yunaska I.
Islands of Four Mountains

ALASKA   MARITIME   NATIONAL   WILDLIFE

⇐ NORTHERN METROPOLIS. Anchorage, established in 1915 as a construction port for the Alaska Railroad, sits in the shadow of the snow-covered Chugach Mountains.

ARCTIC OCEAN

Barrow • Point Barrow ← Northernmost point in the U.S.

BEAUFORT SEA

NUNAVUT

• Point Hope

Prudhoe Bay

ALASKA MARITIME N.W.R.

North Slope

ARCTIC

Meade
Utukok
Colville

NORTHWEST TERRITORIES

BROOKS RANGE

NOATAK N.W.&S.R.
NOATAK NAT. PRESERVE

CAPE KRUSENSTERN NATIONAL MONUMENT

SALMON N.W.&S.R.
KOBUK VALLEY N.P.

GATES OF THE ARCTIC NAT. PARK & PRESERVE

TINAYGUK N.W.&S.R.

IVISHAK N.W.&S.R.

NATIONAL

WILDLIFE

Killik
Savavanirktok

ALATNA N.W.&S.R.
KOYUKUK, NORTH FORK N.W.&S.R.

JOHN N.W.&S.R.

WIND N.W.&S.R.

REFUGE

SHEENJEK N.W.&S.R.

Porcupine

• Kotzebue

KOBUK N.W.&S.R.

SELAWIK NAT. WILDLIFE REF.
SELAWIK N.W.&S.R.
SELAWIK N.W.R.

ARCTIC CIRCLE

Lowest recorded temperature in the U.S. -80°F (-62°C)

YUKON FLATS
Fort Yukon •

KANUTI N.W.R.

NAT. WILDLIFE REF.

LARGEST STATE

BERING LAND BRIDGE NATIONAL PRESERVE

ward

insula

KOYUKUK N.W.R.

Koyukuk

Melozitna

TRANS-ALASKA PIPELINE

BEAVER CREEK N.W.&S.R.

BIRCH CREEK N.W.&S.R.

CHARLEY N.W.&S.R.

YUKON-CHARLEY RIVERS NAT. PRES.

CANADA
U.S.

Alaska

orton Sound

UNALAKLEET N.W.&S.R.

• Galena

INNOKO NAT.

NOWITNA N.W.R.

College •
Yukon

North Pole •

Fairbanks •

FORTYMILE N.W.&S.R.

From the western Aleutians to its southern panhandle, Alaska would extend from coast to coast in the lower 48 states.

• Unalakleet

WILDLIFE

NOWITNA N.W.&S.R.

NAT.

③

Tanana

Tok •

YUKON

Yukon

REFUGE

Aniak •

ANDREAFSKY N.W.&S.R.

TA Yukon

Kuskokwim Mountains

DENALI NATIONAL PARK & PRES.
Mt. McKinley (Denali) +
20,320 ft 6,194 m
Highest point in North America

ALASKA

N. Fk.

DELTA N.W.&S.R.

②

GULKANA N.W.&S.R.

TETLIN N.W.R.

200 miles
200 kilometers

Azimuthal Equidistant Projection

NAL

IDITAROD NATIONAL HISTORIC TRAIL

S. Fk.

RANGE

Susitna

①

Copper

WRANGELL-ST. ELIAS

NATIONAL

ALASKA HIGHWAY

KLONDIKE GOLD RUSH N.H.P.

• Bethel

UGE

MULCHATNA N.W.&S.R.

Wasilla •
• Palmer

Matanuska

Chugach Mts. PARK &

St. Elias Mountains

COAST MOUNTAINS

Skagway •
Haines •

CHILIKADROTNA N.W.&S.R.

LAKE CLARK NAT. PK. & PRESERVE

Anchorage •

Kenai •

Valdez •

PRESERVE

Mt. St. Elias
18,008 ft 5,489 m

BRITISH COLUMBIA

Dillingham •

TLIKAKILA N.W.&S.R.

Kenai
Peninsula

KENAI
KENAI N.W.R.

Cook Inlet

CHUGACH NAT. FOREST

Prince William Sound

Cordova •

MALASPINA GLACIER

TONGASS N.F.

GLACIER BAY NAT. PARK & PRESERVE

Juneau ★

Iliamna Lake

Seward •

Homer •

KENAI FJORDS NATIONAL PARK

Largest glacier in North America

Largest national forest in the U.S.

TONGASS

Chichagof I.
ALEXANDER

ADMIRALTY ISLAND N.M.

Petersburg •

• Naknek

KATMAI NAT. PARK & PRESERVE

KODIAK N.W.R.
Afognak Island

Capital of Russian America until 1867

Sitka •
SITKA N.H.P.

NATIONAL

Bristol
Bay

Becharof L.

BECHAROF N.W.R.

GULF OF ALASKA

Baranof I.

Wrangell •

MISTY FIORDS NAT. MON.

• Kodiak

ANIAKCHAK NAT. MON. & PRESERVE

KODIAK N.W.R.
Kodiak Island

ARCHIPELAGO

Prince of Wales I.

FOREST

Ketchikan •
ANNETTE ISLAND I.R.

REFUGE

ka Peninsula

ANIAKCHAK N.W.&S.R.

Trinity Islands

CANADA
U.S.

Dixon Entrance

Attu I. ALEUTIAN ISLANDS

NEAR IS.

ALASKA MARITIME NATIONAL WILDLIFE REFUGE

Yunaska I.

PACIFIC
OCEAN

Agattu I.

Kiska I.

RAT ISLANDS

Semisopochnoi Island

Tanaga
I.

Garelol I.

Atka I. • Amlia I.

ADAK NAVAL STATION

Adak I.

Seguam I.

ANDREANOF ISLANDS

Amchitka I.

Continuation of the Aleutian Islands at same scale as main map

---

Economy Symbols

Fishing	Vegetables	Mining	Hydro-electricity
Shellfish	Nursery stock	Coal	Food processing
Dairy cows/products	Timber/forest products	Oil/gas	Tourism

THE GOLDEN STATE:
CALIFORNIA

CALIFORNIA REPUBLIC

THE BASICS

STATS

Area
163,696 sq mi (423,972 sq km)

Population
37,253,956

Capital
Sacramento
Population 466,488

Largest city
Los Angeles
Population 3,792,621

Ethnic/racial groups
57.6% white; 13.0% Asian; 6.2% African American; 1.0% Native American. Hispanic (any race) 37.6%.

Industry
Electronic components and equipment, computers and computer software, tourism, food processing, entertainment, clothing

Agriculture
Fruits and vegetables, dairy products, cattle, forest products, commercial fishing

Statehood
September 9, 1850; 31st state

GEO WHIZ

Every December one of the largest gatherings of northern elephant seals in the world converges on the beaches of Año Nuevo State Reserve, south of San Francisco, to rest, mate, and give birth.

The Monterey Bay Aquarium has been working to save endangered sea otters for 20 years. Rescued animals that cannot be rehabilitated for re-release into the wild find a permanent home at the aquarium.

Castroville, known as the Artichoke Capital of the World, crowned future movie legend Marilyn Monroe its first-ever artichoke queen in 1947.

CALIFORNIA QUAIL
GOLDEN POPPY

CALIFORNIA

The coast of what is now California was visited by Spanish and English explorers in the mid-1500s, but colonization did not begin until 1769 when the first of 21 Spanish missions was established at San Diego. The missions, built to bring Christianity to the many native people living in the area, eventually extended up the coast as far as Sonoma along a road known as El Camino Real. The U.S. gained control of California in 1847, following a war with Mexico. The next year gold was discovered near Sutter's Mill, triggering a gold rush and migration from the eastern U.S. and around the world. Today, California is the most populous state, and its economy ranks above that of most of the world's countries. It is a major source of fruits, nuts, and vegetables, accounting for more than half of the U.S. output. The state is an industrial leader, producing jet aircraft, ships, and high-tech equipment. It is also a center for the entertainment industry.

⇧ ENGINEERING WONDER. Stretching more than a mile (1.6 km) across the entrance to San Francisco Bay, the Golden Gate Bridge opened to traffic in 1937. The bridge is painted vermilion orange, a color chosen in part because it is visible in fog.

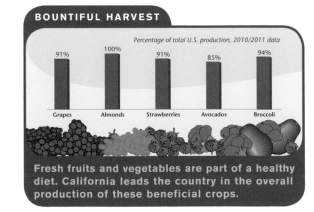

BOUNTIFUL HARVEST

Percentage of total U.S. production, 2010/2011 data

Grapes	Almonds	Strawberries	Avocados	Broccoli
91%	100%	91%	85%	94%

Fresh fruits and vegetables are part of a healthy diet. California leads the country in the overall production of these beneficial crops.

⇦ FOREST GIANT. Sequoias in Yosemite National Park's Mariposa Grove exceed 200 feet (61 m), making them the world's tallest trees. The trees, some of which are 3,000 years old, grow in isolated groves on the western slopes of the Sierra Nevada.

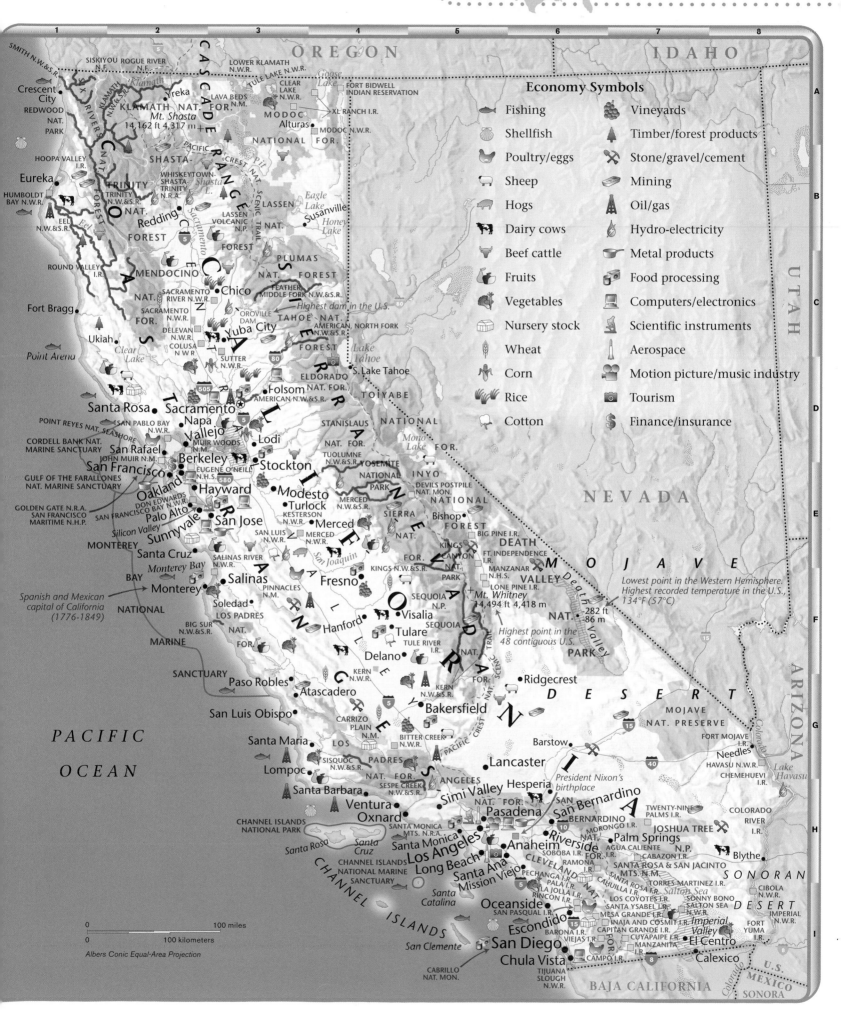

Economy Symbols

- Fishing
- Shellfish
- Poultry/eggs
- Sheep
- Hogs
- Dairy cows
- Beef cattle
- Fruits
- Vegetables
- Nursery stock
- Wheat
- Corn
- Rice
- Cotton
- Vineyards
- Timber/forest products
- Stone/gravel/cement
- Mining
- Oil/gas
- Hydro-electricity
- Metal products
- Food processing
- Computers/electronics
- Scientific instruments
- Aerospace
- Motion picture/music industry
- Tourism
- Finance/insurance

OREGON · IDAHO · UTAH · NEVADA · ARIZONA

PACIFIC OCEAN

Crescent City · Yreka · Mt. Shasta 14,162 ft 4,317 m · Alturas · Modoc
REDWOOD NAT. PARK · KLAMATH NAT. FOR. · LAVA BEDS N.M. · MODOC NATIONAL FOR.
HOOPA VALLEY I.R. · SHASTA-TRINITY NAT. FOREST · FORT BIDWELL INDIAN RESERVATION · XL RANCH I.R.
Eureka · WHISKEYTOWN-SHASTA-TRINITY N.R.A. · LASSEN NAT. FOREST · Susanville
HUMBOLDT BAY N.W.R. · Redding · LASSEN VOLCANIC N.P. · Honey Lake · Eagle Lake
EEL N.W.&S.R. · Eagle Lake
ROUND VALLEY I.R. · MENDOCINO NAT. FOR. · Chico · PLUMAS NAT. FOREST
Fort Bragg · SACRAMENTO RIVER N.W.R. · Highest dam in the U.S. · FEATHER MIDDLE FORK N.W.&S.R.
Ukiah · Clear Lake · Yuba City · OROVILLE DAM · TAHOE NAT. FOREST
Point Arena · DELEVAN N.W.R. · COLUSA N.W.R. · AMERICAN, NORTH FORK N.W.&S.R.
Santa Rosa · Sacramento · Napa · SUTTER N.W.R. · Lake Tahoe · S. Lake Tahoe
POINT REYES NAT. SEASHORE · Vallejo · Lodi · ELDORADO NAT. FOR. · TOIYABE
CORDELL BANK NAT. MARINE SANCTUARY · San Rafael · MUIR WOODS N.M. · STANISLAUS NAT. FOR. · Mono Lake
JOHN MUIR N.M. · Berkeley · EUGENE O'NEILL N.H.S. · TUOLUMNE N.W.&S.R. · INYO NATIONAL FOR.
GULF OF THE FARALLONES NAT. MARINE SANCTUARY · San Francisco · YOSEMITE NATIONAL PARK · DEVILS POSTPILE NAT. MON.
GOLDEN GATE N.R.A. SAN FRANCISCO MARITIME N.H.P. · Oakland · Hayward · Modesto · MERCED N.W.&S.R. · NATIONAL
DON EDWARDS SAN FRANCISCO BAY N.W.R. · Palo Alto · Turlock · KESTERSON N.W.R. · SIERRA NAT. · Bishop · FOREST
Silicon Valley · Sunnyvale · San Jose · Merced · MERCED N.W.R. · San Joaquin · DEATH VALLEY
MONTEREY · Santa Cruz · SALINAS RIVER N.W.R. · KINGS CANYON NAT. PARK · FT. INDEPENDENCE I.R. · MANZANAR N.H.S.
Monterey Bay · PINNACLES N.M. · Salinas · Fresno · KINGS N.W.&S.R. · BIG PINE I.R. · LONE PINE I.R.
Spanish and Mexican capital of California (1776-1849) · Monterey · Soledad · SEQUOIA N.P. · Mt. Whitney 14,494 ft 4,418 m
NATIONAL · LOS PADRES · Visalia · SEQUOIA NAT. FOR. · Lowest point in the Western Hemisphere. Highest recorded temperature in the U.S. 134°F (57°C)
MARINE · BIG SUR NAT. FOR. · Hanford · Tulare · TULE RIVER I.R. · Highest point in the 48 contiguous U.S. · -282 ft -86 m
SANCTUARY · Paso Robles · Delano · KERN N.W.R. · MOJAVE · DESERT · Ridgecrest
Atascadero · CARRIZO PLAIN N.M. · Bakersfield · KERN N.W.&S.R. · MOJAVE NAT. PRESERVE
San Luis Obispo · BITTER CREEK N.W.R. · Barstow · FORT MOJAVE I.R. · Needles
Santa Maria · LOS PADRES NAT. FOR. · LOS ANGELES · Lancaster · HAVASU N.W.R. · CHEMEHUEVI I.R.
Lompoc · SISQUOC N.W.&S.R. · Hesperia · President Nixon's birthplace · Lake Havasu
Santa Barbara · SESPE CREEK N.W.&S.R. · Simi Valley · San Bernardino · TWENTY-NINE PALMS I.R. · COLORADO RIVER · Blythe
Ventura · Oxnard · SANTA MONICA N.R.A. · Pasadena · San Bernardino · JOSHUA TREE N.P. · MORONGO I.R.
CHANNEL ISLANDS NATIONAL PARK · Santa Monica · Los Angeles · Anaheim · Riverside · Palm Springs · AGUA CALIENTE I.R. · CABAZON I.R.
Santa Rosa · Santa Cruz · Long Beach · Santa Ana · Mission Viejo · CLEVELAND NAT. FOR. · SANTA ROSA & SAN JACINTO MTS. N.M. · SOBOBA I.R. · RAMONA · PECHANGA I.R. · PALA I.R.
CHANNEL ISLANDS NATIONAL MARINE SANCTUARY · Santa Catalina · Oceanside · SAN LUIS REY I.R. · RINCON I.R. · LA JOLLA I.R. · TORRES-MARTINEZ I.R. · SALTON SEA · SONNY BONO SALTON SEA N.W.R.
Santa Rosa · SAN PASQUAL I.R. · Escondido · Salton Sea · Imperial Valley · CIBOLA N.W.R. · IMPERIAL N.W.R.
CHANNEL ISLANDS · San Clemente · San Diego · Chula Vista · El Centro · Calexico
CABRILLO NAT. MON. · TIJUANA SLOUGH N.W.R. · Colorado · FORT YUMA I.R.
BAJA CALIFORNIA · MEXICO · SONORA · U.S.

0 — 100 miles
0 — 100 kilometers
Albers Conic Equal-Area Projection

THE BASICS

STATS

Area
104,094 sq mi (269,602 sq km)

Population
5,029,196

Capital
Denver
Population 600,158

Largest city
Denver
Population 600,158

Ethnic/racial groups
81.3% white; 4.0% African American;
2.8% Asian; 1.1% Native American.
Hispanic (any race) 20.7%.

Industry
Real estate, government, durable
goods, communications, health and
other services, nondurable goods,
transportation

Agriculture
Cattle, corn, wheat, dairy products, hay

Statehood
August 1, 1876; 38th state

GEO WHIZ

The Black Canyon of the Gunnison is
one of the newest national parks
in the Rockies. As it flows through
the canyon, the Gunnison River
drops an average of 95 feet (29 m)
per mile—one of the steepest descents
in North America. The craggy rock walls
are a mecca for rock climbers.

Colorado's lynx population is making
a comeback, thanks to a program
that releases wild
cats captured in
Canada into
Colorado's
southern Rockies.
Since the program began in
1999, more than 200 cats have
been released and at least
141 lynx kittens have
been born.

LARK BUNTING
COLUMBINE

COLORADO

Indians were the earliest inhab-itants of present-day Colorado. Some were cliff dwellers; others were plains dwellers. Spanish explorers arrived in Colorado in 1541. In 1803 eastern Colorado became U.S. territory as part of the Louisiana Purchase. Gold was discovered in 1858, and thou-sands were attracted by the prospect of quick wealth. The sudden jump in population led to conflict with native Cheyennes and Arapahos over control of the land, but the settlers prevailed. Completion of the transcontinental railroad in 1869 helped link Colorado to the eastern states and opened its doors for growth. Cattle ranching and farming developed on the High Plains of eastern Colorado, while the mountainous western part of the state focused on mining. Today, mining is still important in Colorado, but the focus has shifted to energy resources—oil, natu-ral gas, and coal. Agriculture is also an important source of income, with cattle accounting for almost half of farm income. And Colorado's majestic moun-tains attract thousands of tourists each year.

⇧ THRILLING SPORT.
Colorado's snow-covered
mountains attract winter
sports enthusiasts from
near and far. In the past
skis were used by gold
prospectors. Today, skiing
and snowboarding are
big moneymakers in the
state's recreation and
tourism industry.

⇦ ANCIENT CULTURE. Ancestral Puebloans lived from about
A.D. 600 to A.D. 1300 in the canyons that today are a part of Mesa
Verde National Park. More than 600 stone structures were built
on protected cliffs of the canyon walls; others were located on
mesas. These dwellings hold many clues to a past way of life.

BROWNS
PARK
N.W.R.

DINOSAUR

NATIONAL

MONUMENT

Rangely   White

UTAH

Grand Valley

70

COLORADO
NAT. MON.   Grand
Junction
GRAND
MESA N.F.

Roan Plateau

Dolores

MANTI-
LA SAL
N.F.

UNC

Uncompahgre

San Miguel

N.

CANYONS OF
THE ANCIENTS
N.M.

SA

HOVENWEEP
N.M.   Cortez

YUCCA HOUSE   MESA
N.M.   VERDE
N.P.

UTE MOUNTAIN I.R.

FOUR
CORNERS

ARIZONA   Only spot in the U.S.
where the borders of
4 states come together

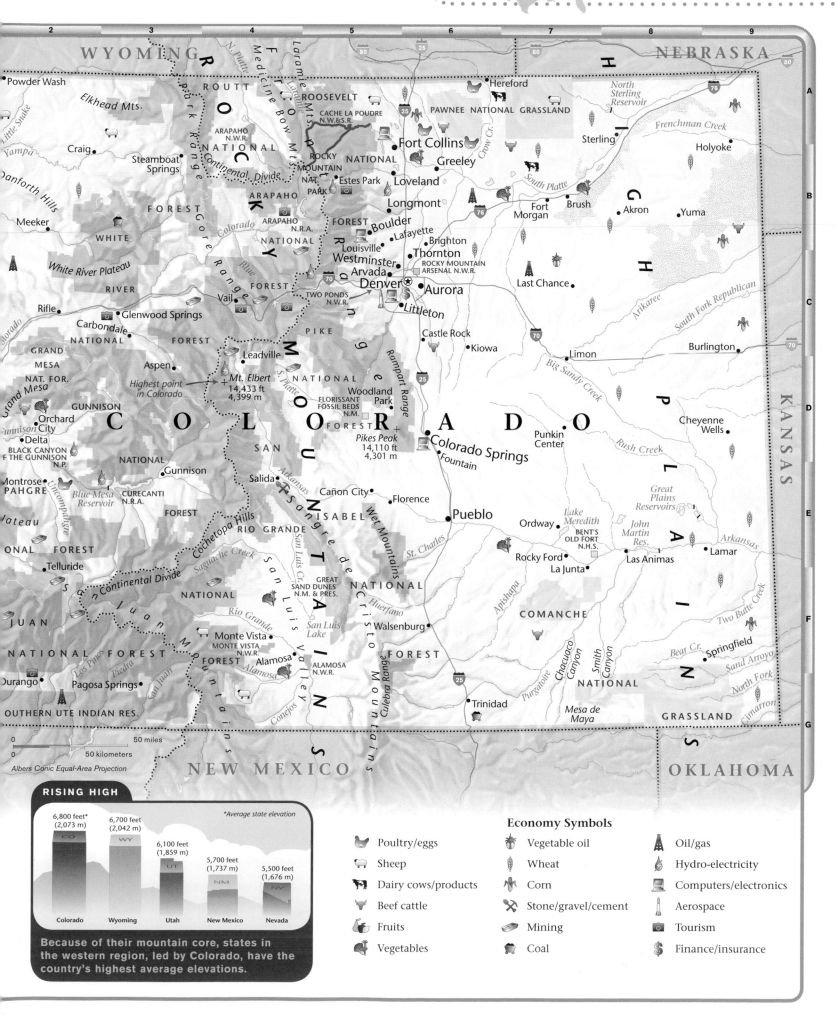

RISING HIGH

6,800 feet* (2,073 m) — Colorado
6,700 feet (2,042 m) — Wyoming
6,100 feet (1,859 m) — Utah
5,700 feet (1,737 m) — New Mexico
5,500 feet (1,676 m) — Nevada

*Average state elevation

Because of their mountain core, states in the western region, led by Colorado, have the country's highest average elevations.

Economy Symbols

- Poultry/eggs
- Sheep
- Dairy cows/products
- Beef cattle
- Fruits
- Vegetables
- Vegetable oil
- Wheat
- Corn
- Stone/gravel/cement
- Mining
- Coal
- Oil/gas
- Hydro-electricity
- Computers/electronics
- Aerospace
- Tourism
- Finance/insurance

HAWAI'I

Some 1,500 years ago, Polynesians traveling in large canoes arrived from the south to settle the volcanic islands that make up Hawai'i. In 1778 Captain James Cook claimed the islands for Britain, and soon Hawai'i became a center of the whaling industry and a major producer of sugarcane. The spread of sugarcane plantations led to the importation of workers from Asia. Hawai'i became a U.S. territory in 1900. Naval installations, established as fueling depots and to protect U.S. interests in the Pacific, were attacked by the Japanese in 1941, an act that officially brought the U.S. into World War II. In 1959 Hawai'i became the 50th state. Tourism, agriculture, and the military, with bases centered on O'ahu's Pearl Harbor, are the cornerstone of Hawai'i's economy today. Jet airline service makes the distant islands accessible to tourists from both the mainland U.S. and Asia as well as from Australia and New Zealand. Hawai'i is still a major producer of sugarcane, along with nursery products and pineapples.

⇧ ISLAND PARADISE. High-rise hotels light up Waikiki, the center of Honolulu's tourist industry. Thousands of visitors flock to the islands each year to enjoy the warm climate, sandy beaches, and rich, multicultural heritage of Hawai'i.

THE BASICS

STATS

Area
10,931 sq mi (28,311 sq km)

Population
1,360,301

Capital
Honolulu
Population 337,256

Largest city
Honolulu
Population 337,256

Ethnic/racial groups
38.6% Asian; 24.7% white; 10.0% Hawaiian/Pacific Islander; 1.6% African American. Hispanic (any race) 10.5%.

Industry
Tourism, trade, finance, food processing, petroleum refining, stone, clay, glass products

Agriculture
Sugarcane, pineapples, nursery stock, tropical fruit, livestock, macadamia nuts

Statehood
August 21, 1959; 50th state

GEO WHIZ

The shallow waters off the coast of Hawai'i are home to some of the world's most interesting sea creatures: marine worms. They were among the first sea animals more than 500 million years ago.

Hawai'i is the most isolated population center on Earth. It is more than 2,300 miles (3,700 km) from California, 3,850 miles (6,196 km) from Japan, and 4,900 miles (7,886 km) from China.

Everywhere else in the world caterpillars feed on plants. In Hawai'i there are 20 species that eat meat. Scientists have recorded the world's only known carnivorous caterpillars munching on ants.

You can ski two different ways on the same day in Hawai'i: on water at the beach and on snow on the slopes of Mauna Kea, a 13,796-foot-high volcano (4,205 m) on the Big Island.

HAWAIIAN GOOSE (NENE)

HIBISCUS

DANGER FROM BELOW

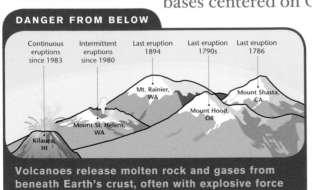

| Continuous eruptions since 1983 | Intermittent eruptions since 1980 | Last eruption 1894 | Last eruption 1790s | Last eruption 1786 |

Mt. Rainier, WA
Mount Shasta, CA
Mount Hood, OR
Mount St. Helens, WA
Kilauea, HI

Volcanoes release molten rock and gases from beneath Earth's crust, often with explosive force that can put people and property at great risk.

One of the world's rainiest spots

KAUA'I
Princeville
KILAUEA POINT N.W.R.
HANALEI N.W.R.
Wai'ale'ale 5,148 ft 1,569 m
Kapa'a
Hanama'ulu
Lehua I.
Kekaha
Lihu'e
Pu'uwai
Kalaheo
NI'IHAU
Kaulakahi Channel

Midway Islands
Kure Atoll
Pearl and Hermes Atoll
Lisianski I.
Laysan I.
NORTHWESTERN HAW
Mar Ree

0   400 miles
0   400 kilometers
Oblique Mercator Projection

1   2

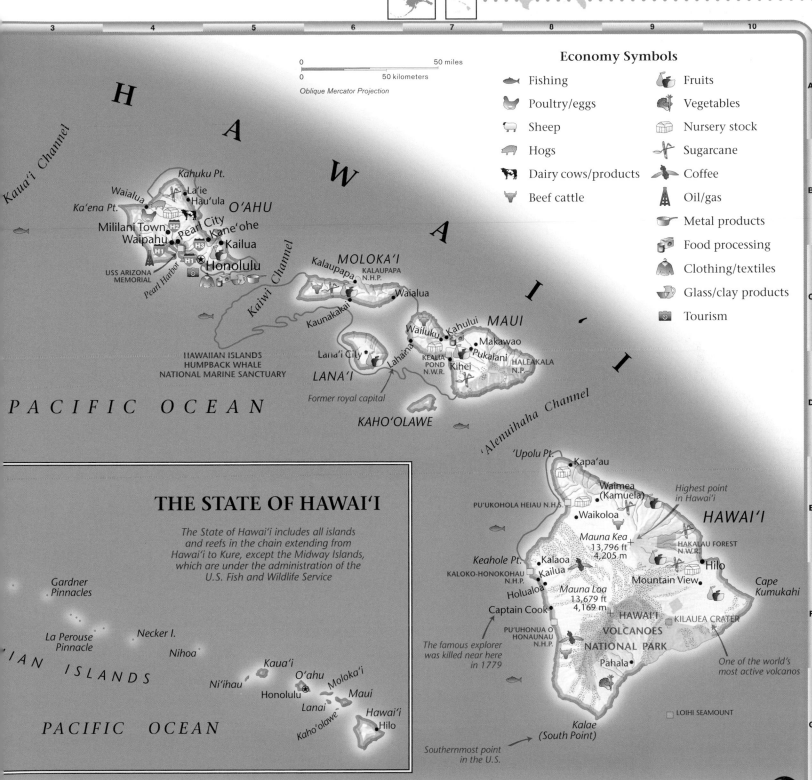

0 ——— 50 miles
0 ——— 50 kilometers
Oblique Mercator Projection

Economy Symbols

🐟 Fishing		🍎 Fruits	
🐔 Poultry/eggs		🥬 Vegetables	
🐑 Sheep		Nursery stock	
🐖 Hogs		Sugarcane	
🐄 Dairy cows/products		Coffee	
🐂 Beef cattle		Oil/gas	
		Metal products	
		Food processing	
		Clothing/textiles	
		Glass/clay products	
		📷 Tourism	

H A W A I ' I

Kaua'i Channel

Kahuku Pt.
Waialua
La'ie
Ka'ena Pt.
Hau'ula
O'AHU
Mililani Town
Pearl City
Kane'ohe
Waipahu
Kailua
Honolulu
USS ARIZONA
MEMORIAL
Pearl Harbor

Kaiwi Channel
Kalaupapa
MOLOKA'I
KALAUPAPA
N.H.P.
Kaunakakai
Waialua

Moloka'i Channel

Kahului
Wailuku
MAUI
Makawao
Lana'i City
Pukalani
Lahaina
KEALIA
POND
N.W.R.
Kihei
HALEAKALA
N.P.
LANA'I
Former royal capital

HAWAIIAN ISLANDS
HUMPBACK WHALE
NATIONAL MARINE SANCTUARY

P A C I F I C   O C E A N

KAHO'OLAWE

'Alenuihaha Channel

'Upolu Pt.
Kapa'au
Waimea
(Kamuela)
Highest point
in Hawai'i
PU'UKOHOLA HEIAU N.H.S.
Waikoloa
HAWAI'I
Mauna Kea
13,796 ft
4,205 m
HAKALAU FOREST
N.W.R.
Keahole Pt.
Kalaoa
Kailua
Hilo
KALOKO-HONOKOHAU
N.H.P.
Mountain View
Cape
Kumukahi
Holualoa
Mauna Loa
13,679 ft
4,169 m
Captain Cook
HAWAI'I
VOLCANOES
PU'UHONUA O
HONAUNAU
N.H.P.
NATIONAL PARK
KILAUEA CRATER
The famous explorer
was killed near here
in 1779
Pahala
One of the world's
most active volcanos

LOIHI SEAMOUNT

Kalae
(South Point)
Southernmost point
in the U.S.

THE STATE OF HAWAI'I

*The State of Hawai'i includes all islands
and reefs in the chain extending from
Hawai'i to Kure, except the Midway Islands,
which are under the administration of the
U.S. Fish and Wildlife Service*

Gardner
Pinnacles

La Perouse
Pinnacle

Necker I.

Nihoa

...IAN   ISLANDS

Kaua'i
Ni'ihau
O'ahu
Moloka'i
Honolulu
Maui
Lanai
Kaho'olawe
Hawai'i
Hilo

P A C I F I C   O C E A N

⇨ **FIERY CREATION.** Hawai'i is the fastest-
growing state in the U.S.—not in people,
but in land. Active volcanoes are constantly
creating new land as lava continues to flow.
The Pu'u 'O'o vent on Kīlauea has added
more than 568 acres (230 ha) of new land
since it began erupting in 1983.

IDAHO

THE BASICS

STATS

Area
83,570 sq mi (216,447 sq km)

Population
1,567,582

Capital
Boise
Population 205,671

Largest city
Boise
Population 205,671

Ethnic/racial groups
89.1% white; 1.4% Native American; 1.2% Asian; .6% African American. Hispanic (any race) 11.2%.

Industry
Electronics and computer equipment, tourism, food processing, forest products, mining, chemicals

Agriculture
Potatoes, dairy products, cattle, wheat, alfalfa hay, sugar beets, barley, trout

Statehood
July 3, 1890; 43rd state

GEO WHIZ

Before the last ice age, mammoths, woolly rhinos, giant ground sloths, and other huge mammal species roamed what is now Idaho. Fossils of these prehistoric creatures are on display at the Museum of Idaho, in Idaho Falls.

Wood duck chicks born in Idaho and other Rocky Mountain states undergo an amazing rite of passage the day after they are born. If they want to eat, they have to jump as much as 60 feet (18 m) from their tree-hole nest to the water below, where their mother waits for them.

In preparation for their mission to the Moon, Apollo astronauts visited Craters of the Moon National Monument to study its volcanic geology and experience firsthand its harsh environment.

MOUNTAIN BLUEBIRD
SYRINGA (MOCK ORANGE)

Some of the earliest Native American sites in what is now Idaho date back 10,000 to 12,000 years. In the 18th and early 19th centuries, contact between native people and Europeans brought not only trade and cultural change but also diseases that wiped out many native groups. Present-day Idaho was part of the 1803 Louisiana Purchase, and in 1805 it was explored during the famous Lewis and Clark expedition. In 1843 wagons crossed into Idaho on the Oregon Trail. The arrival of white settlers brought conflict with the Indians, which continued until 1890 when Idaho became a state. Today, farming plays an important role in Idaho's economy. More than one-fifth of the land is planted with crops, especially wheat, sugar beets, barley, and potatoes. The state supports the use of alternative sources of energy, including geo-thermal, ethanol, wind, and biomass. The economy has diversified to include manufacturing and high-tech industries. The state's rugged natural beauty also attracts tourists year-round.

⇧ WOOLLY RUSH HOUR. Sheep fill a roadway in Idaho's Salmon River Valley. The herds move twice a year. In the spring they migrate north to mountain pastures. In the fall they return to the Snake River plains in the south.

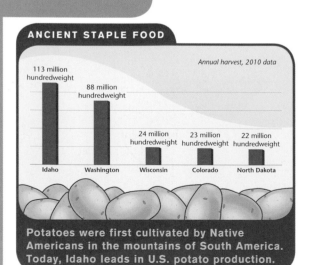

ANCIENT STAPLE FOOD

Annual harvest, 2010 data

113 million hundredweight — Idaho
88 million hundredweight — Washington
24 million hundredweight — Wisconsin
23 million hundredweight — Colorado
22 million hundredweight — North Dakota

Potatoes were first cultivated by Native Americans in the mountains of South America. Today, Idaho leads in U.S. potato production.

⇧ TIMBER! More than 40 percent of Idaho's land area is tree-covered, much of it in national forests. Lumber and paper products, most of which are sold to other states, are important to the state economy.

↓ ROLLING SPUDS. Growing more than 30 varieties of potatoes, Idaho leads the country in production of this staple food crop. About 60 percent of all potatoes grown in the state end up as french fries. Much of the rest goes to fresh-food markets and for making chips.

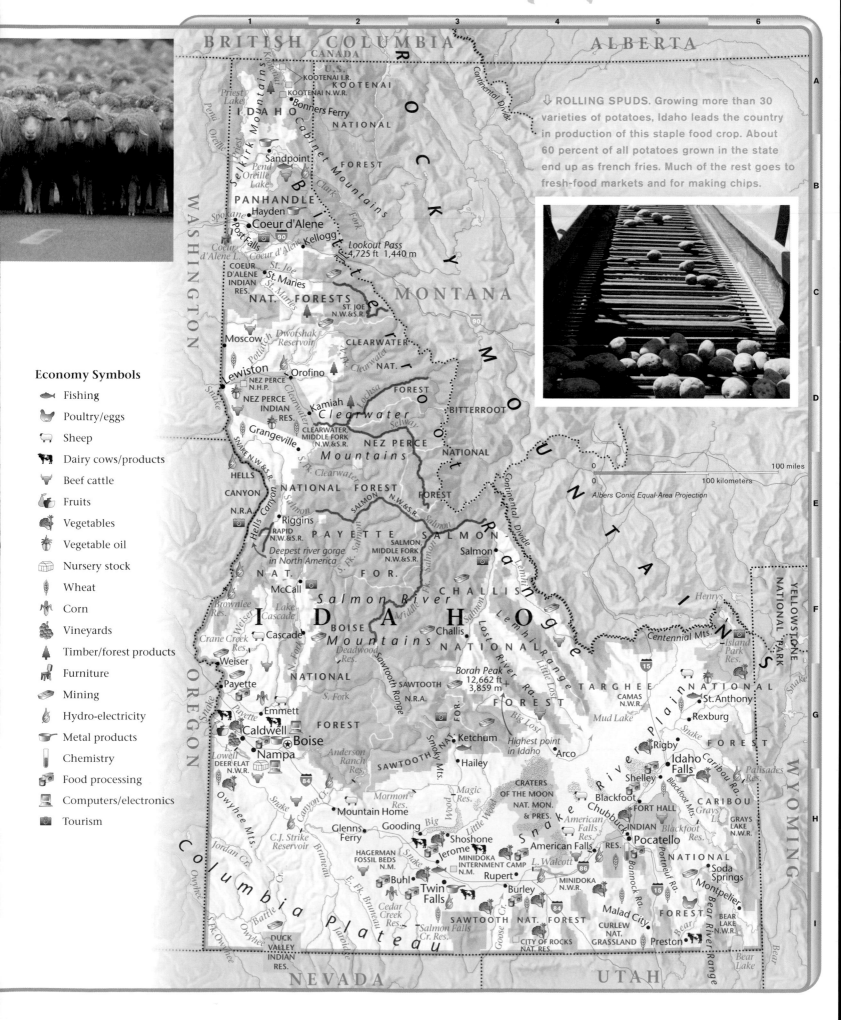

Economy Symbols

- 🐟 Fishing
- 🐓 Poultry/eggs
- 🐑 Sheep
- 🐄 Dairy cows/products
- 🐂 Beef cattle
- 🍑 Fruits
- 🥬 Vegetables
- 🌽 Vegetable oil
- 🏺 Nursery stock
- 🌾 Wheat
- 🌽 Corn
- 🍇 Vineyards
- 🌲 Timber/forest products
- 🪑 Furniture
- ⛏ Mining
- 💧 Hydro-electricity
- 🍳 Metal products
- 🧪 Chemistry
- 📦 Food processing
- 💻 Computers/electronics
- 🏛 Tourism

Map labels

BRITISH COLUMBIA — ALBERTA
CANADA / U.S.
WASHINGTON
OREGON
MONTANA
WYOMING
NEVADA — UTAH
IDAHO

Priest Lake, Kootenai I.R., KOOTENAI N.W.R., Bonners Ferry, KOOTENAI NATIONAL FOREST, Selkirk Mountains, Cabinet Mountains, Pend Oreille Lake, Sandpoint, PANHANDLE, Hayden, Coeur d'Alene, Post Falls, Kellogg, Lookout Pass 4,725 ft 1,440 m, Coeur d'Alene L., St. Joe, St. Maries, COEUR D'ALENE INDIAN RES., NAT. FORESTS, ST. JOE N.W.&S.R., Moscow, Dworshak Reservoir, CLEARWATER NAT. FOREST, BITTERROOT, Lewiston, Orofino, Kamiah, NEZ PERCE N.H.P., NEZ PERCE INDIAN RES., Clearwater Mountains, NEZ PERCE NATIONAL, Grangeville, CLEARWATER, MIDDLE FORK N.W.&S.R., S. Fk. Clearwater, HELLS CANYON N.R.A., NATIONAL FOREST, SALMON N.W.&S.R., Riggins, RAPID N.W.&S.R., Deepest river gorge in North America, PAYETTE, SALMON, MIDDLE FORK N.W.&S.R., Salmon, CHALLIS, McCall, Salmon River, BOISE, Challis, NATIONAL, Brownlee Res., Lake Cascade, Cascade, Deadwood Res., Sawtooth Range, Crane Creek Res., Weiser, Payette, SAWTOOTH N.R.A., Borah Peak 12,662 ft 3,859 m, Emmett, Caldwell, Boise, Nampa, DEER FLAT N.W.R., Anderson Ranch Res., Ketchum, Highest point in Idaho, Arco, Hailey, Smoky Mts., Mormon Res., Magic Res., Mountain Home, Gooding, Glenns Ferry, C.J. Strike Reservoir, CRATERS OF THE MOON NAT. MON. & PRES., Shoshone, Jerome, HAGERMAN FOSSIL BEDS N.M., MINIDOKA INTERNMENT CAMP N.M., Rupert, Buhl, Twin Falls, Burley, Cedar Creek Res., Salmon Falls Cr. Res., SAWTOOTH NAT. FOREST, CITY OF ROCKS NAT. RES., DUCK VALLEY INDIAN RES., American Falls Res., L. Walcott, MINIDOKA N.W.R., Chubbuck, Pocatello, FORT HALL INDIAN RES., American Falls, CAMAS N.W.R., St. Anthony, Rexburg, Mud Lake, Rigby, Idaho Falls, Shelley, Blackfoot, Soda Springs, Montpelier, Malad City, Preston, CURLEW NAT. GRASSLAND, TARGHEE NATIONAL FOREST, CARIBOU NATIONAL FOREST, GRAYS LAKE N.W.R., BEAR LAKE N.W.R., Bear Lake, YELLOWSTONE NATIONAL PARK, Island Park Res., Centennial Mts., Henrys, Palisades Res., Grays L., Bear River Range

ROCKY MOUNTAINS, Bitterroot Mountains, Continental Divide, Lemhi Range, Lost River Range, Snake River Plain, Columbia Plateau, Owyhee Mts., Jordan Cr., Bruneau

0 — 100 miles
0 — 100 kilometers
Albers Conic Equal-Area Projection

MONTANA

THE BASICS

STATS

Area
147,042 sq mi (380,840 sq km)

Population
989,415

Capital
Helena
Population 28,190

Largest city
Billings
Population 104,170

Ethnic/racial groups
89.4% white; 6.3% Native American
.6% Asian; .4% African American.
Hispanic (any race) 2.9%.

Industry
Forest products, food processing,
mining, construction, tourism

Agriculture
Wheat, cattle, barley, hay, sugar beets,
dairy products

Statehood
November 8, 1889; 41st state

GEO WHIZ

The fossil of a dinosaur about the size
of a large turkey is being called the
missing link between Asian and
North American horned dinosaurs.
Paleontologist Jack Horner,
who served as the model for
the character of Alan Grant in the
Jurassic Park movies, discovered the
fossil while sitting on it during a lunch
break at a dig near Choteau.

Montana is the only state with river systems that empty into the Gulf of Mexico,
Hudson Bay, and the Pacific Ocean.

Grasshopper Glacier is
littered with the bodies of
thousands of grasshoppers
that became trapped in the
ice sometime before the
species became extinct
200 years ago.

WESTERN MEADOWLARK
BITTERROOT

MONTANA

Long before the arrival of Europeans, numerous native groups lived and hunted in the plains and mountains of present-day Montana. While contact between European explorers and Native Americans was often peaceful, Montana was the site of the historic 1876 Battle of the Little Bighorn, in which Lakota (Sioux) and Cheyenne warriors defeated George Armstrong Custer's troops. In the mid-19th century the discovery of gold and silver attracted many prospectors, and later cattle ranching became big business, adding to tensions with the Indians. Montana became the 41st state in 1889. Today, Indians still make up more than 6 percent of the state's population—only four other states have a larger percent. Agriculture is an important part of the economy, producing wheat, hay, and barley as well as beef cattle. Mining and timber industries have seen a decline, but service industries and tourism are growing. Montana's natural environment, including Glacier and Yellowstone National Parks, remains one of its greatest resources.

⬆ STEP BACK IN TIME. Just like in the past, Montana ranchers move their cattle herds from low winter pastures to higher elevations for summer grazing. Some ranches allow adventurous tourists to participate in the drives.

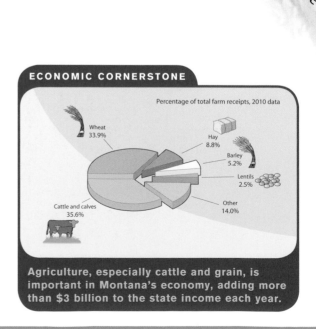

ECONOMIC CORNERSTONE

Percentage of total farm receipts, 2010 data

Wheat 33.9%
Hay 8.8%
Barley 5.2%
Lentils 2.5%
Other 14.0%
Cattle and calves 35.6%

Agriculture, especially cattle and grain, is important in Montana's economy, adding more than $3 billion to the state income each year.

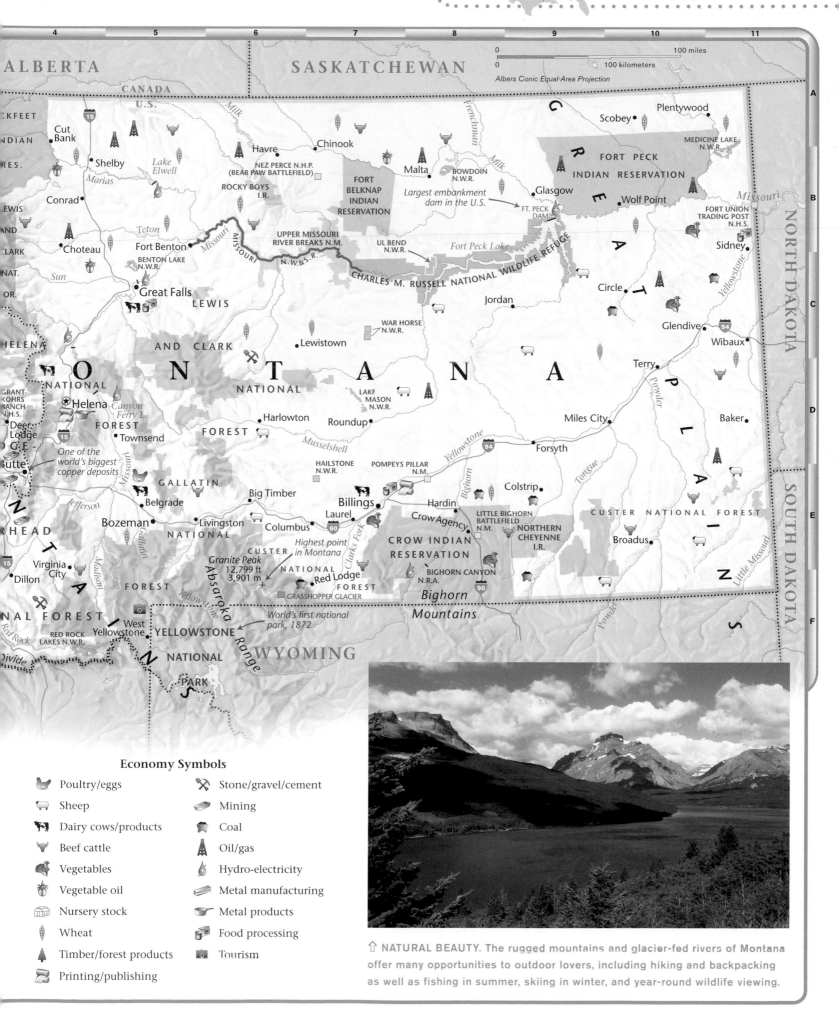

ALBERTA

SASKATCHEWAN

0   100 miles
0   100 kilometers
Albers Conic Equal-Area Projection

CANADA
U.S.

BLACKFEET INDIAN RES.

Cut Bank
Shelby
Conrad
Choteau
Fort Benton
BENTON LAKE N.W.R.
Great Falls

Lake Elwell
Marias
Teton
Sun

LEWIS

Havre
Chinook
Malta
BOWDOIN N.W.R.

Milk
Frenchman
Milk

NEZ PERCE N.H.P. (BEAR PAW BATTLEFIELD)
ROCKY BOYS I.R.

FORT BELKNAP INDIAN RESERVATION

Largest embankment dam in the U.S.

Glasgow
FT. PECK DAM

G R E A T

Scobey
Plentywood

FORT PECK INDIAN RESERVATION

MEDICINE LAKE N.W.R.

Wolf Point

Missouri

FORT UNION TRADING POST N.H.S.

Sidney

UPPER MISSOURI RIVER BREAKS N.M.
N.W.&S.R.
UL BEND N.W.R.

Fort Peck Lake

CHARLES M. RUSSELL NATIONAL WILDLIFE REFUGE

Yellowstone

Circle

Glendive
94
Wibaux

HELENA
GRANT-KOHRS RANCH N.H.S.
Deer Lodge
Butte

NATIONAL

Helena
Canyon Ferry L.

LEWIS
AND CLARK
NATIONAL

FOREST

Townsend

One of the world's biggest copper deposits

Missouri

GALLATIN

Belgrade
Bozeman

M O N T A N A

WAR HORSE N.W.R.
Lewistown

LAKE MASON N.W.R.

Harlowton
Roundup

FOREST

Musselshell

HAILSTONE N.W.R.
POMPEYS PILLAR N.M.

Jordan

Miles City

Terry

Powder

Baker

Forsyth
94

Yellowstone

Bighorn

Colstrip

CUSTER NATIONAL FOREST

Tongue

FOREST
Virginia City
Dillon
15

Jefferson
Gallatin
Madison

Big Timber
Livingston
Columbus
90

Laurel
Billings

Clarks Fork

Hardin
Crow Agency

CROW INDIAN RESERVATION

LITTLE BIGHORN BATTLEFIELD N.M.
NORTHERN CHEYENNE I.R.

Broadus

Red Rock

NATIONAL FOREST

FLATHEAD

M O N T A N A

Highest point in Montana

CUSTER

NATIONAL

Granite Peak 12,799 ft 3,901 m

Red Lodge
GRASSHOPPER GLACIER

FOREST

BIGHORN CANYON N.R.A.

Bighorn Mountains

RED ROCK LAKES N.W.R.
West Yellowstone
YELLOWSTONE

Absaroka Range
Yellowstone

NATIONAL

PARK

World's first national park, 1872

WYOMING

NORTH DAKOTA

SOUTH DAKOTA

Missouri
Little Missouri
Powder
G R E A T   P L A I N S

Economy Symbols

- Poultry/eggs
- Sheep
- Dairy cows/products
- Beef cattle
- Vegetables
- Vegetable oil
- Nursery stock
- Wheat
- Timber/forest products
- Printing/publishing

- Stone/gravel/cement
- Mining
- Coal
- Oil/gas
- Hydro-electricity
- Metal manufacturing
- Metal products
- Food processing
- Tourism

⇧ **NATURAL BEAUTY.** The rugged mountains and glacier-fed rivers of Montana offer many opportunities to outdoor lovers, including hiking and backpacking as well as fishing in summer, skiing in winter, and year-round wildlife viewing.

THE BASICS

STATS

Area
110,561 sq mi (286,352 sq km)

Population
2,700,551

Capital
Carson City
Population 55,274

Largest city
Las Vegas
Population 583,756

Ethnic/racial groups
66.2% white; 8.1% African American;
7.2% Asian; 1.2% Native American.
Hispanic (any race) 26.5%.

Industry
Tourism and gaming, mining, printing
and publishing, food processing,
electrical equipment

Agriculture
Cattle, hay, dairy products

Statehood
October 31, 1864; 36th state

GEO WHIZ

Lehman Caves, in Great Basin
National Park, contains the best
collection of shield, or angel wing,
formations in the country.

The Applegate Trail, named for two
brothers who first traveled it in 1846,
offered a shorter alternative to
the Oregon Trail. The trail
headed south from Idaho,
across Nevada's Black Rock
Desert into northern California
and then north into Oregon.

So many people claim to have seen
extraterrestrials along a 98-mile
(158-km) stretch of Nevada Highway
375 that the state transportation
board named it Extraterrestrial
Highway in 1996.

MOUNTAIN BLUEBIRD
SAGEBRUSH

NEVADA

Nevada's earliest settlers were native people about whom little is known. Around two thousand years ago, they began establishing permanent dwellings of clay and stone perched atop rocky ledges in what is today the state of Nevada. This was what Spanish explorers saw when they arrived in 1776. In years following, many expeditions passing through the area faced challenges of a difficult environment and native groups protecting their land. In the mid-1800s, gold and silver were discovered. In 1861, the Nevada Territory was created, and three years later statehood was granted. Today, the Nevada landscape is dotted with ghost towns—places once prosperous, but now abandoned except for curious tourists. Mining is now overshadowed by other economic activities. Casinos, modern hotels, and lavish entertainment attract thousands of visitors each year. Hoover Dam, on the Colorado River, supplies water and power to much of Nevada as well as two adjoining states. But water promises to be a challenge to Nevada's future growth.

⇧ TURNING BACK TIME. The Luxor, recreating a scene from ancient Egypt, is one of the many hotel-casinos that attract thousands of tourists to the four-mile (7-km) section of Las Vegas known as the Strip.

THIRSTY LAND

Annual precipitation, 1981–2010 averages

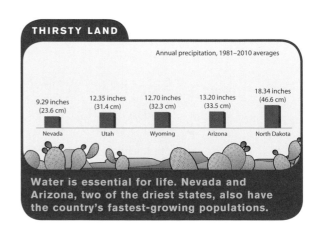

9.29 inches (23.6 cm)	12.35 inches (31.4 cm)	12.70 inches (32.3 cm)	13.20 inches (33.5 cm)	18.34 inches (46.6 cm)
Nevada	Utah	Wyoming	Arizona	North Dakota

Water is essential for life. Nevada and Arizona, two of the driest states, also have the country's fastest-growing populations.

⇦ PRICKLY GARDEN. Nevada's desert environment includes many varieties of cactuses. Saguaro and aloe plants as well as other xerophytes—plants that tolerate very dry conditions—thrive in this rocky garden.

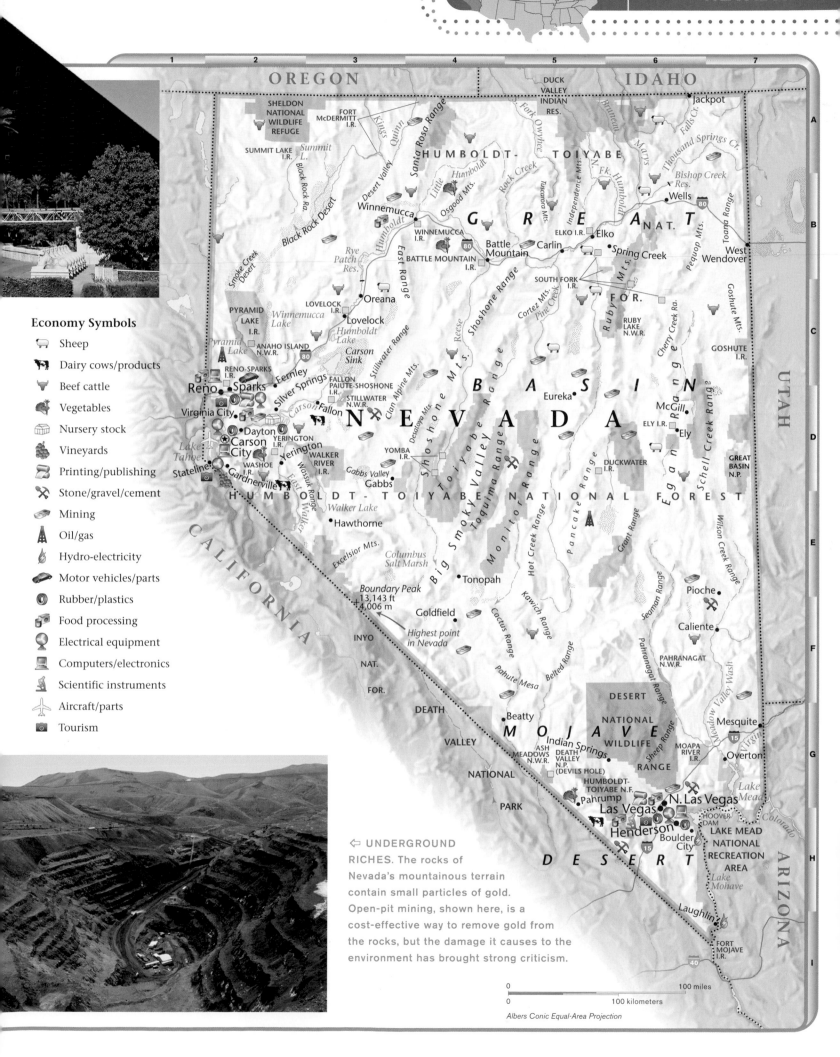

Economy Symbols

- 🐑 Sheep
- 🐄 Dairy cows/products
- 🐂 Beef cattle
- 🥬 Vegetables
- 🏭 Nursery stock
- 🍇 Vineyards
- 🖨 Printing/publishing
- ⚒ Stone/gravel/cement
- 🪨 Mining
- 🛢 Oil/gas
- 💧 Hydro-electricity
- 🚗 Motor vehicles/parts
- ⚙ Rubber/plastics
- 📦 Food processing
- 🔌 Electrical equipment
- 💻 Computers/electronics
- 🔬 Scientific instruments
- ✈ Aircraft/parts
- 📷 Tourism

OREGON IDAHO

SHELDON NATIONAL WILDLIFE REFUGE
FORT McDERMITT I.R.
DUCK VALLEY INDIAN RES.
Jackpot
SUMMIT LAKE I.R.
Summit L.
Santa Rosa Range
HUMBOLDT - TOIYABE
Bishop Creek Res.
Wells
Black Rock Desert
Winnemucca
WINNEMUCCA I.R.
GREAT
Elko
ELKO I.R.
Carlin
Spring Creek
West Wendover
Rye Patch Res.
BATTLE MOUNTAIN I.R.
Battle Mountain
SOUTH FORK I.R.
FOR.
Smoke Creek Desert
Oreana
PYRAMID LAKE I.R.
LOVELOCK I.R.
Lovelock
RUBY LAKE N.W.R.
GOSHUTE I.R.
Pyramid Lake
ANAHO ISLAND N.W.R.
Humboldt Lake
Carson Sink
B A S I N
RENO-SPARKS I.R.
Reno Sparks Fernley
Silver Springs
FALLON PAIUTE-SHOSHONE I.R.
STILLWATER N.W.R.
N E V A D A
Eureka
McGill
Virginia City
Fallon
ELY I.R.
Ely
Carson City
DAYTON
YERINGTON I.R.
Yerington
YOMBA I.R.
DUCKWATER I.R.
GREAT BASIN N.P.
Lake Tahoe
WASHOE I.R.
WALKER RIVER I.R.
Gabbs Valley
Gabbs
Stateline
Gardnerville
HUMBOLDT - TOIYABE NATIONAL FOREST
Walker Lake
Hawthorne
CALIFORNIA
Excelsior Mts.
Columbus Salt Marsh
Pioche
Boundary Peak 13,143 ft 4,006 m
Tonopah
Caliente
Goldfield
INYO NAT. FOR.
Highest point in Nevada
PAHRANAGAT N.W.R.
DEATH
Pahute Mesa
DESERT NATIONAL WILDLIFE RANGE
Beatty
VALLEY
MOJAVE
Mesquite
ASH MEADOWS N.W.R.
Indian Springs
MOAPA RIVER I.R.
Overton
NATIONAL
DEATH VALLEY N.P. (DEVILS HOLE)
HUMBOLDT-TOIYABE N.F.
Pahrump
N. Las Vegas
Lake Mead
PARK
Las Vegas
Henderson
Boulder City
HOOVER DAM
LAKE MEAD NATIONAL RECREATION AREA
DESERT
Laughlin
Lake Mohave
ARIZONA
FORT MOJAVE I.R.
UTAH

⬅ UNDERGROUND
RICHES. The rocks of
Nevada's mountainous terrain
contain small particles of gold.
Open-pit mining, shown here, is a
cost-effective way to remove gold from
the rocks, but the damage it causes to
the environment has brought strong criticism.

0   100 miles
0   100 kilometers

Albers Conic Equal-Area Projection

STATE OF OREGON

1859

THE BASICS

STATS

Area
98,381 sq mi (254,806 sq km)

Population
3,831,074

Capital
Salem
Population 154,637

Largest city
Portland
Population 583,776

Ethnic/racial groups
83.6% white; 3.7% Asian; 1.8% African American; 1.4% Native American. Hispanic (any race) 11.7%.

Industry
Real estate, retail and wholesale trade, electronic equipment, health services, construction, forest products, business services

Agriculture
Nursery stock, hay, cattle, grass seed, wheat, dairy products, potatoes

Statehood
February 14, 1859; 33rd state

GEO WHIZ

To recover wetlands and save two endangered fish species, 100 tons of explosives were used to blast through levees so that water from the Williamson River could again flow into Upper Klamath Lake.

Crater Lake, at 1,943 feet (592 m), is the deepest in the United States. It fills a depression created when an eruption caused the top of a mountain to collapse. Wizard Island, at the center of the 6-mile-wide lake (10 km), is the top of a volcano.

Snow-covered Mount Hood dominates the Portland skyline. The peak is one of the most active volcanoes in the Cascade Range. Its last eruption occurred just a few years before Lewis and Clark reached the region.

WESTERN MEADOWLARK
OREGON GRAPE

OREGON

Long before the Oregon Trail brought settlers from the eastern U.S., Indians fished and hunted in Oregon's coastal waters and forested valleys. Spanish explorers sailed along Oregon's coast in 1543, and in the 18th century fur traders from Europe set up forts in the region. In the mid-1800s settlers began farming the rich soil of the Willamette Valley. Oregon achieved statehood in 1859, and by 1883 Oregon was linked to the East by railroad, and Portland had become an important shipping center. Today, forestry, fishing, and agriculture make up an important part of the state's economy, but Oregon is making an effort to diversify into manufacturing and high-tech industries, as well. Dams on the Columbia River generate inexpensive electricity to support energy-hungry industries, such as aluminum production. Computers, electronics, and research-based industries are expanding. The state's natural beauty—snow-capped volcanoes, old-growth forests, and rocky coastline—makes tourism an important growth industry.

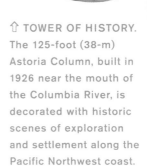

⇧ TOWER OF HISTORY. The 125-foot (38-m) Astoria Column, built in 1926 near the mouth of the Columbia River, is decorated with historic scenes of exploration and settlement along the Pacific Northwest coast.

⇦ CHANGING LANDSCAPE. Oregon's Pacific coast is a lesson on erosion and deposition. Rocky outcrops called sea stacks are leftovers of a former coastline that has been eroded by waves. The sandy beach is a result of eroded material being deposited along the shore.

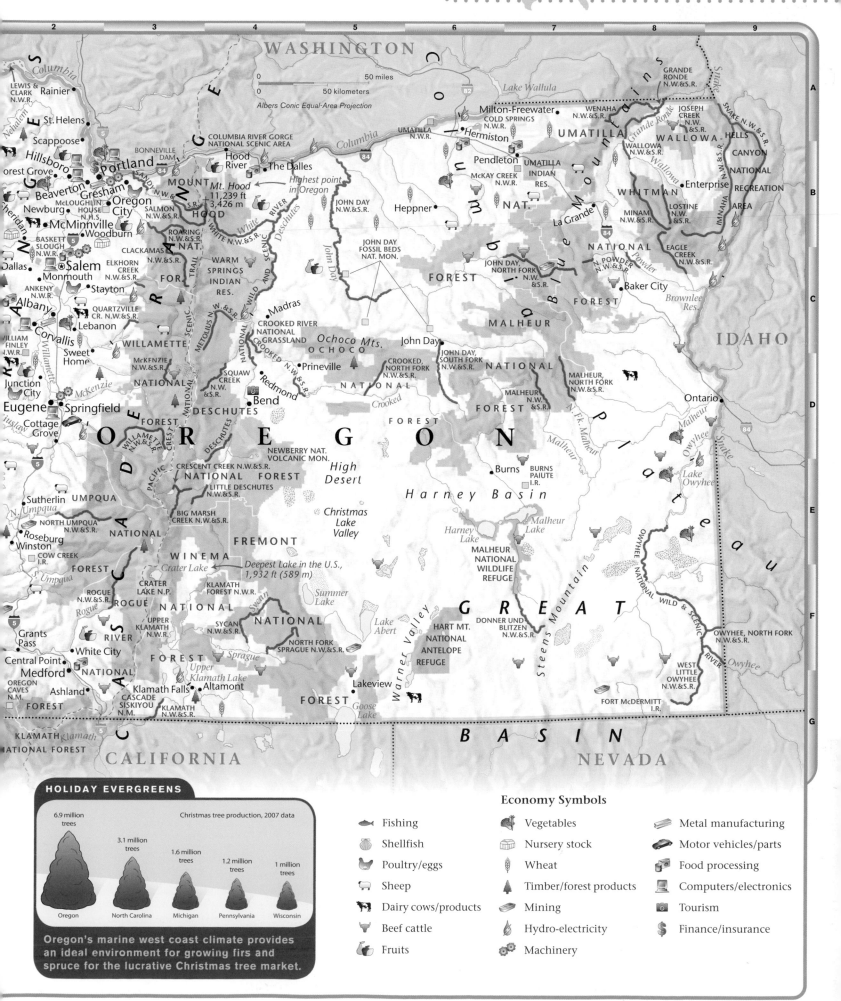

WASHINGTON

50 miles
50 kilometers
Albers Conic Equal-Area Projection

Highest point in Oregon
Mt. Hood
11,239 ft
3,426 m

OREGON

IDAHO

High Desert

Harney Basin

Deepest Lake in the U.S.,
1,932 ft (589 m)

Christmas Lake Valley

GREAT BASIN

CALIFORNIA

NEVADA

HOLIDAY EVERGREENS

6.9 million trees

Christmas tree production, 2007 data

3.1 million trees

1.6 million trees

1.2 million trees

1 million trees

Oregon | North Carolina | Michigan | Pennsylvania | Wisconsin

Oregon's marine west coast climate provides an ideal environment for growing firs and spruce for the lucrative Christmas tree market.

Economy Symbols

- Fishing
- Shellfish
- Poultry/eggs
- Sheep
- Dairy cows/products
- Beef cattle
- Fruits

- Vegetables
- Nursery stock
- Wheat
- Timber/forest products
- Mining
- Hydro-electricity
- Machinery

- Metal manufacturing
- Motor vehicles/parts
- Food processing
- Computers/electronics
- Tourism
- Finance/insurance

UTAH

THE BASICS

STATS

Area
84,899 sq mi (219,888 sq km)

Population
2,763,885

Capital
Salt Lake City
Population 186,440

Largest city
Salt Lake City
Population 186,440

Ethnic/racial groups
86.1% white; 2.0% Asian; 1.2% Native American; 1.1% African American. Hispanic (any race) 13.0%.

Industry
Government, manufacturing, real estate, construction, health services, business services, banking

Agriculture
Cattle, dairy products, hay, poultry and eggs, wheat

Statehood
January 4, 1896; 45th state

GEO WHIZ

A giant, duck-billed dinosaur is among the many kinds of dinosaur fossils that have been found in the Grand Staircase–Escalante National Monument. Scientists think the plant eater was at least 30 feet (9 m) long and had a mouthful of 300 teeth.

Drought has caused the level of Lake Powell to drop by more than 100 feet (30 meters), revealing much of the spectacular scenery of Glen Canyon that was drowned in 1963 when a dam created the lake.

Great Salt Lake is the largest natural lake west of the Mississippi River. The lake, which has a high level of evaporation, is about eight times saltier than the ocean.

CALIFORNIA GULL
SEGO LILY

For thousands of years, present-day Utah was populated by Native Americans living in small hunter-gatherer groups, including the Utes for whom the state is named. Spanish explorers passed through Utah in 1776, and in the early 19th century trappers came from the East searching for beavers. In 1847, the arrival of Mormons seeking freedom to practice their religion marked the beginning of widespread settlement of the territory. They established farms and introduced irrigation. Discovery of precious metals in the 1860s brought miners to the territory. Today, almost 70 percent of Utah's land is set aside by the federal government for use by the military and defense industries and as national parks, which attract large numbers of tourists annually. As a result, government is a leading employer in the state. Another important force in Utah is the Church of Latter-day Saints (Mormons), which has influenced culture and politics in the state for more than a century. More than half the state's population is Mormon.

⇧ NATURE'S HANDIWORK. Arches National Park includes more than 2,000 arches carved by forces of water and ice, extreme temperatures, and the shifting of underground salt beds over a period of 100 million years. Delicate Arch stands on the edge of a canyon, with the La Sal Mountains in the distance.

SPREADING THE FAITH

Mormon Church membership, 2011 data

Utah	California	Idaho	Arizona	Texas
1,910,343	763,370	414,182	387,950	296,141

From a colony of believers who settled in Utah's Salt Lake basin in the 1840s, followers of the Mormon faith have expanded into nearby states.

⇦ MONUMENT TO FAITH. Completed in 1893, the Salt Lake Temple is where Mormons gather to worship and participate in religious ceremonies. Church members regard temples as the most sacred places on Earth.

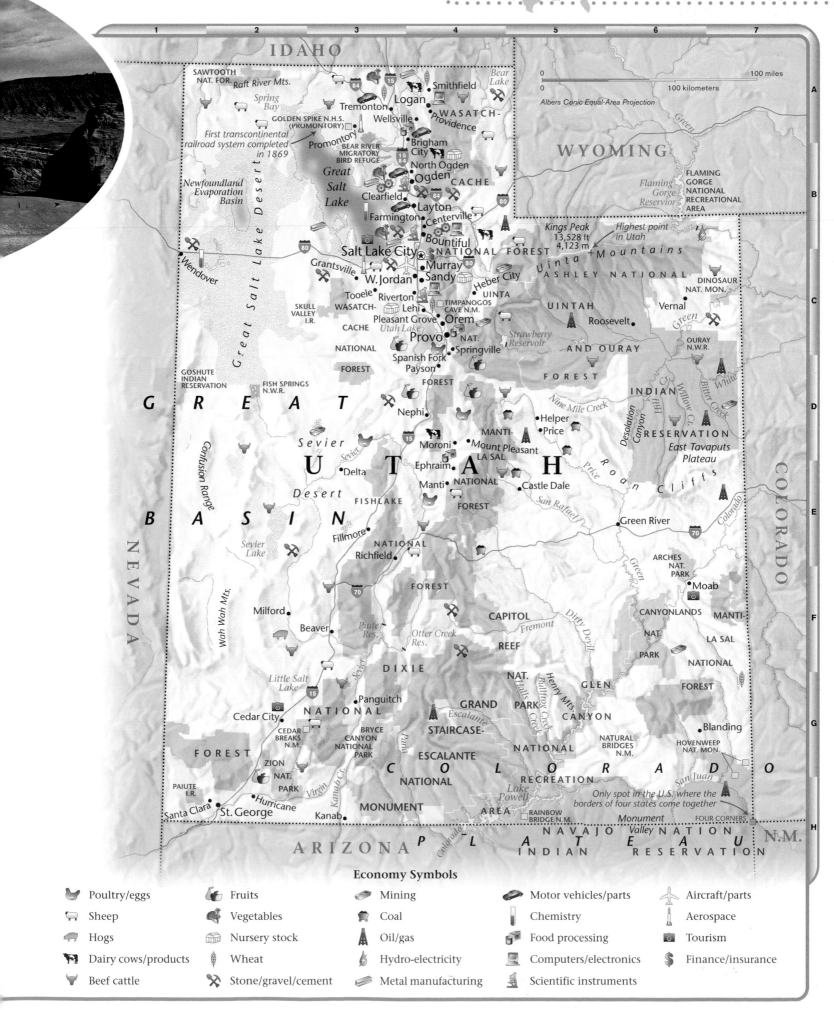

IDAHO

WYOMING

NEVADA

COLORADO

ARIZONA · N.M.

SAWTOOTH NAT. FOR.
Raft River Mts.
Spring Bay
GOLDEN SPIKE N.H.S. (PROMONTORY)
First transcontinental railroad system completed in 1869
Promontory
BEAR RIVER MIGRATORY BIRD REFUGE
Newfoundland Evaporation Basin
Great Salt Lake
Great Salt Lake Desert
Tremonton
Logan
Smithfield
WASATCH-
Providence
Wellsville
Brigham City
North Ogden
Ogden
CACHE
Clearfield
Layton
Centerville
Farmington
Bountiful
NATIONAL FOREST
Salt Lake City
Murray
Sandy
Grantsville
W. Jordan
Heber City
Wendover
Tooele
Riverton
UINTA
Lehi
TIMPANOGOS CAVE N.M.
WASATCH-
Pleasant Grove
Orem
CACHE
Utah Lake
Provo
NATIONAL
Springville
NAT.
FOREST
Spanish Fork
Payson
GOSHUTE INDIAN RESERVATION
SKULL VALLEY I.R.
FISH SPRINGS N.W.R.
FOREST
Nephi

Kings Peak 13,528 ft 4,123 m
Highest point in Utah
Uinta Mountains
ASHLEY NATIONAL
UINTAH
Strawberry Reservoir
AND OURAY
FOREST
Roosevelt
Vernal
DINOSAUR NAT. MON.
OURAY N.W.R.
INDIAN
Nine Mile Creek
Desolation Canyon
RESERVATION
East Tavaputs Plateau
Roan Cliffs
Bitter Creek
Willow Cr.
White

G R E A T

Sevier
UTAH
Sevier
Desert
Confusion Range
Sevier Lake
FISHLAKE
Delta
Ephraim
Manti
NATIONAL
FOREST
Moroni
MANTI
Mount Pleasant
LA SAL
Castle Dale
San Rafael
Helper
Price
Green River

B A S I N

Fillmore
NATIONAL
Richfield
FOREST
Milford
Beaver
Piute Res.
Otter Creek Res.
CAPITOL
REEF
Fremont
Dirty Devil
ARCHES NAT. PARK
Moab
CANYONLANDS
NAT.
PARK
MANTI
LA SAL
NATIONAL
FOREST
Wah Wah Mts.

DIXIE
Little Salt Lake
Sevier
Panguitch
Cedar City
CEDAR BREAKS N.M.
NATIONAL
BRYCE CANYON NATIONAL PARK
GRAND STAIRCASE-
ESCALANTE
Escalante
Paria
NAT.
PARK
Henry Mts.
Bullfrog Creek
GLEN
CANYON
NATURAL BRIDGES N.M.
Blanding
HOVENWEEP NAT. MON.

FOREST
ZION NAT. PARK
Virgin
Kanab Cr.
NATIONAL
COLORADO
RECREATION
Lake Powell
San Juan
Only spot in the U.S. where the borders of four states come together
PAIUTE I.R.
Santa Clara
St. George
Hurricane
Kanab
MONUMENT
RAINBOW BRIDGE N.M.
AREA
Monument Valley
FOUR CORNERS

ARIZONA P L A T E A U
NAVAJO NATION
INDIAN RESERVATION
Colorado

Bear Lake
Flaming Gorge Reservoir
Green
FLAMING GORGE NATIONAL RECREATIONAL AREA

0   100 miles
0   100 kilometers
Albers Conic Equal-Area Projection

Economy Symbols

Poultry/eggs Fruits Mining Motor vehicles/parts Aircraft/parts
Sheep Vegetables Coal Chemistry Aerospace
Hogs Nursery stock Oil/gas Food processing Tourism
Dairy cows/products Wheat Hydro-electricity Computers/electronics Finance/insurance
Beef cattle Stone/gravel/cement Metal manufacturing Scientific instruments

THE EVERGREEN STATE:
WASHINGTON

THE BASICS

STATS

Area
71,300 sq mi (184,666 sq km)

Population
6,724,540

Capital
Olympia
Population 46,478

Largest city
Seattle
Population 608,660

Ethnic/racial groups
77.3% white; 7.2% Asian; 3.6% African American; 1.5% Native American. Hispanic (any race) 11.2%.

Industry
Aerospace, tourism, food processing, forest products, paper products, industrial machinery, printing and publishing, metals, computer software

Agriculture
Seafood, apples, dairy products, wheat, cattle, potatoes, hay

Statehood
November 11, 1889; 42nd state

GEO WHIZ

The forests of the Olympic Peninsula are among the world's rainiest places. The Hoh Rain Forest is one of the planet's few temperate rain forests.

Mount St. Helens, the most active volcano in the lower 48 states, is close to both Seattle and Portland, Oregon. The eruption in May 1980 reduced its elevation by 1,314 feet (401 m), triggering the largest landslide in recorded history.

Orcas, also known as killer whales, are the world's largest dolphins. The 90 or so that call the waters of Puget Sound home have been placed on the government's Endangered Species List.

AMERICAN GOLDFINCH

COAST RHODODENDRON

WASHINGTON

Long before Europeans explored the coast of the Pacific Northwest, Native Americans inhabited the area, living mainly off abundant seafood found in coastal waters and rivers. In the late 18th century, first Spanish sailors and then British explorers, including Captain James Cook, visited the region. Under treaties with Spain (1819) and Britain (1846), the U.S. gained control of the land, and in 1853 the Washington Territory was formally separated from the Oregon Territory. Settlers soon based their livelihood on fishing, farming, and lumbering. Washington became the 42nd state in 1889. The 20th century was a time of growth and development in Washington. Seattle became a major Pacific seaport. The Grand Coulee Dam, completed in 1941, provided the region with inexpensive electricity. Today, manufacturing, led by Boeing and Microsoft, is a mainstay of the economy. Washington leads the country in production of apples and sweet cherries, and the state is home to the headquarters of the popular Starbucks chain of coffee shops.

⇓ HARVEST TIME. Once a semiarid grassland, the Palouse region north of the Snake River in eastern Washington is now a major wheat-producing area.

⇧ PACIFIC GATEWAY. The city of Seattle, easily recognizable by its distinctive Space Needle tower, is a major West Coast port and home to the North Pacific fishing fleet.

THE EVERGREEN STATE: WASHINGTON

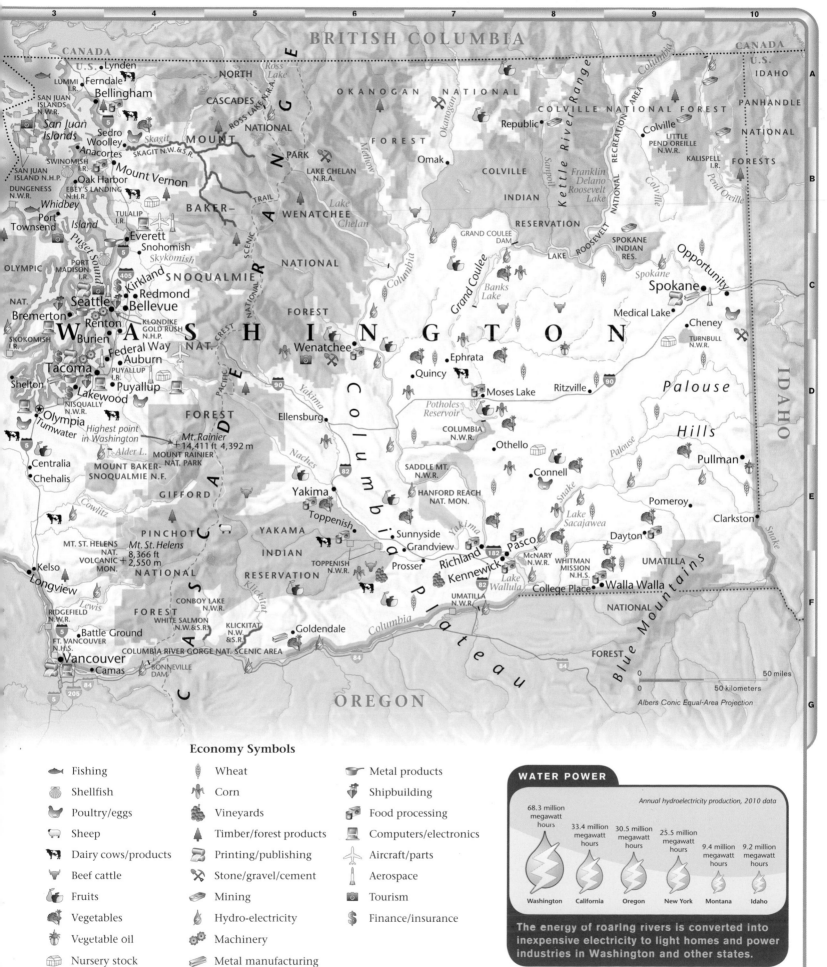

Economy Symbols

- Fishing
- Shellfish
- Poultry/eggs
- Sheep
- Dairy cows/products
- Beef cattle
- Fruits
- Vegetables
- Vegetable oil
- Nursery stock

- Wheat
- Corn
- Vineyards
- Timber/forest products
- Printing/publishing
- Stone/gravel/cement
- Mining
- Hydro-electricity
- Machinery
- Metal manufacturing

- Metal products
- Shipbuilding
- Food processing
- Computers/electronics
- Aircraft/parts
- Aerospace
- Tourism
- Finance/insurance

WATER POWER

Annual hydroelectricity production, 2010 data

Washington	California	Oregon	New York	Montana	Idaho
68.3 million megawatt hours	33.4 million megawatt hours	30.5 million megawatt hours	25.5 million megawatt hours	9.4 million megawatt hours	9.2 million megawatt hours

The energy of roaring rivers is converted into inexpensive electricity to light homes and power industries in Washington and other states.

THE EQUALITY STATE:
WYOMING

WYOMING

When Europeans arrived in the 18th century in what would become Wyoming, various native groups were already there, living as nomads following herds of deer and bison across the plains. In the early 19th century fur traders moved into Wyoming, and settlers followed later along the Oregon Trail. Laramie and many of the state's other towns developed around old army forts built to protect wagon trains traveling through Wyoming. Today, fewer than 600,000 people live in all of Wyoming. The state's economy is based on agriculture—mainly grain and livestock production—and mining, especially energy resources. The state has some of the world's largest surface coal mines. In addition, it produces petroleum, natural gas, industrial metals, and precious gems. The natural environment is also a major resource. People come to Wyoming for fishing and hunting, for rodeos, and for the state's majestic mountains and parks. Yellowstone, established in 1872, was the world's first national park.

⇧ WANT TO RACE? Unique to the High Plains of the West, the pronghorn can sprint up to 60 miles per hour (97 kmph).

⇩ DRAMATIC LANDSCAPE. Rising more than 13,000 feet (3,900 m), the jagged peaks of the Tetons, one of the youngest mountain ranges of the West, tower over a barn on the valley floor.

THE BASICS

STATS

Area
97,814 sq mi (253,337 sq km)

Population
563,626

Capital
Cheyenne
Population 59,466

Largest city
Cheyenne
Population 59,466

Ethnic/racial groups
90.7% white; 2.4% Native American; .8% African American; .8% Asian. Hispanic (any race) 8.9%.

Industry
Oil and natural gas, mining, generation of electricity, chemicals, tourism

Agriculture
Cattle, sugar beets, sheep, hay, wheat

Statehood
July 10, 1890; 44th state

GEO WHIZ

The successful reintroduction of wolves into Yellowstone National Park, a program that began in the mid-1990s, has become a model for saving endangered carnivores around the world. In 2010 there were almost 350 wolves in 45 packs living in the Northern Rockies of Wyoming.

The National Elk Refuge, in Jackson Hole, provides a winter home for some 5,000 elk. The herd's migration from the refuge to their summer home in Yellowstone National Park is the longest elk herd migration in the lower 48 states.

Devils Tower, a huge formation of igneous rock near Sundance, was the country's first national monument. It was featured in the science-fiction classic *Close Encounters of the Third Kind*.

WESTERN MEADOWLARK
INDIAN PAINTBRUSH

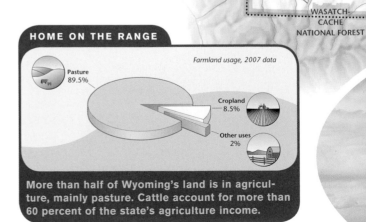

HOME ON THE RANGE

Farmland usage, 2007 data

Pasture 89.5%

Cropland 8.5%

Other uses 2%

More than half of Wyoming's land is in agriculture, mainly pasture. Cattle account for more than 60 percent of the state's agriculture income.

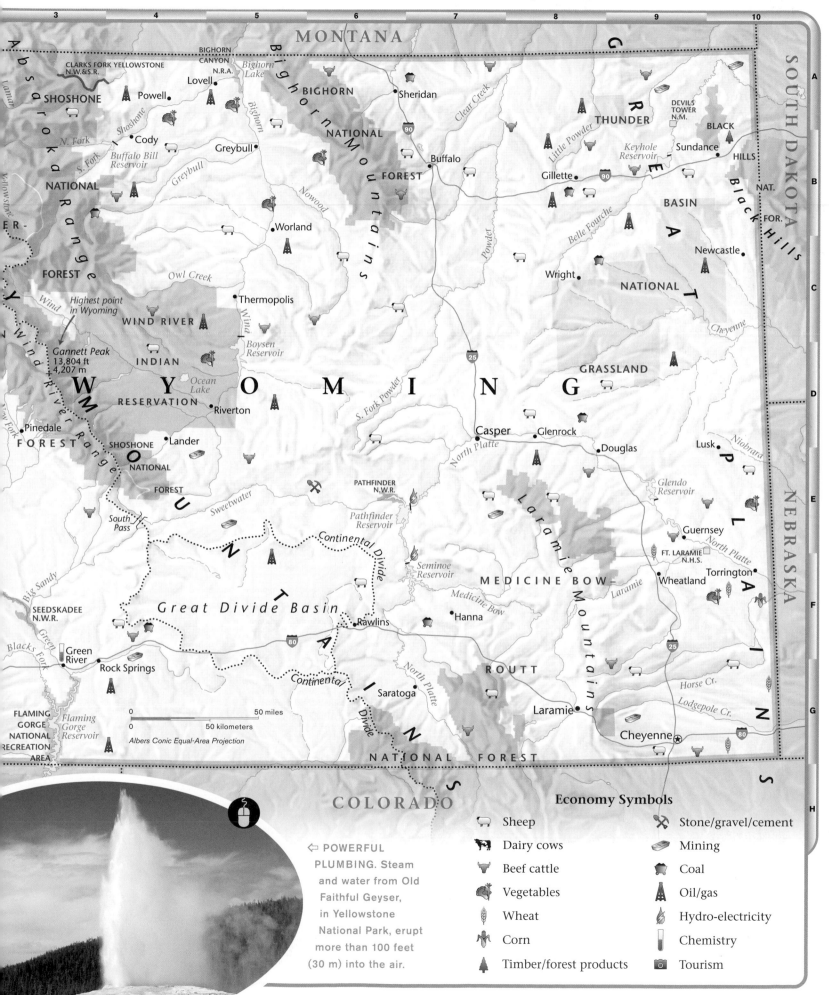

MONTANA

3 4 5 6 7 8 9 10

Absaroka Range

SHOSHONE

CLARKS FORK YELLOWSTONE
N.W.&S.R.

Lamar

Yellowstone

Powell • Lovell

BIGHORN CANYON N.R.A.

Bighorn Lake

Sheridan •

BIGHORN

NATIONAL

Bighorn Mountains

FOREST

Clear Creek

I-90

GREAT

THUNDER

DEVILS TOWER N.M.

BLACK

HILLS

NAT.

FOR.

• Cody

Shoshone

Greybull •

Bighorn

Buffalo •

Little Powder

Keyhole Reservoir

Sundance •

N. Fork

S. Fork

Buffalo Bill Reservoir

Greybull

Nowood

Gillette •

I-90

Belle Fourche

BASIN

Newcastle •

NATIONAL

NATIONAL

RANGE

FOREST

Worland •

Owl Creek

Powell

Wright •

Wind

Highest point in Wyoming

Thermopolis •

WIND RIVER

Wina

Cheyenne

Gannett Peak
13,804 ft
4,207 m

INDIAN

Boysen Reservoir

GRASSLAND

Wind River Range

Ocean Lake

WYOMING

New Fork

Pinedale •

RESERVATION

Riverton •

S. Fork Powder

Casper • Glenrock •

PLAINS

FOREST

SHOSHONE

Lander •

Douglas •

Lusk •

Niobrara

MOUNTAINS

NATIONAL

North Platte

Glendo Reservoir

FOREST

South Pass

Sweetwater

PATHFINDER N.W.R.

Laramie Mountains

Guernsey •

Continental Divide

Pathfinder Reservoir

FT. LARAMIE N.H.S.

North Platte

Big Sandy

Seminoe Reservoir

MEDICINE BOW

Laramie

Torrington •

SEEDSKADEE N.W.R.

Green

Great Divide Basin

Rawlins •

Medicine Bow

Wheatland •

Blacks Fork

I-80

Hanna •

Green River

Rock Springs •

Continental

ROUTT

North Platte

Horse Cr.

Divide

Saratoga •

Lodgepole Cr.

FLAMING GORGE NATIONAL RECREATION AREA

Flaming Gorge Reservoir

Laramie •

0 50 miles

0 50 kilometers

Albers Conic Equal-Area Projection

Cheyenne ★

I-80

NATIONAL FOREST

COLORADO

SOUTH DAKOTA

Black Hills

NEBRASKA

⟸ POWERFUL
PLUMBING. Steam
and water from Old
Faithful Geyser,
in Yellowstone
National Park, erupt
more than 100 feet
(30 m) into the air.

Economy Symbols

Sheep	Stone/gravel/cement
Dairy cows	Mining
Beef cattle	Coal
Vegetables	Oil/gas
Wheat	Hydro-electricity
Corn	Chemistry
Timber/forest products	Tourism

The Territories

ACROSS TWO SEAS

Listed below are the 5 largest of the 14 U.S. territories, along with their flags and key information. Two of these are in the Caribbean Sea, and the other three are in the Pacific Ocean. Can you find the other 9 U.S. territories on the map?

U.S. CARIBBEAN TERRITORIES

PUERTO RICO

Area: 3,508 sq mi (9,086 sq km)

Population: 3,989,133

Capital: San Juan
Population 2,730,000

Languages: Spanish, English

U.S. VIRGIN ISLANDS

Area: 149 sq mi (386 sq km)

Population: 109,666

Capital: Charlotte Amalie
Population 54,000

Languages: English, Spanish or Spanish Creole, French or French Creole

U.S. PACIFIC TERRITORIES

AMERICAN SAMOA

Area: 77 sq mi (199 sq km)

Population: 67,242

Capital: Pago Pago
Population 60,000

Language: Samoan

GUAM

Area: 217 sq mi (561 sq km)

Population: 183,286

Capital: Hagåtña (Agana)
Population 153,000

Languages: English, Chamorro, Philippine languages

NORTHERN MARIANA ISLANDS

Area: 184 sq mi (477 sq km)

Population: 46,050

Capital: Saipan (Capitol Hill)
Population 1,500

Languages: Philippine languages, Chinese, Chamorro, English

OTHER U.S. TERRITORIES

Baker Island, Howland Island, Jarvis Island, Johnston Atoll, Kingman Reef, Midway Islands, Navassa Island, Palmyra Atoll, Wake Island

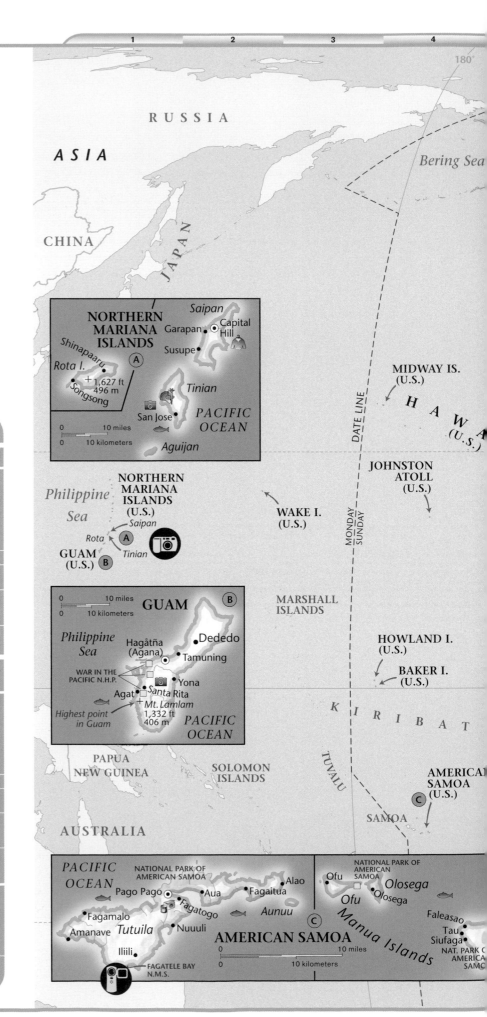

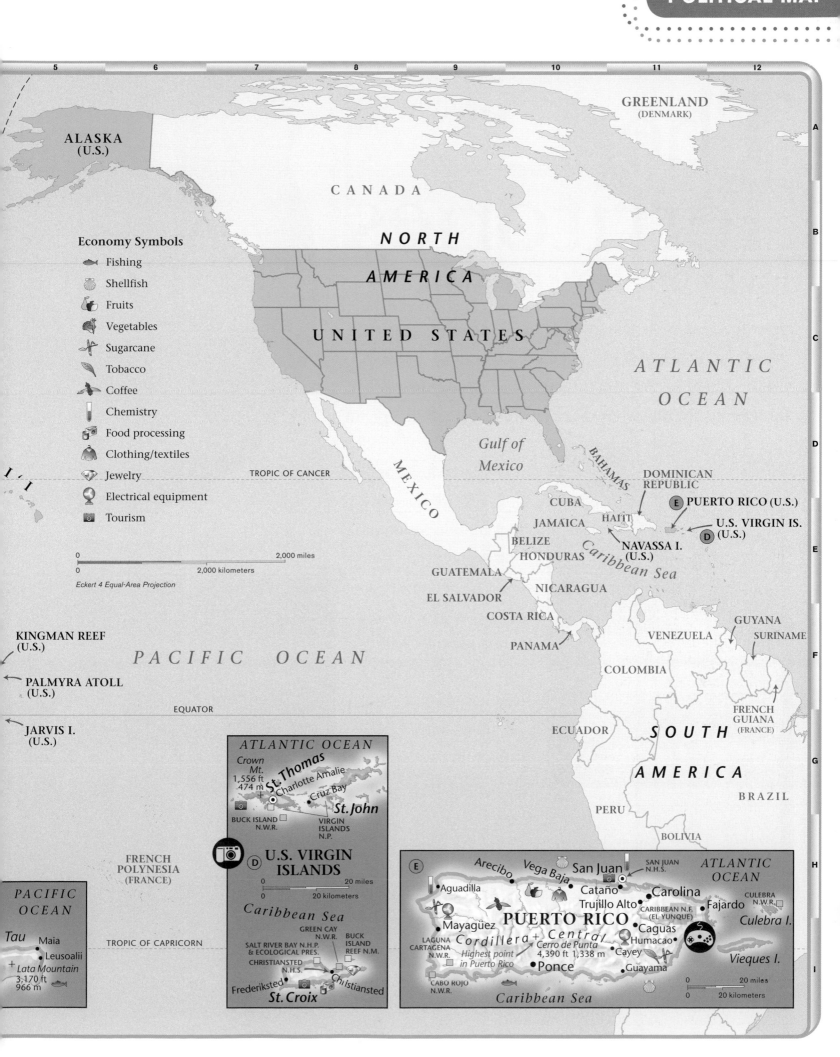

Economy Symbols

- Fishing
- Shellfish
- Fruits
- Vegetables
- Sugarcane
- Tobacco
- Coffee
- Chemistry
- Food processing
- Clothing/textiles
- Jewelry
- Electrical equipment
- Tourism

0   2,000 miles
0   2,000 kilometers

Eckert 4 Equal-Area Projection

GREENLAND
(DENMARK)

ALASKA
(U.S.)

CANADA

NORTH

AMERICA

UNITED STATES

ATLANTIC

OCEAN

Gulf of Mexico

MEXICO

TROPIC OF CANCER

BAHAMAS

DOMINICAN
REPUBLIC

CUBA

(E) PUERTO RICO (U.S.)

JAMAICA

HAITI

U.S. VIRGIN IS.
(U.S.) (D)

BELIZE

NAVASSA I.
(U.S.)

Caribbean Sea

GUATEMALA

HONDURAS

EL SALVADOR

NICARAGUA

COSTA RICA

KINGMAN REEF
(U.S.)

PACIFIC   OCEAN

PANAMA

VENEZUELA

GUYANA

SURINAME

COLOMBIA

PALMYRA ATOLL
(U.S.)

EQUATOR

FRENCH
GUIANA
(FRANCE)

JARVIS I.
(U.S.)

ECUADOR

SOUTH

AMERICA

PERU

BRAZIL

BOLIVIA

U.S. VIRGIN ISLANDS (D)

ATLANTIC OCEAN

Crown Mt.
1,556 ft
474 m

St. Thomas

Charlotte Amalie

Cruz Bay

St. John

BUCK ISLAND
N.W.R.

VIRGIN
ISLANDS
N.P.

Caribbean Sea

0   20 miles
0   20 kilometers

GREEN CAY
N.W.R.

BUCK
ISLAND
REEF N.M.

SALT RIVER BAY N.H.P.
& ECOLOGICAL PRES.

CHRISTIANSTED
N.H.S.

Frederiksted

Christiansted

St. Croix

FRENCH
POLYNESIA
(FRANCE)

PACIFIC
OCEAN

Tau   Maia

Leusoalii

Lata Mountain
3,170 ft
966 m

TROPIC OF CAPRICORN

PUERTO RICO (E)

Arecibo   Vega Baja   San Juan

SAN JUAN
N.H.S.

ATLANTIC
OCEAN

Aguadilla

Cataño

Carolina

Trujillo Alto

CULEBRA
N.W.R.

CARIBBEAN N.F.
(EL YUNQUE)

Fajardo

Culebra I.

Mayagüez

Caguas

LAGUNA
CARTAGENA
N.W.R.

Cordillera   *Central*

Humacao

Vieques I.

Cerro de Punta
4,390 ft 1,338 m
*Highest point
in Puerto Rico*

Cayey

Ponce

Guayama

CABO ROJO
N.W.R.

0   20 miles
0   20 kilometers

Caribbean Sea

⇨ PRESERVING TRADITION. Young dancers from American Samoa, dressed in costumes of feathers and pandanus leaves, prepare to perform in the Pacific Arts Festival, which is held once every four years to promote Pacific cultures.

The Territories

ISLANDS IN THE FAMILY

Fourteen territories and commonwealths scattered across the Pacific and Caribbean came under U.S. influence after wars or various international agreements. Because they are neither states nor independent countries, the U.S. government provides economic and military aid. Puerto Rico's nearly four million residents give it a population greater than that of 24 U.S. states. Many tourists seeking sunny beaches visit the Virgin Islands, purchased from Denmark for $25 million in 1917. American Samoa, Guam, and the Northern Mariana Islands in the Pacific have sizable populations, but several tiny atolls have no civilian residents and are administered by the U.S. military or government departments. In most cases, citizens of these territories are also eligible for American citizenship.

⇧ RELIC OF THE PAST. Sugar mill ruins on St. John, in the U.S. Virgin Islands, recall a way of life that dominated the Caribbean in the 18th and 19th centuries. Plantations used slave labor to grow cane and make it into sugar and molasses.

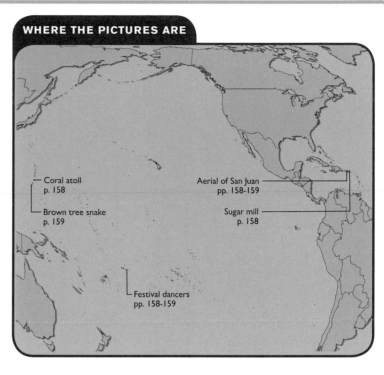

WHERE THE PICTURES ARE

Coral atoll
p. 158

Brown tree snake
p. 159

Aerial of San Juan
pp. 158-159

Sugar mill
p. 158

Festival dancers
pp. 158-159

⇐ PACIFIC JEWEL. Managaha Island sits in the blue-green waters of a lagoon formed by a long reef along Saipan's western coast. Marine biologists fear that portions of the reef are dying due to pollution. The lagoon holds wrecks from battles fought in Northern Mariana waters during World War II.

⇐ ATLANTIC PLAYGROUND. Modern hotels, catering to more than 3 million tourists annually, rise above sandy beaches in San Juan, Puerto Rico. Founded in 1521, the city has one of the best natural harbors in the Caribbean.

⇓ UNWELCOME STOWAWAY. The brown tree snake probably arrived in Guam on cargo ships in the 1950s. The snake has greatly reduced the island's bird and small mammal populations and causes power outages when it climbs electric poles.

BACK OF THE BOOK

U.S. FACTS & FIGURES

THE COUNTRY

STATS

Founding
1776

Area
3,794,083 sq mi (9,826,675 sq km)

Population (December 2011)
312,782,167

Capital
Washington, D.C.

Population
601,723

Largest city
New York

Population
8,782,166

Ethnic/racial groups
72.4% white; 12.6% African American; 4.8% Asian; .9% Native American. Hispanic (any race) 16.3%.

Languages
(most widely spoken)
English, Spanish

Economy
Services: 76.7% of GDP
Industry: 22.2% of GDP
Agriculture: 1.2% of GDP

BALD EAGLE, NATIONAL SYMBOL

Top States

Listed below are major farm products, fish, and minerals and the states that currently lead in their production. Following each list is a ranking of the top states in each category.

Farm Products

Cattle and calves: Texas, Kansas, Nebraska, Iowa
Dairy products: California, Wisconsin, New York, Pennsylvania
Soybeans: Iowa, Illinois, Minnesota, Nebraska
Corn for grain: Iowa, Illinois, Nebraska, Minnesota
Hogs and pigs: Iowa, North Carolina, Minnesota, Illinois
Broiler chickens: Georgia, Arkansas, Alabama, North Carolina
Wheat: North Dakota, Kansas, Montana, Washington
Cotton: Texas, Georgia, North Carolina, Arkansas
Eggs: Iowa, Ohio, Pennsylvania, Indiana
Hay: Texas, California, Missouri, South Dakota
Tobacco: North Carolina, Kentucky, Tennessee, Virginia
Turkeys: Minnesota, North Carolina, Missouri, Indiana
Oranges: Florida, California, Texas, Arizona
Potatoes: Idaho, Washington, Wisconsin, Colorado
Grapes: California, Washington, New York
Tomatoes (processed): Florida, Georgia, California

Rice: Arkansas, California, Louisiana, Mississippi

Top Ten in Farm Products
(by net farm income)

1. California
2. Iowa
3. Illinois
4. Nebraska
5. Minnesota
6. North Carolina
7. Indiana
8. South Dakota
9. Kansas
10. Georgia

Fish

Shrimp: Louisiana, Texas, Florida, Alabama
Crabs: Alaska, Louisiana, Oregon, Maryland, California
Lobsters: Maine, Massachusetts, Florida, Rhode Island
Salmon: Alaska, Washington, Oregon, California
Pollock: Alaska, Massachusetts, Maine, New Hampshire

Top Five in Fisheries
(by value of catch)

1. Alaska
2. Massachusetts
3. Maine
4. Louisiana
5. Washington

Minerals

Crude oil: Texas, Alaska, California, North Dakota, New Mexico
Natural gas: Texas, Wyoming, Oklahoma, Louisiana, Colorado
Coal: Wyoming, West Virginia, Kentucky, Pennsylvania, Montana
Crushed stone: Texas, Pennsylvania, Missouri, Illinois, Florida
Copper: Arizona, Utah, Nevada, New Mexico, Montana
Cement: Texas, California, Missouri, Pennsylvania, Alabama
Construction sand and gravel: Texas, California, Arizona, Colorado, Wisconsin
Gold: Nevada, Alaska, Utah, Colorado, California
Iron ore: Michigan, Minnesota
Clay: Georgia, Wyoming, Alabama, Texas, North Carolina
Phosphate rock: Florida, North Carolina, Idaho, Utah
Lime: Alabama, Kentucky, Missouri, Nevada, Ohio
Salt: Louisiana, Texas, New York, Kansas, Utah
Sulfur: Louisiana, Texas

Top Ten in Minerals

1. Nevada
2. Arizona
3. Florida
4. Utah
5. California
6. Texas
7. Alaska
8. Minnesota
9. Missouri
10. Wyoming

Extremes

World's Strongest Surface Wind
231 mph (372 kmph), Mount Washington, New Hampshire, April 12, 1934

World's Tallest Living Tree
"Hyperion," a coast redwood in Redwood National Park, California, 379.1 ft (115.55 m) high

World's Oldest Living Tree
Methuselah bristlecone pine, California; 4,789 years old

World's Largest Gorge
Grand Canyon, Arizona; 290 mi (466 km) long, 600 ft to 18 mi (183 m to 29 km) wide, 1 mile (1.6 km) deep

Highest Temperature in U.S.
134°F (56.6°C), Death Valley, California, July 10, 1913

Lowest Temperature in U.S.
Minus 80°F (-62.2°C) at Prospect Creek, Alaska, January 23, 1971

Highest Point in U.S.
Mount McKinley (Denali), Alaska; 20,320 ft (6,194 m)

Lowest Point in U.S.
Death Valley, California; 282 feet (86 m) below sea level

Longest River System in U.S.
Mississippi-Missouri; 3,710 mi (5,971 km) long

Rainiest Spot in U.S.
Wai'ale'ale (mountain), Hawai'i: average annual rainfall 460 in (1,168 cm)

Metropolitan Areas With More Than Five Million People
A metropolitan area is a city and its surrounding suburban areas. (2010 data)

1. New York, pop. 18,897,109
2. Los Angeles, pop. 12,828,837
3. Chicago, pop. 9,461,105
4. Dallas–Fort Worth, pop. 6,371,773
5. Philadelphia, pop. 5,965,343
6. Houston, pop. 5,946,800
7. Washington, D.C., pop. 5,582,170
8. Miami, pop. 5,564,635
9. Atlanta, pop. 5,268,860

GLOSSARY

aquaculture raising fish or shellfish in controlled ponds or waterways for commercial use

atoll a circular coral reef enclosing a tropical lagoon

arid climate type of dry climate in which annual precipitation is often less than 10 inches (25 cm)

biomass total weight of all organisms found in a given area

bituminous coal a soft form of coal used in industries and power plants

bog a poorly drained area with wet, spongy ground

broadleaf forest trees with wide leaves that are shed during the winter season

butte a high, steep-sided rock formation created by the erosion of a mesa

canal an artificial waterway that is used by ships or to carry water for irrigation

center-pivot irrigation an irrigation system that rotates around a piped water source at its middle, often resulting in circular field patterns

continental climate temperature extremes with long cold winters and heavy snowfall

continental divide an elevated area that separates rivers flowing toward opposite sides of a continent; in the U.S. this divide follows the crest of the Rocky Mountains

copra dried coconut meat from which oil is extracted to make a variety of products, including soap, candles, and cosmetics

Creole a simplified or modified form of a language, such as French or Spanish, used for communication between two groups; spoken in some Caribbean islands

delta lowland formed by silt, sand, and gravel deposited by a river at its mouth

desert vegetation plants such as cactus and dry shrubs that have adapted to conditions of low, often irregular precipitation

fork in a river, the place where two streams join

Fortune 500 company ranking of the top 500 U.S. companies based on total revenue

fossil remains of or an impression left by the remains of plants or animals preserved in rock

geothermal energy a clean, renewable form of energy derived from heat that flows continuously from Earth's interior

grassland areas with medium to short grasses; found where precipitation is not sufficient to support tree growth

gross domestic product (GDP) the total value of goods and services produced in a country in a year

highland climate found in association with high mountains where elevation affects temperature and precipitation

hundredweight in the U.S., a commercial unit of measure equal to 100 pounds

ice age a very long period of cold climate when glaciers often cover large areas of land

intermittent river/lake a stream or lake that contains water only part of the time, usually after heavy rain or snowmelt

lava molten rock from Earth's interior that flows out on the surface during volcanic activity

levee an embankment, usually earth or concrete, built to prevent a river from overflowing

lignite low-grade coal used mainly to produce heat in thermal-electric generators

marine west coast climate type of mild climate found on the mid-latitude West Coast of the U.S.

Mediterranean climate type of mild climate found on the West Coast of the U.S., south of the marine west coast climate

mesa an eroded plateau, broader than it is high, that is found in arid or semiarid regions

metropolitan area a city and its surrounding suburbs or communities

mild climate moderate temperatures with distinct seasons and ample precipitation

nursery stock young plants, including fruits, vegetables, shrubs, and trees, raised in a greenhouse or nursery

pinnacle a tall pillar of rock standing alone or on a summit

plain a large area of relatively flat land that is often covered with grasses

plateau a relatively flat area, larger than a mesa, that rises above the surrounding landscape

population density the average number of people living on each square mile or square kilometer of a specific land area

precipitate process of depositing dissolved minerals as water evaporates, as in limestone caves

rangeland areas of grass prairie that are used for grazing livestock

reactor a device that uses controlled nuclear fission to divide an atomic nucleus to generate power

Richter scale ranking of the power of an earthquake; the higher the number, the stronger the quake

Rust Belt a region made up of northeastern and midwestern states that have experienced a decline in heavy industry and an out-migration of population

scale on a map, a means of explaining the relationship between distances on the map and actual distances on Earth's surface

stalactite column of limestone hanging from the ceiling of a cave that forms as underground water drips down and evaporates, leaving dissolved minerals behind

stalagmite column of limestone that forms on the floor of a cave when underground water drips down and evaporates, leaving dissolved minerals behind

staple main item in an economy; also, main food for domestic consumption

Sunbelt a region made up of southern and western states that are experiencing major in-migration of population and rapid economic growth

territory land that is under the jurisdiction of a country but that is not a state or a province

tropical zone the area bounded by the Tropic of Cancer and the Tropic of Capricorn, where it is usually warm year-round

tundra vegetation plants, often stunted in size, that have adapted to periods of extreme cold and a short growing season; found in polar regions and high elevations

urban areas in which natural vegetation has been replaced by towns or cities, where the main economic activity is nonagricultural

volcanic pipe a vertical opening beneath a volcano through which molten rock has passed

wetland land that is either covered with or saturated by water; includes swamps, marshes, and bogs

OUTSIDE WEB SITES

The following Web sites will provide you with additional valuable information about various topics discussed in this atlas. You can find direct links to each by going to the atlas URL (www.nationalgeographic.com/kids-usa-atlas) and clicking on "Resources."

General information:
States: www.state.al.us (This is for Alabama; for each state insert the two-letter state abbreviation where "al" is now.)

D.C. and the Territories:
Washington, D.C.: kids.dc.gov/kids_main_content.html
American Samoa: www.samoanet.com
Guam: ns.gov.gu
Northern Marianas: www.saipan.com/gov
Puerto Rico: www.prstar.net
U.S. Virgin Islands: www.gov.vi

Natural Environment:
Biomes: www.blueplanetbiomes.org
Climate: www.eoearth.org
Global Warming: www.nrdc.org/globalWarming

Climate:
www.noaa.gov/climate.html
www.worldclimate.com (for cities)
www.cpc.noaa.gov

Natural Hazards:
General: www.usgs.gov/hazards
Droughts: www.drought.unl.edu/DM/monitor.html
Earthquakes: earthquake.usgs.gov
Hurricanes: hurricanes.noaa.gov
Tornadoes: www.tornadoproject.com
Tsunamis: www.noaa.gov/tsunamis.html
Volcanoes: www.geo.mtu.edu/volcanoes
Wildfires: www.nifc.gov/ and www.fs.fed.us/fire

Population:
States: quickfacts.census.gov/qfd
Cities: www.city-data.com
Population migration: www.census.gov/prod/2001pubs/p23-204.pdf
Hispanic population: www.census.gov/prod/2003pubs/p20-545.pdf

Getting Green:
www.epa.gov/
www.earthday.org
www.footprintnetwork.org/index.php

Bird sounds:
www.animalbehaviorarchive.org/loginPublic.do

Mapping site:
earth.google.com

PLACE-NAME INDEX

Map references are in boldface (**50**) type. Letters and numbers following in lightface (D12) locate the place-names using the map grid. (Refer to page 7 for more details.)

Beulah — Cascade

Cascade Range — Crossville

Crow Agency — Fall

Fall Line — Green River

Green River — Jamestown

Jamestown — Little Deschutes N.W.&S.R.

Little Diomede Island — Mio

Mishawaka — Odessa

Odessa — Potomac

Potomac — Sandstone

Stockbridge — Waikoloa

Wailuku — Zuni

Published by the National Geographic Society

John M. Fahey, Jr.
Chairman of the Board and Chief Executive Officer

Timothy T. Kelly
President

Declan Moore
President, Publishing and Digital Media

Melina Gerosa Bellows
Executive Vice President; Chief Creative Officer,
Books, Kids, and Family

Prepared by the Book Division

Hector Sierra, Senior Vice President and General Manager
Nancy Laties Feresten,
Senior Vice President, Editor in Chief, Children's Books
Jonathan Halling, Design Director, Books and Children's Publishing
Jay Sumner, Director of Photography, Children's Publishing
Jennifer Emmett, Editorial Director, Children's Books
Eva Absher-Schantz, Managing Art Director, Children's Publishing
Carl Mehler, Director of Maps
R. Gary Colbert, Production Director
Jennifer A. Thornton, Director of Managing Editorial

Staff for this book

Priyanka Lamichhane, Project Editor
David Seager, Art Director
Sven M. Dolling, Laura McCormick, Thomas L. Gray,
Nicholas P. Rosenbach, Map Editors
Matt Chwastyk, Sven M. Dolling, Steven D. Gardner,
Michael McNey, Gregory Ugiansky, Mapping Specialists, and
XNR Productions, Map Research and Production
Tibor G. Tóth, Map Relief
Lori Epstein, Senior Illustrations Editor
Martha B. Sharma, Consultant
Martha B. Sharma, Timothy J. Hill, Writers
Stuart Armstrong, Graphics Illustrator
Michelle R. Harris, Researcher
Dan Sherman, Web Page Design
Jennifer Kirkpatrick, Web Page Editor
Kathryn Robbins, Design Production Assistant
Stacy Gold, Nadia Hughes, Illustrations Research Editors
Kate Olesin, Assistant Editor
Lewis R. Bassford, Production Manager
Grace Hill, Associate Managing Editor
Joan Gossett, Production Editor
Susan Borke, Legal and Business Affairs

Manufacturing and Quality Management

Christopher A. Liedel, Chief Financial Officer
Phillip L. Schlosser, Senior Vice President
Chris Brown, Vice President
Nicole Elliott, Manager
Rachel Faulise, Manager
Robert L. Barr, Manager

The National Geographic Society is one of the world's largest nonprofit
scientific and educational organizations. Founded in 1888 to "increase and
diffuse geographic knowledge," the Society works to inspire people to care
about the planet. National Geographic reflects the world through its magazines,
television programs, films, music and radio, books, DVDs, maps, exhibitions,
live events, school publishing programs, interactive media and merchandise.
National Geographic magazine, the Society's official journal, published in
English and 33 local-language editions, is read by more than 38 million people
each month. The National Geographic Channel reaches 320 million households
in 34 languages in 166 countries. National Geographic Digital Media receives
more than 15 million visitors a month. National Geographic has funded more
than 9,400 scientific research, conservation and exploration projects and
supports an education program promoting geography literacy. For more
information, visit nationalgeographic.com.

For more information, please call 1-800-NGS LINE (647-5463) or write to the
following address:

NATIONAL GEOGRAPHIC SOCIETY
1145 17th Street N.W., Washington, D.C. 20036-4688 U.S.A.

Visit us online at www.nationalgeographic.com/books

For teachers and librarians: ngchildrensbooks.org

For information about special discounts for bulk purchases, please contact
National Geographic Books Special Sales: ngspecsales@ngs.org

For rights or permissions inquiries, please contact National Geographic Books
Subsidiary Rights: ngbookrights@ngs.org

Printed in the United States of America

13/RRDW-LPH/1

Illustrations Credits

Abbreviations for terms appearing below: (t)-top; (b)-bottom; (l)-left; (r)-right; NGS = National Geographic Image
Collection; iS = iStockphoto.com; SH = Shutterstock.com

Art for state flowers and state birds by Robert E. Hynes

Locator globe page 16 created by Theophilus Britt Griswold

Front cover, Tibor G. Tóth; (sunflower), Shutterstock; (Mt. Rushmore), Digital Stock; (Statue of Liberty), Punchstock;
(eagle), Shutterstock

Back cover (t–b), FloridaStock/SH, Peder Digre/SH, Lou Ann M. Aepelbacher/SH, Olga Lyubkina/SH

Front of the Book
2 (l–r), Freerk Brouwer/SH; PhotoDisc; Brandon Laufenberg/iS; Richard Nowitz/NGS; 3 (l–r), Joel Sartore/NGS; Jeremy
Edwards/iS; Eileen Hart/iS; PhotoDisc; 4 (l), PhotoDisc; 4 (r), Brian J. Skerry/NGS; 4–5, Lenice Harms/SH; 5 (l), italian-
estro/SH; 5 (r), James Davis Photography/Alamy; 5 (b), Digital Stock; 11 (t–b), Lane V. Erickson/SH; Elena Elisseeva/SH;
SNEHIT/SH; Nic Watson/SH; FloridaStock/SH; Sai Yeung Chan/SH; TTphoto/SH; 12 (l) Lowell Georgia/NGS; 12 (r),
NASA; 14 (l–r), George F. Mobley/NGS; Skip Brown/NGS; Jan Brons/SH; Michelle Pacitto/SH; Tammy Bryngelson/
iS; 15 (l–r), Carsten Peter/NGS; Mark Thiessen/NGS; Michael Nichols/NGS; Steven Collins/SH; Robert Madden/
NGS; 18, Ira Block/NGS; 20 (t), Penny de los Santos; 20 (bl), Steven Clevenger/Corbis; 20–21, Sarah Leen/NGS; 22 (l),
Marcelo Piotti/iS; 22–23, Jim Richardson/NGS; 23 (r), Sorin Alb/iS; 24, PhotoDisc; 24–25, PhotoDisc; 25 (t), L. Kragt
Bakker/SH; 25 (b), Lori Epstein/National Geographic Stock.

The Northeast
30 (bl), Rudi Von Briel/Photo Edit; 30 (br), Les Byerley/SH; 30–31 (t), Michael Melford/NGS; 30–31 (b), Tim Laman/
NGS; 31 (t), Donald Swartz/iS; 32 (both), David L. Arnold/NGS; 33, Catherine Karnow/NGS; 34 (bl),
Kevin Fleming/NGS; 34 (br), Stephen R. Brown/NGS; 34–35, Stephen St. John/NGS; 36 (b), iS; 36–37, PhotoDisc;
37 (b), Roy Toft/NGS; 38 (t), Jeremy Edwards/iS; 38 (b), Justine Gecewicz/iS; 39, James L. Stanfield/NGS; 40 (t), Sarah
Leen/NGS; 40 (b), Tim Laman/NGS; 41, Darlyne A. Murawski/NGS; 42 (t), Medford Taylor/NGS; 42–43, Steven
Phraner/iS; 43 (t), Richard Nowitz/NGS; 44 (t), Richard Nowitz/NGS; 44 (bl), Iconica/Getty Images; 44 (br), Matt
Rainey/Star Ledger/Corbis; 44–45, Mike Derer/Associated Press; 46 (t), Glenn Taylor/iS; 46 (b), James P. Blair/NGS;
47, Kenneth Garrett/NGS; 48 (t), Kenneth Garrett/NGS; 48 (b), Jeremy Edwards/iS; 49, William Albert Allard/NGS;
50 (t), Todd Gipstein/NGS; 50 (b), Onne van der Wal/Corbis; 50–51, Ira Block/NGS; 52, Michael S. Yamashita/NGS;
52–53, David McLain/Aurora/Getty Images; 53, Daniel W. Slocum/SH.

The Southeast
58 (t), Klaus Nigge/NGS; 58 (bl), Tyrone Turner/NGS; 58 (br), Richard Nowitz/Corbis; 58–59, Skip Brown/NGS; 59
(t), Raymond Gehman/NGS; 59 (b), Robert Clark/NGS; 60 (t), Raymond Gehman/NGS; 60 (b), Richard Nowitz/
NGS; 62 (t), Harrison Shull/Aurora/Getty Images; 62 (b), Joel Sartore/NGS; 63, Cary Wolinsky/NGS; 64 (t), David
Burnett/NGS; 64 (b), Brian J. Skerry/NGS; 64–65, NASA; 66 (tl), NGS; 66 (tr), PhotoDisc; 66 (b), Michael Melford/
NGS; 68, Melissa Farlow/NGS; 69, Randy Olson/NGS; 70 (t), Tyrone Turner/NGS; 70 (b), Jason Major/iS; 72 (t),
William Albert Allard/NGS; 72 (b), Ira Block/NGS; 73, Elena Vdovina/iS; 74 (l), Jack Fletcher/NGS; 74 (r), Pete Souza/
NGS; 75, Raymond Gehman/NGS; 76, Terry Healy/iS; 76–77, Annie Griffiths Belt/NGS; 77, Raymond Gehman/
NGS; 78, Melissa Farlow/NGS; 79 (t), Dennis R. Dimick/NGS; 79 (b), Jodi Cobb/NGS; 80 (t), Robert Clark/NGS; 80
(b), Richard Nowitz/NGS; 80–81, Medford Taylor/NGS; 82 (t), James L. Stanfield/NGS; 82 (b), Joel Sartore/NGS; 83,
Robert Pernell/SH.

The Midwest
88 (t), James L. Stanfield/NGS; 88 (b), Jim Richardson/NGS; 88–89, NGS; 89 (tl), Nadia M. B. Hughes/NGS;
89 (tr), Sean Martin/iS; 89 (b), Aga/SH; 90 (t), Chas/SH; 90 (b), Jenny Solomon/SH; 90–91 (t), Lenice Harms/SH;
92–93 (t), iS; 92–93 (b), Melissa Farlow/NGS; 94 (t), Joel Sartore/NGS; 94 (b), Madeleine Openshaw/SH; 95, Tom Bean/
NGS; 96, Cotton Coulson/NGS; 97, Phil Schermeister/NGS; 98 (t), Kevin Fleming/Corbis; 98 (b), Vince Ruffa/SH;
99, Geoffrey Kuchera/SH; 100 (t), Joel Sartore/NGS; 100 (b), Medford Taylor/NGS; 101, Lawrence Sawyer/iS; 102, Phil
Schermeister/NGS; 102–103 (b), PhotoDisc; 103, Sarah Leen/NGS; 104 (both), Joel Sartore/NGS; 105, Sarah Leen/
NGS; 106 (t), Farrell Grehan/NGS; 106 (b), Beverley Vycital/iS; 107, Annie Griffiths Belt/NGS; 108 (t), PhotoDisc; 108
(bl), Weldon Schloneger/SH; 108 (br), Robert J. Daveant/SH; 110, Peter Digre/SH; 111, Dan Westergren/NGS; 112 (t),
Paul Damien/NGS; 112 (b), PhotoDisc; 112–113 Medford Taylor/NGS.

The Southwest
118 (t), Joseph H. Bailey/NGS; 118 (b), Penny de los Santos; 118–119, Anton Folton/iS; 119 (t), Chih Hsueh Tseng/SH; 119
(b), Joel Sartore/NGS; 120 (t), Joel Sartore/NGS; 120 (b), George Burba/SH; 122 (tl), James P. Blair/NGS; 122 (tr), italian-
estro/SH; 122 (b), Lynn Johnson/NGS; 124, Joel Sartore/NGS; 125, Annie Griffiths Belt/NGS;
126 (t), Sarah Leen/NGS; 126–127, Diane Cook & Len Jenshel/NGS.

The West
132 (both), PhotoDisc; 132–133, Digital Stock; 133 (t), Phillip Holland/SH; 133 (bl), Joel Sartore/NGS; 133 (br), Digital
Stock; 134 (t), Joel Sartore/NGS; 134 (b), PhotoDisc; 136 (t), PhotoDisc; 136 (b), Randy Olson/NGS; 138 (both),
PhotoDisc; 140, PhotoDisc; 141, Frans Lanting/NGS; 142 (b), Joel Sartore/NGS; 142–143, Michael Melford/NGS; 143
(r), J. Cameron Gull/SH; 144 (b), William Albert Allard/NGS; 145, NGS; 146 (b), Sam Abell/NGS; 146–147, Andy Z./SH;
147 (b), Raymond Gehman/NGS; 148 (t), Jennifer Lynn Arnold/NGS; 148 (b), Peter Kunasz/SH; 150 (b), Digital Stock;
150–151, PhotoDisc; 152 (l), PhotoDisc; 152 (r), Digital Stock; 154 (t), Michael Rubin/SH; 154 (b), Digital Stock; 155,
PhotoDisc.

The Territories and Back of the Book
158 (l), Kendra Nielsam/SH; 158–159 (t), James Davis Photography/Alamy; 158–159 (b), Ira Block/NGS; 159 (t),
VisionsofParadise.com/Alamy; 159 (b), Gerry Ellis/Minden/Getty Images; 160, SH.

Map Acknowledgments
2–3, 26–27, 54–55, 84–85, 114–115, 128–129, Blue Marble: Next Generation NASA Earth Observatory; 12–13, climate
data adapted from Peel, M. C., Finlayson, B. L., and McMahon, T. A.: Updated world map of the Köppen-Geiger climate classification, Hydrol. Earth Syst. Sci., 11, 1633–1644, 2007; 14–15, data from Billion Dollar Weather Disasters
1980–2007 (map), NOAA's National Climatic Data Center (NCDC); 18–19, data from Center for International Earth
Science Information Network (CIESIN), Columbia University, and Centro Internacional de Agricultura Tropical
(CIAT), 2005. Gridded Population of the World Version 3 (GPWv3): Population Density Grids—World Population
Density, 2005 (map). Palisades, New York: Socioeconomic Data and Applications Center (SEDAC), Columbia
University. Accessed October 2007. Available at sedac.ciesin.columbia.edu/gpw; 20–21, United States Atlas of
Renewable Resources, National Renewable Energy Laboratory; 22–23, U.S. Census Bureau, Census 2000 Redistricting
Data (PL 94–171) Summary File, Population Division.

Copyright © 2008, 2012 National Geographic Society

Published by the National Geographic Society, 1145 17th St. N.W., Washington, D.C. 20036-4688.
All rights reserved. Reproduction of the whole or any part of the contents without written permission
from the publisher is prohibited.

Paperback ISBN: 978-1-4263-1052-2

ISBNs for 2008 editions, titled United States Atlas for Young Explorers, 3rd ed.: 978-1-4263-0255-8 (hardcover); 978-1-4263-0271-8
(Direct Mail Expanded Edition); 978-1-4263-0272-5 (Deluxe Direct Mail Expanded Edition)